SPORTS ON TELEVISION

Dennis Deninger takes the reader through every aspect of the medium: from its simple beginnings to its rich and complex present, behind cameras, inside board rooms, explaining everything from TV rights to TV wrongs. This serves as a fine guidebook for anyone who wishes to understand the many layered dimensions and decisions that shape and affect how sports comes through the screen and into our homes.

Mary Carillo, television commentator

In *Sports on Television*, Dennis Deninger provides an all-encompassing view of the sports television industry. He progresses from the need for this book, to the history of the industry and discipline, to the pioneering events of sports broadcasting and sports television, to a nuts-and bolts, behind-the-scenes look at a sports television production. All the while, he examines the impact that sports and the mass media have had (and are continuing to have) on one another and on society.

Dennis Deninger is an Emmy-award winning television producer and educator who has produced television programs from six continents and across the USA. He spent 25 years at ESPN leading production teams for studio programming, live remote events and digital video platforms. He now teaches at Syracuse University and serves as president and executive producer of Deninger Media, USA, a consulting and production firm based in Cheshire, Connecticut.

SPORTS ON TELEVISION

THE HOW AND WHY BEHIND WHAT YOU SEE

DENNIS DENINGER

Routledge
Taylor & Francis Group

NEW YORK AND LONDON

First published 2012
by Routledge
711 Third Avenue, New York, NY 10017

Simultaneously published in the UK
by Routledge
2 Park Square, Milton Park, Abingdon, Oxon OX14 4RN

Routledge is an imprint of the Taylor & Francis Group, an informa business

Library of Congress Cataloging in Publication Data
Deninger, Dennis.
   Sports on television: the how and why behind what you see/
   Dennis Deninger.
   p. cm.
   1. Television and sports.   2. Television broadcasting of sports.
   3. Mass media and sports.   I. Title.
   GV742.3.D44 2012
   070.4'49796—dc23
   2012005528

ISBN: 978-0-415-89675-7 (hbk)
ISBN: 978-0-415-89676-4 (pbk)
ISBN: 978-0-203-10751-5 (ebk)

Typeset in Joanna and Dax
by Florence Production Ltd, Stoodleigh, Devon

Certified Sourcing
www.sfiprogram.org
SFI-00453

Printed and bound in the United States of America
by Edwards Brothers, Inc.

To Gail,
who has watched more than her share of sports on television with me.

And to our sons Matthew and Kevin, who grew up as sports fans.

Contents

Foreword

The US hockey team's Miracle on Ice. David Tyree's acrobatic Super Bowl catch for the New York Giants. Landon Donovan's extra-time, game-winning goal in the 2010 FIFA World Cup. Few things in life match the exhilarating excitement of sports and moments like these.

This unique human drama stokes people's emotions unlike any other entertainment genre, and, because a majority of fans can't be in the stadium or arena to witness most events first-hand, they consume sports primarily through television—it's how they fulfill their sports passions.

Sports is even more compelling because of the "power of live," sharing in real time the elation of your favorite team's victory or even the emptiness after they suffer through what *ABC's Wide World of Sports* dubbed "the agony of defeat." Watching a sporting event after the fact is just not the same as watching it live.

When ESPN launched in 1979, conventional wisdom questioned whether there would be enough interest to sustain a twenty-four-hour sports network, much less a dedicated hour-long sports news and information program like *SportsCenter*. Today, ESPN has eight domestic networks in the United States and fifteen localized versions of *SportsCenter* around the world. And, beyond ESPN, there are countless other networks and programs devoted to sports.

The astonishing growth of sports television over the past three decades has been fueled by fans and their unquenchable thirst for sports, and we haven't even approached the saturation point.

While digital media continues to grow substantially, television remains the driving force in sports media with its ability to reach a mass audience. High definition has transformed the viewing experience, and 3D quite possibly could do the same. Beyond TV, the industry is constantly evolving, with new technologies and innovative platforms emerging before our eyes.

Sports video content is available on a plethora of digital platforms, computers, phones, tablets, etc. There has never been a better time to be a sports fan or a more exciting time to be taking a course on sports television.

That you are reading this textbook demonstrates not only your passion for sports but also your curiosity about this industry.

Dennis Deninger spent twenty-five years at ESPN. He understands the industry—what makes it unique and how it has evolved. I know you will enjoy his perspective and the special insights he brings to the chapters within this book.

George Bodenheimer
Executive Chairman, ESPN

Acknowledgements

I want to thank my mother, who first got me excited about her beloved Brooklyn Dodgers. And thanks to everyone along the way who has given me the opportunity to learn about broadcasting and to grow as a professional. From Charles D. Henderson, who hired me when I was still a senior in high school to do the morning news on WLEA Radio in Hornell, New York, to all of the generous mentors who have taken the time to share their knowledge and expertise.

Michael Schoonmaker, Dona Hayes, and David Rubin gave me the chance to start teaching at Syracuse University, and share the lessons I have learned with new generations of young professionals. The encouragement and support I've received from all my Syracuse colleagues, Michael Veley and Rick Burton in particular, have been invaluable in this project.

Special thanks go to my publisher at Routledge, John Szilagyi, who led the way for this first-time author, and to Arlin Kauffman and Kristen Shilton, for their enthusiastic and expert research and clearance assistance.

I also want to acknowledge the generosity and contributions of Chris LaPlaca at ESPN and David Plaut at NFL Films.

And thanks to all my students, who inspire me to keep learning right along with them.

Dennis Deninger

1 TELEVISION THAT MATTERS

Why do you watch sports on TV? For most people the answer includes one or more of these factors:

- To see your favorite team.

- To follow and admire favorite players.

- To see competition, collisions, and confrontation.

- To see performances by individuals who are the best in the world at what they do.

- To see human drama that is unscripted.

- To see how a story will end, to see who wins and who loses. (If you have wagered on the game or event, or if you play fantasy sports, you want to see if you will be the winner or loser.)

Substitute the words "actors" for "players" and "shows" for "teams," and the first four of these reasons for watching could just as easily be the answer to, "Why do you watch scripted entertainment shows on television?" The critical differences are in the unscripted nature of sports, and the fact that the results of the games and events *matter* to you.

Watch any fictional entertainment or non-fiction "reality" show on television and you will always find a set of stories, some more obvious than others, that will be resolved by the end of the episode or the season. But does that resolution matter to you? Do you carry with you what happened to a character in a drama, or is it important to you who is voted the best dancer or who goes off to live "happily ever after" with "The Bachelor" or "The Bachelorette?" Probably not.

Compare that to how you feel when your team wins the Super Bowl, the World Series, the NCAA championship, the NBA Finals, the Stanley Cup, or even a regular season game against a long-time rival. The results mean something to us. The plot of the story may seem apparent, especially when a big favorite faces a decided underdog, but the ending is always in suspense because the drama is unscripted.

The same can be said for the unforeseen stories that almost always provide layers of texture and multiple plot lines within each live event. The commentators may tell us before the game begins which stars to watch for and why, but there is no guarantee that they will be at their best, that they won't run into a defense they cannot overcome, that they won't be injured in the first few minutes and spend the rest of the day on the bench. Unheralded second-string players may step forward and become the stars of the contest; a veteran past his or her prime may rise to the occasion and temporarily recapture the form and fame of old.

Every sporting event is filled with human narratives of hardships endured, commitments made, dedication to family or mentors, goals achieved or yet to be attained. These are all stories we can relate to, they drive our interest and build audience. There are real consequences to the events we watch each week: starting positions will be gained or lost, players will be traded or released, and coaches will be fired or hired based upon the results of their seasons. And then there's the money. The unscripted outcomes of events will determine which athletes top the money list, who will get the most lucrative endorsements, which teams and leagues will succeed, be forced to move, or fail, and how large the next television rights deal will be.

The money generated by sports on television fuels a set of businesses from television networks and distributors to the sales of high-definition and 3D televisions, the manufacture and sales of sneakers and jerseys, and a lot in between. Big money and large audiences create power. And power always attracts politicians.

Sports is television that matters to people in ways that no other entertainment can.

AN AUDIENCE THAT MATTERS

In the first decade of the 21st century the top-ten rated television shows in the United States were all Super Bowls. The Nielsen Company reports that the most-watched single program in the history of American television was Super Bowl XLV on February 6, 2011. An average of 111,041,000 viewers were watching the Green Bay Packers play the Pittsburgh Steelers every minute of the telecast on CBS. That represents a rating of 46.0, which means just short of half the television homes in the nation were watching. The share of the televisions that were in use on that day and were tuned to FOX TV for the Super Bowl was 68 percent. It is very likely that successive Super Bowls after the publication of this text will surpass Super Bowl XLV and move into that all-time number one position.

If every Packers fan and every Steelers fan in America were the only people watching Super Bowl XLV as Green Bay won 31–17 at Cowboys Stadium in Texas, the total television audience would have been only a fraction of the record-breaking total. Clearly the collective stories that developed over the course of the entire NFL season, regardless of which of the thirty-two teams was a fan's favorite, drove audience to the Super Bowl. Add to that the attraction that Americans have for big events like championship games, the Olympics, and the Oscars, and you get an enormous number of viewers who care about the outcome and want to see the event live.

An audience of over 110,000,000 people on commercial television will see a lot of commercials from sponsors who are willing to pay very high rates to deliver their messages to the masses. There were 115 ads during the Super Bowl XLV game telecast on FOX, occupying forty-eight minutes of air time. The commercials sold for approximately $3 million per thirty-second spot. That put the cost of reaching 1000 viewers in Super Bowl XLV at roughly $27.27. The value of television advertising is measured in cost per thousand (CPM). Shortly after Super Bowl XLV, NBC announced that it would start selling thirty-second commercials in Super Bowl

Figure 1.1 The Super Bowl is the most-watched American television show year after year. The game is fed to over 180 countries and territories in thirty different languages

XLVI at $3.5 million each, the highest price ever charged for a half minute of advertising on American television.

When you add the commercials that aired in the four hours of the FOX pre-game show, plus the post-game show, you get a sense of how Super Bowl Sunday has become one of the most important advertising days of the year in the United States. The agreement that FOX has with the NFL gives the network the exclusive rights to televise the Super Bowl every three years in rotation with NBC and CBS. But the network with the game is by no means the only network covering, or generating advertising revenue from, the Super Bowl. For example, ESPN originates a week of "surround" programming each year from the Super Bowl for its networks as well as ESPN.com and ESPN Radio. The NFL Network blankets its schedule leading up to the Super Bowl with over one hundred hours of content related to the upcoming game. NBC has hosted *The Today Show* from the Super Bowl site and a variety of networks create and produce programs that connect with fans and/or the host city. Sports and general interest publications and web sites cover the preparations and the game as do radio networks and stations.

All of these platforms sell advertising, and all of those dollars piled together represent a major economic impact from this one televised NFL football game. Sports has not banished scripted or reality entertainment shows from the television universe. Those programs in prime time and throughout the day and night continue to draw millions of viewers and bring in billions of dollars in advertising, but, when reaching the absolute largest audience of the year matters, the answer is a televised sporting event, the Super Bowl.

Table 1.1 Top ten most watched US television shows, 2000–11

	Program	Avg. Viewers per Minute	Rating	Share	Date	Network
1	Super Bowl XLV (Green Bay Packers vs. Pittsburgh Steelers)	111,041,000	46.0	69%	2/6/11	FOX
2	Super Bowl XLIV (New Orleans Saints vs. Indianapolis Colts)	106,480,000	46.4	68%	2/7/10	CBS
3	Super Bowl XLIII (Pittsburgh Steelers vs. Arizona Cardinals)	98.7 million	42.1	65%	2/1/09	NBC
4	Super Bowl XLII (New York Giants vs. New England Patriots)	97.5 million	43.3	65%	2/3/08	FOX
5	Super Bowl XLI (Indianapolis Colts vs. Chicago Bears)	93.2 million	42.6	64%	2/4/07	CBS
6	Super Bowl XL (Pittsburgh Steelers vs. Seattle Seahawks)	90.7 million	41.6	62%	2/5/06	ABC
7	Super Bowl XXXVIII (New England Patriots vs. Carolina Panthers)	88.4 million	41.4	63%	2/1/04	CBS
8	Super Bowl XXXIX (New England Patriots vs. Philadelphia Eagles)	86.1 million	41.1	62%	2/6/05	FOX
9	Super Bowl XXXVII (Tampa Bay Buccaneers vs. Oakland Raiders)	88.6 million	40.7	61%	1/26/03	ABC
10	Super Bowl XXXIV (St. Louis Rams vs. Tennessee Titans)	88.5 million	43.3	63%	1/30/00	ABC

Source: copyrighted information of Nielsen, licensed for use herein.

When the stakes are this high, the pressure on everyone involved in the production, programming, promotion, and sponsorship of the television event is multiplied. We will examine each of these functions and identify the sets of skills and attributes required of these individuals in the coming chapters.

BUSINESS MATTERS

Sports is big business in the United States, providing a livelihood for hundreds of thousands of people far beyond the celebrity athletes with the multi-million dollar contracts and endorsement deals. Research by PricewaterhouseCoopers for the *Sports Business Journal* and by the Sporting Goods Manufacturers Association (SGMA) shows that, in the year 2009, the sports sector of the economy totaled $235 billion. If you add the $27.33 billion that Americans spent in 2009 on recreational transportation—bicycles, snowmobiles, motorcycles, pleasure boats, and RVs—the total would come to $262.3 billion, over a quarter of a trillion dollars.

It would be impossible to extrapolate how much of that money is attributable to the fact that sports is on television every day of the year, reaching millions of consumers who buy the shoes, hats, and jerseys they see worn by athletes, buy the Gatorade and other foods the athletes consume, pay the monthly fees charged by the cable, digital, or satellite providers who deliver the live programs to their homes, or who buy tickets and travel packages to future games to be played by the teams they follow on TV. In the early years of television many leagues and teams feared that live television coverage would result in fewer people attending games in person because they could sit home and watch, never having to open their wallets. But

Table 1.2 The sports business in the US, 2009

Advertising	$27.43 billion
Spectator spending	$26.17 billion
Operating expenses	$22.98 billion
Gambling	$18.90 billion
Professional services	$15.25 billion
Travel	$16.06 billion
Medical spending	$12.60 billion
Licensed goods	$10.50 billion
Media broadcast rights	$6.99 billion
Sponsorships	$6.40 billion
Facility construction	$2.48 billion
Multimedia	$2.12 billion
Endorsements	$0.897 billion
Internet ads/subscribers	$0.239 billion
Sporting goods	
Sports apparel	$28.17 billion
Sporting goods equipment	$20.2 billion
Athletic footwear	$12.3 billion
Exercise equipment	$4.2 billion
Team uniforms	$1.13 billion
Total	$235 billion

Source: *Sports Business Journal* media kit.

the reverse has proven to be true: a lack of television exposure can consign a league or team to anonymity and red ink.

The economics, advertising, and power of sports television are major topics that we will be covering in depth later in this book. However, when billions of dollars are changing hands it's abundantly clear that there is far more at stake than the latest "scores and highlights."

A MATTER OF IDENTITY

Each year I have assigned my students to write a short "self-portrait" explaining how televised sport has influenced who they are, what they wear, the expressions they use in everyday speech, their perceptions of races other than their own, and how they spend their time. These "self-portraits" have been most revealing both to me and to the students who take the time to think about the things that define them as individuals. "My life would be considerably different if I didn't have televised sport in my life," wrote one 21-year-old male. "Actually, I can't even imagine what my life would be like. I ask my dad from time to time what it was like when he was growing up" when there was far less sports on television. The young man's father responded that he "didn't really know," but that it must be like remembering how we all existed before there were cell phones.

A woman who was a junior wrote about how she remembered watching the 1996 Summer Olympics when American gymnast Kerri Strug injured her ankle on her first vault and battled through the pain to land her second vault, helping the US women's team win the gold medal in Atlanta. "The determination and courage displayed by these women throughout the entire 1996 Olympic Games," she said, "served as my inspiration and commitment to athletics, leadership, and willingness to succeed in any endeavor." Many others have said how the games they saw on television influenced one of the most important choices they will make in their entire lives—which college they would attend.

Young men and women from small towns in New Hampshire, Delaware, and upstate New York have all described how sports on television provided their first opportunity to learn about and see the amazing accomplishments of African-Americans, Hispanic-Americans, and players from foreign countries. They said it helped broaden their understanding of humanity and prepared them for the diversity of people on campus and in the world outside their home towns.

A senior from Seattle echoed the observations of many when he wrote that "televised sport has provided me with the ability to connect and share experiences with others, even absolute strangers." He said that, "I truly believe sport in any form, but especially at the collegiate and professional levels, is a form of social currency."

Sports on television matters to each of these young people far more than it ever did to generations of Americans who preceded them. To find out how the increased availability and mass distribution of live television sports has changed us we need to go back to the years before World War II when the United States was a very different place.

DISCUSSION TOPICS/ASSIGNMENTS

1 Do your own "self-portrait" describing how sports on television has affected who you are, what you wear, how you speak, and how you spend your time.

2   Take your favorite team or sport and research its current economic health. Include television rights deals for local, regional, and national distribution. Has the size of the television audience for this team or sport increased or decreased in the past five years? Who are the biggest sponsors? What are their attendance and ticket pricing trends?

3   If you were an investor, which sport would you buy into now? What factors would you have to know before making your decision?

4   What is your first memory of watching sports on television? Why is it memorable? Who were you with? Has it affected your sport preferences or team loyalty to this day?

2 BEGINNINGS

THE DECADES OF EXPERIMENTATION AND FULFILLMENT

It is with a feeling of humbleness that I come to this moment of announcing the birth in this country of a new art so important in its implications that it is bound to affect all society. It is an art which shines like a torch of hope in a troubled world. It is a creative force which we must learn to utilize for the benefit of mankind.

(David Sarnoff, RCA President, April 30, 1939)

With these words, David Sarnoff introduced television to the American public at the opening of the RCA exhibit at the New York World's Fair in 1939. RCA's station W2XBS (XBS for "experimental broadcast station") began the first regular schedule of television service on that date in April with President Franklin D. Roosevelt's speech at the opening of the World's Fair.

"Now we add sight to sound," said Sarnoff, whose RCA owned the NBC Red and Blue radio networks. Millions of people each day tuned in for the entertainment and news programs on these networks using radio sets built and sold by RCA. The more appealing the product that NBC could create and broadcast, the more demand they could generate for the radios they manufactured. RCA's development of a television station and regularly scheduled broadcasts followed the same formula: give Americans a reason to buy one of the new RCA television receivers that the company was also introducing at the World's Fair.

It is estimated that there were less than 400 operating television sets in New York City that could receive the inaugural transmission. But it could be seen on the new sets in the RCA World's Fair pavilion, where visitors were able to walk in front of a television camera and see themselves on a tiny black and white screen.

THE FIRST TELEVISED GAME

Less than three weeks after the World Fair opened, live sports made its debut on American television. On May 17, 1939, W2XBS took one camera to Columbia University's Baker Field and placed this camera on top of a twelve foot high platform that was built for the occasion on the third-base side of home plate. The event was the second game of a college baseball doubleheader, Princeton at Columbia. Scheduling on W2XBS was obviously very flexible in those days of television's infancy: there was no way to predict how long the first game of the doubleheader would last, so the start time for game two could be early or late.

Bill Stern became America's first television sportscaster when he opened the show, saying, "Good afternoon ladies and gentlemen. Welcome to the first telecast of a sporting event. I'm not sure what it is we're doing here, but I certainly hope

Figure 2.1 The first televised sporting event in the United States. NBC camera at Columbia University's Baker Field, May 17, 1939
Source: courtesy of University Archives, Columbia University in the City of New York

it turns out well for you people who are watching." Bill Stern was the host of NBC Radio's *Bill Stern's Sports Reel*, a show that began in 1937 and ran until 1956.

Stern knew radio, but his uncertainty with live television was warranted: no one had ever done live TV sports in the United States, and he had no way of seeing what was going out on the telecast to the small number of television sets in use in the New York City area. He had no monitor, just the microphone in front of him into which he gave his commentary of the game. Princeton won 2–1 in ten innings to sweep the doubleheader. They had won the first game 8–6.

Figure 2.2 Bill Stern
Source: courtesy American Sportscasters Association

3   THE MODERN ERA BEGINS

Spanning the globe to bring you the constant variety of sport. The thrill of victory and the agony of defeat.

(ABC's Wide World of Sports open)

Table 3.1 Chapter 3: The Rundown

- A new football league: Lamar Hunt and the AFL.
- The first national TV contract: the AFL on ABC.
- The Sports Broadcasting Act of 1961.
- ABC changes sports coverage.
- The Olympics come to American television.
- *ABC's Wide World of Sports.*
- The first instant replay.
- Cameras in the sky.

A NEW FOOTBALL LEAGUE

Watching the 1958 NFL Championship Game in his Houston, Texas, hotel room was Lamar Hunt, a 26-year-old former backup receiver for SMU and, more importantly, the son of oil billionaire H.L. Hunt. Lamar was in Houston to attend the Southwest Conference Holiday Basketball Tournament that December. He had spent a good portion of 1958 exploring the possibility of investing in either a professional baseball or football team, and what he saw on television in that hotel put him on a course that would change the sports landscape in the United States in less than ten years.

In the spring of 1958, Hunt had contacted NFL Commissioner Bert Bell and told him that he was interested in bringing an NFL franchise to Dallas. At the time the NFL was a twelve-team league, and Bell explained that his owners were not interested in expanding beyond that number until they could sort out their problems in Chicago where the league had two teams: the Bears and the Cardinals. The problem was that the Cardinals were perennial losers on the field (they averaged ten losses per season for the decade of the 1950s), and they were losing money. Bell suggested that Hunt contact the Cardinals' owners, Walter Wolfner and his wife, Violet Bidwill Wolfner, to see if they might be interested in selling the team to Hunt who could then move it to Dallas.

Mrs. Bidwill had inherited the Cardinals in 1947, when her first husband Charles Bidwill died. She married Wolfner, a St. Louis businessman, in 1949. Hunt talked with the Wolfners a number of times in 1958, but nothing substantive ever developed. The Wolfners did eventually stop trying to fight George Halas and his Chicago Bears for the hearts and wallets of Chicagoans, but not until two years later when they moved the Cardinals to Walter's home town of St. Louis in 1960. (The Cardinals subsequently left St. Louis in 1988 to play in Arizona, and their ownership has remained in the Bidwill family.)

Lamar Hunt had traveled to New York in the fall of 1958 to hear Branch Rickey, the former president and general manager of the Dodgers, talk about his plans to launch a third baseball league. Rickey was the man who had signed Jackie Robinson in 1947, to break the color barrier in major league baseball. Lamar Hunt never did invest in a baseball team, but he came away from those New York meetings with one very important concept: revenue sharing. Bill Veeck, who was the Chicago White Sox owner, and before that had owned the Cleveland Indians, raised the idea of revenue sharing. He said that any new league should pool all of its earnings, including all television rights payments, and divide the total among its clubs to keep them all profitable. That idea would resonate in Hunt's head and pay dividends in the very near future.

After watching "the Greatest Game Ever Played" on a black and white TV in his hotel room that Sunday night in late December, Hunt realized that his mind was made up. "My interest emotionally was always more in football," he said, "but clearly the '58 Colts–Giants game, sort of in my mind made me say, 'Well that's it. This sport has everything and it televises well.'" Lamar Hunt had a good sense of how important "televising well" would be for any American sport in the years to come, and had he not moved forward with the formation of a second professional

Figure 3.1 AFL founder Lamar Hunt, 1932–2006
Source: reprinted with permission of Getty Images

football league in the United States, the Super Bowl would have never come to be. The ultimate season-ending game would have remained the NFL Championship Game.

Hunt set up one last meeting with Walter Wolfner in February 1959, hoping against hope that he could convince him to sell the Cardinals, allowing the team to move to Texas. The meeting was in Florida where the Wolfners had a winter home. The surroundings may have been sunnier than Chicago, but, for Hunt, the result was the same: Walter Wolfner said he would not sell the team. He told Hunt that in fact a number of other wealthy investors including Bud Adams from Houston had approached him about selling the Cardinals, but that he had refused them all.

On his flight from Miami back to Dallas Hunt said, "A light bulb came on!" If there were all these investors who wanted to buy an NFL team for their home cities but who had been turned down, why not contact them and together start a new football league with all new teams? Hunt said that he asked a flight attendant for some paper, and before the plane landed in Dallas he had sketched out a document on three pages of American Airlines stationery that he called "Original 6 and First Year's Operations." It is the plan that would launch the American Football League. Hunt, the son of a billionaire with millions to spend on a professional football team, was flying coach.

Even though he now had his plan for a new league on paper, Lamar Hunt reached out once more to NFL Commissioner Bert Bell. This time Bell recommended that Hunt call Chicago Bears founder and owner George Halas. He was part of an NFL committee on expansion that had been formed in 1958, but never met. Halas told Hunt that expanding the NFL beyond twelve teams "is probably a long way off."

At that point Lamar Hunt started calling the list of investors he called his "Original 6" to suggest that if they couldn't get NFL franchises they should consider forming a new league with him. He convinced Bud Adams and four others to join him in what Hunt called "The Foolish Club," foolish for going up against the long established NFL that had gained new momentum from the success of the 1958 championship. Before their first league meeting on August 14, 1959, in Chicago, each prospective new owner had to put up just $100,000 as a performance bond and back that up with another $25,000 in earnest money. The six original cities would be Dallas, where Hunt would finally get his professional team, plus Houston, Denver, Los Angeles, New York, and Minneapolis. The only two of these that had NFL franchises at the time were Los Angeles and New York. The Los Angeles owner was Barron Hilton of the Hilton Hotel chain who named his team the "Chargers" because Hilton owned the Carte Blanche *charge* card company. The Chargers played just one season in Los Angeles before moving to San Diego in 1961.

A week later the original six christened their new venture the "American Football League." Ralph Wilson of Buffalo signed on as the league's seventh franchise on October 28, 1959, and William Sullivan of Boston became the league's eighth owner on November 22, 1958, the date of the AFL's first player draft. The draft went thirty-three rounds and was held in secret. Each of the eight teams got one territorial pick to select a top college player from their area who could draw ticket-buying fans, plus up to thirty-two other players who they would attempt to sign.

When the NFL saw how serious Hunt was with his plans for a rival league, they did offer him an expansion franchise for Dallas. However, by that time, late in 1959,

Hunt said he had "sunk too much money into this," and had made too many commitments to his fellow "Foolish Club" owners to consider accepting an NFL offer. So the NFL granted their Dallas franchise to Clint Murchison and Bedford Wynne, who founded the Cowboys franchise that would begin play in the fall of 1960 and compete against Lamar Hunt's Dallas Texans.

The NFL couldn't derail Hunt from moving ahead with the American Football League, but the older league did entice the AFL ownership group in Minneapolis to take an NFL franchise instead. So on January 27, 1960, that group backed out of the AFL and one day later at the NFL owners meeting in Miami was granted a charter as the Minnesota Vikings. It didn't take the AFL long to find a replacement to keep the league at eight teams: on January 30, 1959, a group from Oakland, California, headed by cement contractor Y. Charles "Chet" Soda signed up. The nickname they chose for the team was the Oakland Señors, but that was quickly dropped in favor of "Raiders."

THE FIRST NATIONAL TV CONTRACT: THE AFL ON ABC

The single most important factor in making the AFL's inaugural season in 1960 a reality was the rights agreement the new league made with the ABC television network. Signed on June 9, 1960, it was for five years of weekly live games plus the AFL Championship Game and an AFL All-Star game. ABC contracted to pay a total of $8.5 million dollars over five years to the AFL, which divided the revenue equally among its eight clubs in accordance with the revenue-sharing concept Lamar Hunt had begun considering after his baseball meeting back in 1958. That came to just $1.7 million dollars per year for the league. Divided eight ways each team got $212,500 per season, enough when combined with ticket sales and other revenue to make the AFL solvent in its first year.

This was the first television football contract between an American network and a professional league, not with the individual teams, for a full season or more of games. At that point in time each NFL team was negotiating its own local, regional, and national television packages, some in concert with one or two other teams. For example the New York Giants, in the NFL's largest market, were making $350,000 per year in television revenue each year, ten times the $35,000 that the Green Bay Packers earned in TV rights in the league's smallest market.

The NFL owners were sold on the wisdom of also adopting the revenue-sharing model by their new commissioner, Pete Rozelle, who in 1961 signed a two-year, $9.3 million contract with CBS that would share television monies equally among the fourteen NFL franchises. (The league had grown from twelve to fourteen teams with the addition of the Dallas Cowboys and the Minnesota Vikings.) However, the contract with CBS was challenged and later nullified in federal court for violating provisions of the Sherman Antitrust Act, which was interpreted as effectively blocking individually owned teams from uniting as one entity to negotiate a television contract. Each team was an independent company not owned by the NFL, and the local TV stations that had separate deals with teams did not like the idea of being left out of the rights equation.

The AFL television rights contract with ABC was not challenged in court even though it was exactly the same type of agreement: a contract for sponsored broadcasts between a league of individually owned teams and a television network. The difference however was that no AFL teams existed before the contract with ABC was executed, and none had any pre-existing agreements with local television stations to broadcast their games. So there were no claims of antitrust violations because no station would lose any of its existing business to ABC as a result of a network rights contract.

To make the new NFL contract with CBS a reality, Commissioner Rozelle would have to take the extra step of lobbying Congress to grant professional leagues, his in particular, an exemption from antitrust laws for all television rights agreements.

THE SPORTS BROADCASTING ACT OF 1961

Backed by the considerable political clout of his powerful team owners, Pete Rozelle's lobbying mission to Washington was a quick success. Less than three months after his efforts began, both the House and Senate had approved Public Law 87–331 and sent it to President John F. Kennedy for signature in September of 1961.

The Sports Broadcasting Act of 1961, as it came to be known, exempted any professional football, baseball, basketball, or hockey league in the United States from antitrust regulation, in any contracts they would make for the "sponsored telecasting" of their games. In 1966, the Act was amended to also cover the mergers of two or more professional football leagues as long as the combination of their operations would increase and not decrease the total number of clubs operating. This helped pave the way for the merger of the NFL and AFL later in the decade that made the Super Bowl possible.

In a *New York Times* article following Rozelle's death in 1996, former Cleveland Browns owner Art Modell said, "Congress sanctioning the single network deal is the most significant thing Pete ever did."

Armed with the new antitrust exemption, Pete Rozelle went back to CBS in the fall of 1961, and they crafted a new television contract that would begin in the 1962–63 season and pay the NFL $4.65 million for the first year's rights. That swelled to $14.1 million for the 1964–65 season. The money and national exposure that this contract with CBS brought the league is arguably one of the most important milestones that made the NFL the hugely successful business that it is today.

Additional sections of and amendments to the Sports Broadcasting Act of 1961 allowed professional leagues to "black out" television broadcasts in the home markets of their teams, addressing the fears of team owners who thought that people would choose to sit at home and watch games on television instead of buying tickets. The Act also states that any professional football league that may choose to televise its games on Friday nights or Saturdays, thereby competing with high school or college football, would no longer be covered by the antitrust exemption.

EXCERPTS FROM THE SPORTS BROADCASTING ACT OF 1961

The antitrust laws, as defined in section 1 of the Act of October 15, 1914, as amended (38 Stat. 730) [15 U.S.C. 12], or in the Federal Trade Commission Act, as amended (38 Stat. 717) [15 U.S.C. 41 et seq.], shall not apply to any joint agreement by or among persons engaging in or conducting the organized professional team sports of football, baseball, basketball, or hockey, by which any league of clubs participating in professional football, baseball, basketball, or hockey contests sells or otherwise transfers all or any part of the rights of such league's member clubs in the sponsored telecasting of the games of football, baseball, basketball, or hockey, as the case may be, engaged in or conducted by such clubs.

(In addition, such laws shall not apply to a joint agreement by which the member clubs of two or more professional football leagues, which are exempt from income tax under section 501(c)(6) of the Internal Revenue Code of 1986 [26 U.S.C. 501 (c)(6)], combine their operations in expanded single league so exempt from income tax, if such agreement increases rather than decreases the number of professional football clubs so operating, and the provisions of which are directly relevant thereto.)

Intercollegiate and Interscholastic Football Contest Limitations

The first sentence of section 1291 of this title shall not apply to any joint agreement described in such section which permits the telecasting of all or a substantial part of any professional football game on any Friday after six o'clock postmeridian or on any Saturday during the period beginning on the second Friday in September and ending on the second Saturday in December in any year from any telecasting station located within seventy-five miles of the game site of any intercollegiate or interscholastic football contest scheduled to be played on such a date if—

1 such intercollegiate football contest is between institutions of higher learning both of which confer degrees upon students following completion of sufficient credit hours to equal a four-year course, or

2 in the case of an interscholastic football contest, such contest is between secondary schools, both of which are accredited or certified under the laws of the State or States in which they are situated and offer courses continuing through the twelfth grade of the standard school curriculum, or the equivalent, and

3 such intercollegiate or interscholastic football contest and such game site were announced through publication in a newspaper of general circulation prior to August 1 of such year as being regularly scheduled for such day and place.

ABC CHANGES SPORTS COVERAGE

The AFL proved to be the innovator in many more ways than how they structured their television contracts. "We were selling excitement and entertainment," said league founder Lamar Hunt, "we had to be different. We couldn't afford to be dull." So when the AFL began play on September 9, 1960, with the Denver Broncos visiting the Boston Patriots at Boston University's Nickerson Field, the league set out to differentiate itself from the NFL. (The Broncos won that inaugural game 13–10 over the Patriots before an announced crowd of 27,597.)

The AFL incorporated the two-point conversion as an option after touchdowns. The NFL didn't add this element of drama and decision-making to its games until 1994. They also put their players' names on the backs of jerseys to help fans identify who was carrying the ball or had just made the tackle, without having to consult a printed program. And perhaps more important than any innovation or rules change, the AFL opened its arms to talented African-American players in far greater numbers than the NFL teams of the era had done up to that point. This helped create what sportswriters of the day described as a "wide open" style of play that favored speed and athleticism, and that in turn made for a more exciting television product.

The ABC television network developed its own style of "AFL coverage" in conjunction with the league that emphasized excitement and entertainment. The sparse crowds of the early years would be grouped around the 50-yard line so that

THE OLYMPICS COME TO AMERICAN TELEVISION

The Olympics has become such an overwhelming and powerful television presence in the past several decades that it may seem hard to believe that the Games were not televised in the United States until 1960. The Winter Olympics were staged in Squaw Valley, California, that year and ABC signed a contract with the organizers to purchase the US television rights for $50,000. But ABC stepped away from the deal, choosing not to spend the additional money it would take to produce coverage from a remote ski resort and transmit the programs from there to San Francisco for broadcast on the network.

CBS picked up the rights and televised thirteen hours of coverage from Thursday February 18 through Sunday February 28, 1960. The first show was a half-hour of the opening ceremonies; fifteen minutes of edited highlights were shown each weeknight at 11:15 p.m. Eastern, and CBS was live for one to three hours per weekend day and for the women's figure skating finals on Tuesday evening, February 23. The shows were hosted by Walter Cronkite, the CBS News reporter who was still two years away from being named anchorman of *The CBS Evening News with Walter Cronkite*, a position he held until 1981, becoming known during that tenure as "the most trusted man in America." The reporters CBS assigned to join Cronkite were Jim McKay, who had not yet left to join ABC where he would become the face of Olympics telecasts in the United States; Harry Reasoner, who would later host *60 Minutes* for CBS and then anchor the nightly news on ABC; and Olympic figure skating champion Dick Button, who won gold medals in 1948 and 1952. In 2010 at the age of 80, Dick Button continued his Olympic commentary at the Winter Games in Vancouver on NBC.

CBS originally had no overt interest in covering an international winter sports competition: the chairman of the network William S. Paley stepped in to replace ABC as the American broadcaster only as a favor to an old friend, Walt Disney. The Squaw Valley Olympic organizers had asked Disney to provide entertainment for the event, and then sought his company's additional help with ticketing, parking, and security, expertise that the Walt Disney Company had gained in operating Disneyland since 1955. It was Disney who approached Paley when ABC backed out, helping to ensure that there would be television coverage of the event, including of course the ceremonies that Disney was producing for the Winter Games.

The fourteen shows that CBS broadcast from Squaw Valley in February, 1960, were enough to open the network's eyes to the possibilities that the Olympics presented for compelling programming, and to whet the appetite of American viewers. The great potential for the success of the Olympics on television was hinted at by the *New York Times*, which wrote on February 21, 1960, that spectators at Squaw Valley had a "more dramatic over-all view of the ski jumping" than anyone watching on television, but that "the slalom provided more effective close-ups on the screen than were available to the crowds lining the slopes." "More effective close-ups" of American and international athletes in action speaks to the ability of television to tell stories and bring pictures into your home that would be otherwise inaccessible.

Encouraged by how well their shows from Squaw Valley had been received, CBS paid $394,000 for the rights to televise the Summer Olympics from Rome in August and September of 1960. That's nearly eight times the $50,000 price paid for the Winter Olympic rights earlier in the year, but they were rewarded with plenty of stories to tell. Wilma Rudolph, a polio victim at an early age and the twentieth child in a family of twenty-two from Tennessee, won three gold medals in the 100 meters, 200 meters and 4 × 100 meter relay; Cassius Clay, who would go on to win the world heavyweight boxing championship as Muhammad Ali, was eighteen years old when he won the gold medal in Rome in the light heavyweight division; American Rafer Johnson won the Olympic decathlon in the 1960 Games; and the American men's basketball team led by Oscar Robertson, Jerry West, and Jerry Lucas crushed the competition and won gold.

CBS programmed twenty hours of Olympic coverage from Rome, all of it hosted by Jim McKay, who wasn't even in Italy. A CBS crew of approximately forty was in Rome producing the events and recording them to videotapes that were flown out of Rome every night to New York's Idlewild Airport (now JFK International), where a messenger would pick them up and deliver them still cold from the plane's cargo hold to Grand Central Station. There McKay wrote his leads and recorded the show opens, bridges, and closes needed for each evening's telecast. No shows from the Rome Olympics were live—there were no commercial communications satellites orbiting the earth in 1960.

Roone Arledge, who would become the president of ABC Sports and ABC News, was 28 years old in 1960. He had not yet gotten his first job at ABC, but he became enthralled with the Olympics. In his autobiography *Roone*, Arledge said that, while watching the CBS shows from Squaw Valley, he sensed that "there was a magic in seeing the divided world come together in sport." He said he particularly took note of the figure skating competition with its "spotlight on single performers, the limited time spans, and the suspense of waiting for the judge's decisions . . . that made figure skating a made-for-television event."

Roone Arledge was producing the Shari Lewis puppet show on the local NBC station in New York when he was hired by Ed Scherick at Sports Programs, Inc. to work on the new NCAA football package that Scherick was producing for ABC in 1960. A year later Scherick sold his company to ABC, bringing with him Chester R. "Chet" Simmons, who had worked with him since he founded the company in 1957, and Arledge. The small Sports Programs, Inc. group became ABC Sports, Scherick was rewarded with an appointment as ABC's vice president of sales, and Simmons became the first executive producer of the new ABC sports. Later in his career, Chet Simmons became president of ESPN in its early years, then commissioner of the now-defunct USFL.

Despite the fiasco that ABC had caused by backing out of the Squaw Valley deal in 1960, Arledge was convinced that ABC had to get into the Olympics business to secure the future of its fledgling sports division. In 1962, Arledge and Simmons convinced the network's vice president of programming, Tom Moore, that they should bid for the 1964 Winter Olympics in Innsbruck, Austria.

Together Arledge and Simmons boarded a plane for Austria and returned with a broadcast rights agreement for $500,000, which the Austrians insisted had to be secured with a bank guarantee because of how ABC had backed out of its 1960 Olympic commitment. Arledge and Simmons got the necessary approval from the ABC board of directors, opening the door for ABC to become the "network of the Olympics" from 1964 through to 1988. During that stretch, ABC Sports televised six Winter Games and four Summer Olympics, concluding with 94.5 hours of coverage from the 1988 Winter Olympics at Calgary for which the network paid $309 million in broadcast rights. In the years since, NBC has taken on the Olympic mantle, and the US television rights fees have continued to soar, reaching

Figure 3.3 ABC Sports innovator, Roone Arledge, 1931–2002
Source: reprinted with permission of Getty Images

a combined $2.2 billion for the 2010 Winter Games in Vancouver and the 2012 Summer Games in London. Compare that figure with the combined $444,000 that CBS paid for the Winter and Summer Games in 1960, and you can begin to assess how the power of the Olympics as television programming has grown.

The 1964 Olympic Summer Games in Tokyo marked a major milestone for all of sports television. It became the first major sporting event carried live via satellite around the world. Less than two months before the Tokyo games' opening ceremony on October 10, 1964, NASA had launched the Syncom 3 communications satellite, which was built by Hughes Aircraft. It was the first ever to be placed into a geo-stationary orbit, which meant it would orbit the earth once per day, keeping pace with the earth rotating below its position 22,300 miles above the Pacific Ocean at 180 degrees longitude. As a fixed point in the sky, television signals could be continuously transmitted to it from Japan or any uplink in Asia, and received on the West Coast of the US for re-transmission and broadcast. The transmission worked the same from North America to Asia.

A year later, in 1965, Intelsat 1, nicknamed Early Bird, was placed in geo-synchronous orbit over the Atlantic, making live television and telephone communications possible between North American and Europe. Also built by Hughes Aircraft technology, Early Bird was used to transmit ABC's live coverage of the 1968 Olympic Winter Games in Grenoble, France.

Once television audiences in the United States and around the world got to see the Olympics, the stature and nature of the event changed. It became an international spectacle of sportsmanship and politics with a huge economic impact from the world television and sponsorship rights. Because of the millions upon millions of viewers it would reach, the Olympics also became a platform for those who might want to make their political messages heard in virtually every country of the world. It would never again be a simple gathering of athletes from a relatively small number of nations whose sole purpose was athletic competition. (We'll have more about the political and economic impact of the Olympics in later chapters.)

ABC'S WIDE WORLD OF SPORTS

International sports events would become the backbone of a new series that ABC launched in 1961 as a twenty-week summer fill-in show. Over the next four decades, *ABC's Wide World of Sports* would introduce Americans to the World Cup soccer final, the Indianapolis 500, the Daytona 500, British Open golf, the 24 Hours of Le Mans, the Iditarod Sled Dog Race, along with international figure skating, gymnastics, track and field, and world championship boxing events. In its run, which ended in 1998, the series did 4967 events in over one hundred different sports from fifty-three countries and forty-six states.

It was Ed Scherick's idea to do a series with a unique flavor that would feature a myriad of events from around the world, the lesser known and the unfamiliar athletic competitions that were outside the realm of football, baseball, basketball, and hockey. It would help fill ABC's need for some summer sports programming for 1961. The NCAA football package filled Saturday afternoons and the new AFL games were the anchor on Sundays in the fall, but the only sports ABC had after football season were a Dodgers and Giants baseball package, *Saturday Night Fights*, and a bowling series called *Make that Spare*. Scherick put the concept in Roone Arledge's hands, and he ran with it.

When Arledge was producing the puppet show for the local NBC television station he had learned that NBC's corporate library kept the *New York Times* archive on microfilm. His idea was to go through the archive to find all the obscure sporting events that he could find results for in the newspaper, but that weren't being televised in the United States. Arledge feared that he might be recognized if he visited his former employers, so he sent his young production assistant, Chuck Howard, over to NBC's 30 Rockefeller Plaza headquarters to scan through the microfilm. Within forty-eight hours he had Howard's list, a "compendium of worldwide sporting events" with their dates and locales.

With the mantra "if something is visually exciting, let's try it," Arledge set off on a quest for the television rights to everything from baton twirling to Irish hurling.

One of his first stops near the end of 1960 was just a few blocks away in Manhattan at the New York Athletic Club, where the Amateur Athletic Union (AAU) was holding its annual meeting. For a small fee upfront and a guarantee of $50,000 after the series debuted, Arledge bought the exclusive US rights to televise every AAU competition to be held in 1961, including the US vs. Soviet Union track and field meet scheduled for that July in Moscow.

The premiere of *ABC's Wide World of Sports* on the Saturday afternoon of April 29, 1961, combined live coverage of two AAU track and field events: the Penn Relays in Philadelphia and the Drake Relays from Des Moines, Iowa. Making his ABC debut as the host at the Penn Relays was Jim McKay, who Arledge had hired away from CBS for $1000 per episode.

Jim McKay recalled that day while taping the *ABC's Wide World of Sports 30th Anniversary Special*, a show that aired on ESPN in 1991. He said, "It was an overcast day in Philadelphia at Franklin Field. Rain the night before had knocked out half of our black and white cameras. The track in those days was made of cinders at the Penn Relays."

"Half the cameras" meant that only three of ABC's six were working. No producer or director who has worked in the last three decades would ever try to cover an event the size of an outdoor track and field meet with just three cameras, but ABC had no choice that day, and they made it work.

The show was going to be called *ABC's World of Sports*, but six days before its premiere, "Wide" was added to the title. "Wide" certainly did not describe its audience in its first several weeks in May and June of 1961; the show just wasn't attracting very many viewers, and McKay said, "I think we were close to being taken off the air." But the event that helped the series turn the corner was that US–Soviet track and field competition from Moscow in late July that was part of the AAU package Roone Arledge had negotiated several months earlier.

Figure 3.4 *ABC's Wide World of Sports* debuted in 1961 and was a presence on Saturday afternoons until 1998

Source: reprinted with permission of ABC Television Group

It was the height of the Cold War between the United States and the Soviet Union in 1961. An American U2 high-altitude spy plane had been shot down in Russian air space in May of 1960, and its pilot, Francis Gary Powers, was being held prisoner in the USSR. At the United Nations General Assembly in New York in October of 1960, Soviet Premier Nikita Khrushchev took off his shoe and pounded it on a table shouting "we will bury you!" The "Iron Curtain" was a heavily guarded border between the Eastern European countries that were under Soviet military control, and the republics and democracies of Western Europe. The very fact that American athletes could go "behind the Iron Curtain" to compete in Moscow was international news, and the ability to see them in the Soviet capital, to get a rare glimpse into what was considered "enemy territory," attracted attention in the US among sports fans and average citizens alike to the coverage on ABC's Wide World of Sports.

When ABC's team of twenty-five producers and technicians arrived in Moscow with their twenty tons of television equipment, however, they found that the AAU had apparently not told the Soviet organizers that an American television network would be televising the event back to the states. Arledge credits the political and sports connections of their Russian guide Roman Kislev for working out the agreement that allowed the broadcast to proceed.

The critical and ratings success of this US vs. Soviet event convinced ABC to renew Wide World for a full fifty-two weeks in 1962. And when the new season debuted, the show came on the air with a new open that captured its essential mission and has been remembered by generations of viewers:

Spanning the globe to bring you the constant variety of sport. The thrill of victory and the agony of defeat. This is ABC's Wide World of Sports.

Roone Arledge said that he wrote the script on a flight back to New York from an assignment in London in late 1961. It replaced the original show open, which wasn't nearly as poetic or gender-neutral:

Sports, in its unending variety, unfolds on ABC's Wide World of Sports. Capturing the sight and sound, the emotion, the beauty and history-making achievements, wherever men gather to compete in this great wide world of athletics.

Over its thirty-eight years the "constant variety" of Wide World included sumo wrestling, figure-eight stock car racing, demolition derbies, the Cheyenne Frontier Days Rodeo, ice skaters jumping over barrels, and one of the favorites that became a hallmark of the series, the Acapulco cliff diving competition. Roone Arledge said that he first heard about this event when he and Jim McKay were in Mexico in 1961 to cover a tennis event. Arledge met with the promoter of the cliff diving who said he would sell the US television rights to ABC for $100,000. That figure was double what had been paid in 1960 for the rights to the entire Winter Olympics, so Arledge flew home to New York.

McKay stayed behind to complete the tennis show, and a few days later he called Arledge to say, "We got the cliff diving." McKay explained that he had gone directly to the divers themselves, and they had agreed to appear on TV for ten dollars a dive.

There were countless milestones along the way in the thirty-eight years of ABC's Wide World of Sports, including the first underwater camera at a swimming event—

the 1961 National AAU Swimming and Diving Championships; the first European sports event televised live via satellite to the US—the 24 Hour Grand Prix of Endurance from Le Mans, France, in 1965; the first live boxing championship from Europe—Muhammad Ali vs. Henry Cooper from London in 1966 for the world heavyweight title; the first sports coverage from Cuba since Fidel Castro's takeover twelve years earlier—the US vs. Cuba volleyball matches from Havana in 1971; and, also in 1971, the "ping pong diplomacy" table tennis matches from Beijing, China, that were a hallmark of then President Richard Nixon's efforts to open avenues of communication between the US and China.

The impact that *ABC's Wide World of Sports* made on American television cannot be underestimated. For millions who knew only the major sports, it broadened their horizons and interests. It helped increase awareness and curiosity about what people in different states and different countries did for competition and entertainment. One of the universal truths that make sports popular across the generations is that people care about people. And *Wide World* emphasized the personalities of individual athletes in each event. The people-oriented commentary that Roone Arledge developed on *Wide World* came to be known as "Up Close and Personal," which has been an important thread in the coverage of the Olympics and many other sports telecasts large and small ever since.

THE FIRST INSTANT REPLAY

The defining technology of the sports we now watch on television is arguably "instant replay." We count on replays from multiple angles to immediately tell us if a receiver was in or out of bounds, if an outfielder made the catch or trapped the ball, or what caused a massive wreck in an auto race. Replay settles arguments and starts new ones. It is a fixture in every sports broadcast of every sport. But not one event that aired on American television from 1939 until the end of 1963 ever included one instant replay. Twenty-four years of sports broadcasts and zero replays.

The first videotape machines that were introduced by the Ampex Corporation in 1956 had serious limitations. For example, you could play a tape back only on the machine that had recorded the video. At first tapes weren't interchangeable because different machines had incompatible speeds and record/playback heads that were not perfectly matched. To play any video back, the two-inch reel-to-reel machines required a ten second "pre-roll" in order for the picture and audio to lock up. Built from two huge pieces the size of a large freezer that weighed 1200 pounds, they were anything but portable, making their use anywhere but in a studio control room all but impossible.

The first time a taped replay was used in an American sports telecast was on November 25, 1961, during halftime of the Syracuse vs. Boston College football game, which was part of ABC's new live NCAA football package. A highlight from the first half of play was rolled in during the halftime studio report from the ABC control room in New York. Roone Arledge said that when he saw that video play back, even though it was primitive, "you could see the future."

Credit for the first instant replay goes to Tony Verna, who was the director of the Army–Navy football game on CBS on December 7, 1963. Verna had been a free-lancer on the CBS crew that produced the 1960 Summer Olympics from Rome, and it was there that the seed of his idea began to germinate. In his book *Instant Replay: The Day that Changed Sports Forever*, Tony Verna explains how he learned to use the second audio track on the tapes being recorded in Rome as a way to leave cues for the technicians and producers to whom the day's coverage was shipped by airplane every night. His goal was to make it easier for the New York crew to find the right scenes and edit the shows for air, because there were no digital time-code readers on the machines, only mechanical tape counters. Verna said however that most of the technicians at CBS ignored his audio cues and just searched through the tapes themselves.

Just three years later at age 29, he was directing college football games for CBS, and was searching for a way to improve the shows for viewers at home in the dead time between plays. He convinced his bosses to let him take one of the fourteen videotape machines that CBS had in its New York control room with him to Philadelphia for the Army–Navy game at Franklin Field. His idea was to have the tape operator in his truck put one audio tone on the second audio channel (which could be heard only in the TV truck, not at home) when the team with the ball went into its huddle, and two quick tones on the tape when they broke the huddle. Verna figured that, when he heard the two tones on playback, there would be just about ten seconds before the snap, the ten seconds he needed for the video on the tape to lock up so he could put it on the air.

Tony Verna told his producer, Bill Creasy, about his plan on the train ride to Philadelphia. The Army–Navy game had increased importance that season: a special tribute to President John F. Kennedy was being produced as part of the day's coverage. The president had planned to attend the traditional rivalry game between the service academies, but he was assassinated in Dallas on November 22, 1963, and the Army–Navy contest had been postponed until the first week of December out of respect for the fallen leader and to allow for network coverage of his state funeral.

The play-by-play commentator assigned to the game, Lindsey Nelson, says he didn't hear about Verna's replay idea until they were in a cab together on the way to the stadium. Verna says Nelson's first reaction upon hearing the plan was, "What? You're going to do what?" It would be Nelson's job to explain what the audience was seeing for the very first time, helping them comprehend that the same team hadn't scored again on the very next play.

Verna wasn't surprised that the CBS technicians in New York had shipped him the least reliable of their fourteen videotape machines, but he was troubled by the quality of the only reel of tape they sent. It had leaders physically spliced into it for I Love Lucy shows and lots of Duz detergent ads. Apparently, at $300 per reel, CBS was unwilling to give their young college football director a new tape.

During the game Verna was keyed on the Navy quarterback, Roger Staubach, who was an All American and destined for a hall of fame career in the NFL. But Staubach didn't have a very good game, and the technicians in the CBS truck were having so many problems with the tape machine and the used tape, that it was impossible to get anything cued up that could be played back into the live telecast. Finally in the fourth quarter the Army quarterback, Rollie Stichweh, ran off tackle for a touchdown, and Verna told his play-by-play commentator, "Lindsey we've got it. Go!" The truck cut to the black and white replay in real time, not slow motion, and Nelson said, "This is not live. Ladies and gentlemen, Army did not score again!"

That was the only replay they were able to manage in the entire game, but Tony Verna and his team had changed sports television. A month later he was directing the 1964 Cotton Bowl and his lead commentator was Pat Summerall, the former

New York Giants kicker who was doing his first play by play assignment. It was during that Cotton Bowl telecast on CBS that Summerall coined the term, "instant replay." No sports telecast has ever been the same since.

CAMERAS IN THE SKY

One of the distinctions that set the major sporting events apart from all the rest can be identified by just looking up. Today it's a given that, if there's a blimp overhead, you are at one of the very special events that will be attracting huge audiences, at the venue and on television.

The tradition began at the 1960 Orange Bowl Classic in Miami, and it was the idea of CBS producer Frank Chirkinian who had one of the most innovative minds in sports television. "There was already a blimp flying over the Orange Bowl," said Chirkinian, "so I thought what if I get a camera up there?" He said that when he sought approval for the added expense, the president of CBS Sports asked him how long he planned to use the shot from the blimp. "When I said ten seconds, he said 'are you crazy?' And I said 'yes, that's why you hired me!'"

Chirkinian's first producing assignment had been the 1958 PGA Championship on CBS, and, in 1959, he produced his first of thirty-eight consecutive years of The Masters, all on CBS. He incorporated cameras on blimps into his golf coverage along with cameras mounted on cranes, roving reporters, and microphones everywhere. It was Chirkinian's idea to have the inside of the cup at every hole painted white so it could be seen better on television. And it wasn't until he suggested it that golf scores were listed relative to how many strokes they were below or above par. Before Frank Chirkinian all golf scores were presented as total strokes for the round or tournament.

Frank Chirkinian was elected to the World Golf Hall of Fame shortly before his death at age 84 in March of 2011.

Figure 3.5 Frank Chirkinian, 1926–2011
Source: CBS/David Russell/Landov

SUMMARY

The founding of the American Football League by Lamar Hunt helped launch a new era for sports television in the 1960s. The AFL signed the first national television contract with a network, the league instituted the sharing of TV revenues equally among owners, which protected small market teams, and the innovations that it developed with its first TV partner, ABC Sports, made for more exciting, entertaining programs.

The NFL followed suit and signed a network television package with CBS for the 1961 season, but the deal was found to be in violation of antitrust rules against independently owned companies (the teams) functioning as a single entity in contract negotiations. An all-out lobbying blitz by NFL Commissioner Pete Rozelle led to passage of the Sports Broadcasting Act of 1961, which exempts professional football, baseball, basketball, and hockey leagues from antitrust complaints when their respective teams work together as one on television rights contracts.

The first Olympic coverage on American television was in 1960 from the Winter Olympics in Squaw Valley, California and the Summer Games in Rome. The extent of the programming was minimal and the rights fees were small, but the potential for great stories and dramatic competition was immediately evident to visionaries like Roone Arledge, who was one of the founding producers of ABC Sports. Arledge also reached beyond America's borders to add variety and interest to ABC's *Wide World of Sports*, which he created in 1961.

The early 1960s was when sports fans saw the first instant replay on television, during the annual Army–Navy football game in December of 1963, and the first live pictures from a blimp, at the 1960 Orange Bowl Classic in Miami.

DISCUSSION TOPICS/ASSIGNMENTS

1   Compare the contributions of the following sports television innovators and describe how each has played a role in the development of the sports programs you watch today:

Roone Arledge
Chet Simmons
Tony Verna
Frank Chirkinian

2   Do a short biography on one of the innovators listed above, including how your subject got his start in television.

3   Discuss how different the NFL would be today if the league had granted Lamar Hunt the expansion franchise he originally wanted, and Hunt had not founded the AFL. Would there be as many teams? In the same or different cities? Would the NFL Championship Game have any or all of the characteristics of the Super Bowl?

4   Study the development of Major League Baseball, the NBA, the NHL, boxing, tennis, or golf as television sports in the 1960s. How did coverage of the sport evolve and who were the pioneers who made lasting changes?

4 THE PRO FOOTBALL ASCENDANCY

Football, as the pros go at it, is a game of special brilliance, played by brilliant specialists. . . . So precise is the teamwork that a single mistake by one man can destroy the handiwork of ten. . . . Action piles upon action, thrill upon guaranteed thrill, and all with such a bewildering speed that at the end the fans are literally limp. . . . No other sport offers so much to so many. Boxing's heroes are papier mache champions, hockey is gang warfare, basketball is for gamblers and Australia is too far to travel to see a decent tennis match. Even baseball, the sportswriters' "national pastime," can be a slow-motion bore.

(Time Magazine, December 21, 1962)

Table 4.1 Chapter 4: The Rundown

- Pro football becomes America's favorite sport.
- NFL–AFL merger creates the Super Bowl.
- Horse-trading on Capitol Hill creates a new NFL team.
- The first Super Bowl airs on CBS and NBC.
- The lasting impact of the New York Jets victory in Super Bowl III.
- The infamous "Heidi game" on NBC.
- The birth of NFL *Monday Night Football*.
- The NFL *Today* changes sports studio shows forever.
- NFL Films: the best promotional vehicle in the history of sports TV.
- The NFL and television were made for each other.

Time Magazine called professional football "the sport of the '60's" in its December, 1962, cover story that featured Green Bay Packers' head coach Vince Lombardi. This proclamation came at the end of the first season of the National Football League's new contract with CBS and after the American Football League had been televised by ABC for three consecutive seasons. The sport was being embraced by millions who watched each Sunday in the fall to see teams of "brilliant specialists" meeting in high-stakes struggles filled with drama, intensity, good guys vs. bad guys, and personal stories of achievement, disappointment, and redemption.

Professional football was making its move to center stage in the early 1960s when the other American sports referred to in the *Time* Magazine article were not at their strongest, and did not have the regular national television exposure on two networks that the NFL and AFL were receiving. Boxing would have to wait until 1964 for Muhammad Ali, its most charismatic and controversial champion, to re-light its spark by winning the world heavyweight championship. He, Joe Frazier, and George Foreman would prove to be more than "papier mache champions." Bobby Orr and Wayne Gretzky made hockey much more than "gang warfare," but Orr didn't play his first NHL game until 1966, and Gretzky debuted twelve years later. Basketball in the early 1960s was emerging from the college game-fixing scandals of the 1950s. The Boston Celtics' string of consecutive NBA titles, which reached four in 1962 and would extend to eight in a row, was helping basketball turn the page. In tennis, Australian men did dominate the late 1950s and 60s. After Tony Trabert had won the US Open in 1955, there was a sixteen year stretch before another American man would win: Stan Smith in 1971. And American tennis fans would have to wait until 1966 for Californian Billie Jean King to win Wimbledon and become the world's top-ranked woman player.

Baseball had the biggest names in all of sport during the 1960s. The 1961 home run race between Yankee teammates Roger Maris and Mickey Mantle had captured the nation's imagination. Willie Mays, Henry Aaron, Duke Snider, Stan Musial, and Sandy Koufax were just a few of the stars who were household names in the 1960s. But NBC's *Game of the Week* was the only national spotlight for live baseball action, and it was just one game every Saturday that rotated among all the teams. That meant that you might see one of the big stars one weekend, then not again for several weeks. And, on television, the pace and visual impact of baseball could not compete with professional football.

In October 1965, the Harris Poll asked a sampling of Americans "What is your favorite sport?" The answer came back "pro football," and it has remained at the top every year since, expanding its margin over every other sport. In surveys prior to the fall of 1965, baseball had always been at the top. This polling result signaled a sea change in the passions and preferences of American sports fans that was fueled by the "action piling upon action," the "thrill upon guaranteed thrill," and the "bewildering speed" of the NFL and AFL on television.

THE NFL–AFL MERGER CREATES THE SUPER BOWL

The NFL and the AFL had a tenuous co-existence during the early 1960s, each league with its own television contract, its own separate draft, and its own growing legion of fans. The NFL may actually have inadvertently provided the AFL with an opportunity to attract a larger audience because of its TV blackout policy. The NFL never televised a team's home games in that team's home television market. That meant the only game fans in and around those NFL blackout cities could watch on a Sunday afternoon was the AFL game on ABC, then on NBC from 1964 onward. New viewers became new fans.

The two leagues competed for stars coming out of college, which gave the players more bargaining power. Teams with high draft choices adopted the practice of "baby-sitting" the players they intended to select, sending assistant coaches or representatives to be at their side on draft day to make sure they didn't sign with the team from the rival league that was also drafting them. However, once a player did sign there was an unwritten rule that the leagues would not raid each other's rosters for talent that was under contract.

The competition between the AFL and the NFL was most noticeable in the two metropolitan areas in which each league had a team: New York with the NFL Giants and AFL Jets, and the San Francisco Bay Area where the NFL 49ers competed for fans with the AFL Oakland Raiders. Every other team in each league had pro football exclusivity in its home market. In fact, when the idea of combining the two leagues was first raised among NFL owners, one of their pre-conditions was that the AFL would have to move the Jets and Raiders to other cities in order to restore the Giants' and 49ers' market exclusivity in New York and the San Francisco Bay Area respectively.

Any hopes that the NFL owners had of forcing AFL franchises to move were dashed by the growing popularity of the Jets and Raiders in their regions, and, in the case of New York, by two other important factors. The Jets moved into brand-new Shea Stadium in September of 1964, and Jets owner Sonny Werblin, a noted impresario who had been a talent agent with MCA, signed Joe Namath in 1965. Shea Stadium had five tiers that sat close to 60,000 fans for football, and at the time it was the most modern football stadium in the United States. Namath became such a sensation in New York that the Giants ownership admitted that any move by them to force the Jets to leave New York would have been met with public outcry and general derision.

Namath's three-year, $427,000 contract made it clear to owners in both the AFL and NFL that only the richest teams would be able to sign the best players, and that the weaker teams may face going out of business. To avoid that fate, secret negotiations began in 1965 between Carroll Rosenbloom, owner of the NFL Baltimore Colts, and Ralph Wilson, the owner of the AFL Buffalo Bills. These talks did not reach a merger agreement because the AFL balked at the NFL's insistence upon market exclusivity, which would have forced the Jets and Raiders to move, and at the price tag the NFL put on membership for all eight AFL clubs combined: a reported $50 million.

Dallas Cowboys' general manager Tex Schramm knew that success, if not survival itself, required a merger of the two professional football leagues, although he said years later that he would have liked nothing better at the time than to kill the AFL. He contacted Commissioner Rozelle in the spring of 1966, and said he wanted to work on a merger. Rozelle gave Schramm the green light as long as he kept all meetings secret and that he work with only one representative of the rival league.

So on April 4, 1966, Tex Schramm of the Dallas Cowboys called Lamar Hunt, owner of the team the Cowboys had driven out of Dallas to Kansas City, and asked if Hunt "might be able to come to Dallas to discuss a matter of mutual importance." Two days later Hunt got off a plane at Dallas's Love Field and climbed into Schramm's Oldsmobile. They sat in the car parked at the airport talking for forty-five minutes. Hunt recalled Schramm saying "I think the time has come to talk about a merger if you'd be interested in that." Hunt replied, "Fine, I'm interested."

The conditions Schramm laid out included admitting all the existing AFL franchises into the NFL with Pete Rozelle as commissioner. The two men agreed to talk again in a few weeks about a more detailed framework for the merger.

Two days after the secret session in the Oldsmobile, the AFL owners' meeting got underway in Houston. It was April 8, 1966, and AFL Commissioner Joe Foss opened the meeting by submitting his resignation. To replace him, the league ownership elected Al Davis of the Oakland Raiders as commissioner. Davis relished the idea of taking on the NFL and waging an all-out battle for players and fans. He knew nothing about Lamar Hunt's merger talks.

On May 3, Tex Schramm got back to Lamar Hunt after having discussed the NFL's position with Rozelle. The NFL would admit each of the original eight AFL franchises for a fee of $2 million each, plus another $2 million from the expansion

Miami Dolphins who were scheduled to begin play in the 1966 season. That came to a total of $18 million. A week later Hunt responded by telling Schramm that an agreement could be reached.

The friction between the two leagues increased however that same week, when the New York Giants appeared to violate the unwritten agreement not to poach players from the rival league. The Giants signed Pete Gogolak, the AFL Buffalo Bills' placekicker, to a three-year contract. Gogolak had played out his option year with the Bills and was a free agent, which made him fair game in the eyes of the Giants ownership. News of the signing came out at the NFL owners' meeting May 16 in Washington, D.C. where it was feared that a bidding war with the AFL would result, and that would cost each NFL owner a lot of money. AFL Commissioner Al Davis reacted by immediately drawing up a plan to target the NFL's top ten players.

Tex Schramm called Lamar Hunt from the NFL meetings to assure him that, despite the outcry over the signing of Pete Gogolak, the merger plans that they had discussed were still on track. The NFL owners would be called to a meeting in New York in a few weeks, and there the details of the merger proposal would be explained.

Only two NFL owners opposed the plan: the San Francisco 49ers and the New York Giants, the two teams that faced home market competition from AFL franchises. But they changed their "nays" to "yeas" when the other NFL owners voted to take the $18 million in AFL entry fees and give $10 million to the Giants and the remaining $8 million to the 49ers.

The opposition Lamar Hunt heard when he pitched the merger to his fellow AFL owners on June 1, 1966, was to the $2 million dollar payment each would have to make as a condition of joining the NFL. These complaints evaporated when Hunt explained that he had worked out a deal that allowed each AFL owner twenty years to pay off the $2 million fee.

On June 8, 1966, the following joint statement from the two leagues was released to the public:

The NFL and AFL today announced plans to join in an expanded major professional football league. It will consist of 26 teams in 25 cities—with expectations of additional teams in the near future.
The main points of the agreement were listed:

* Pete Rozelle will be the commissioner.
* A world championship game this season.
* All existing franchises retained.
* No franchises transferred from present locations.
* Two new franchises no later than 1968.
* Two more teams as soon thereafter as practical.
* Inter-league pre-season games in 1967.
* Single league schedule in 1970.
* A common draft next January.
* Continued two-network TV coverage.

Neither CBS nor NBC had been party to the merger discussions. The first that they heard about the combination of the two leagues was the day the joint statement was made, and neither network was happy. Each had paid for exclusive rights to a league championship game, and that game would now become a virtual semi-final game, less important than the new "world championship game" announced by the two leagues. And this new final game was to be played following the regular season, which would kick off just three months hence. It is further testament to Pete Rozelle's skills as commissioner that he was able to get both CBS and NBC to pay the NFL an additional $1 million dollars each for the rights to jointly televise the game that would become the first Super Bowl.

HORSE-TRADING ON CAPITOL HILL

The only hurdle left for the AFL–NFL merger would need to be cleared in Congress. The Sports Broadcasting Act of 1961 had to be amended to extend the antitrust exemption each league had been granted for the negotiation of broadcast rights, to cover the combination of two previously competing leagues. The proposed legislation went to the House Judiciary Committee, and that's where it may have died.

The committee chairman was Representative Emanuel Celler, a Democrat from New York who at age seventy-eight was in his forty-third year in Congress. Celler was a strong proponent of antitrust laws, and he had no intention of expanding any exemptions. Chairman Celler made his stand abundantly clear at a Judiciary Committee hearing on October 11, 1966, which he adjourned before Commissioner Pete Rozelle or league counsel Hamilton Carothers even had a chance to testify. In the prepared opening statement Rozelle had planned to deliver he said he would recommend that NFL owners scrap plans for the merger with the AFL if Congress did not approve the exemption.

The commissioner feared that, without an antitrust exemption, the league would be open to costly antitrust lawsuits, the sum of which he said, "could easily be larger than the total value and net assets of all the existing franchises." He also said that if Congress didn't approve the merger before the following January, plans for any expansion teams would also probably die.

In mid-October the 1966 NFL and AFL seasons were already a month old, and time was growing short. Immediately after being stone-walled at the House Judiciary Committee, Pete Rozelle reached out for some lobbying help. He called David Dixon, a mutual friend of his and House Majority Leader Hale Boggs of Louisiana. Dixon and Boggs had been fraternity brothers at Tulane.

Through Dixon, the NFL, which had already been considering New Orleans as the site for one of its planned expansion franchises, made it known that a new team in Louisiana would have no problem getting league approval if Boggs could assist in the passage of the extended antitrust exemption. The majority leader saw the political value in his home district and the overall value for his state, and he promptly attached the exemption to a budget bill that he knew would pass both houses of Congress.

In his book *America's Game*, Michael MacCambridge set the scene October 21, 1966, the day that final approval would be put to a vote in the House of Representatives. On his way up the steps to the Capitol rotunda, Commissioner Rozelle said, "Congressman Boggs, I don't know how I can ever thank you enough for this. This is a terrific thing you've done."

Boggs replied, "What do you mean you *don't know* how to thank me? New Orleans gets an immediate franchise in the NFL."

Rozelle's reported response was, "I'm going to do everything I can to make that happen." Boggs turned around as if heading back to the committee room and said, "Well, we can always call off the vote while you—"

Figure 4.1 NFL Commissioner Pete Rozelle, at podium, announces that New Orleans has been awarded the league's 16th franchise during a news conference in New Orleans, November 1, 1966. To the right of Rozelle is Louisiana Rep. Hale Boggs, who helped push the pro-merger bill through the House and at far right is Louisiana Gov. John McKeithen
Source: reprinted with permission of AP Images

At that the NFL Commissioner said, "It's a deal Congressman. You'll get your franchise."

The New Orleans Saints made their NFL debut less than a year later, in September of 1967. And the NFL got approval for the amendment to the Sports Broadcasting Act that would allow all the teams of the AFL and NFL to negotiate as a single league entity for all future television rights after the merger.

It sounds like a classic case of political horse-trading, and Hale Boggs' son Thomas, himself a prominent Washington lobbyist, confirmed years later that it "definitely was a quid pro quo." He said his father deserved credit for bringing the Saints to New Orleans, along with former Louisiana Senator Russell Long, who served with the elder Boggs on the same House–Senate conference committee that attached the NFL's antitrust exemption to the budget bill.

THE FIRST SUPER BOWL

Lamar Hunt's three young children each had a "Super Ball," a toy from Wham-O Inc. that was a rage in the 1960s. Seeing them play with it, Hunt got the idea for a short nickname he could use in discussions about the new world championship game that the merger would create. In a note to Pete Rozelle, Hunt said "I've been calling it the Super Bowl, which obviously can be improved upon." Rozelle didn't like the term "super," which he equated with other empty superlatives like "neat," "fabulous," or "fantastic." He wanted a title with sophistication like "The Championship."

So when the NFL champion Green Bay Packers met the AFL champion Kansas City Chiefs on January 15, 1967, at the Los Angeles Memorial Coliseum, the game

Figure 4.2 The game program for the first "World Championship Game" between the AFL and NFL champions, January 15, 1967. It would later be universally referred to as "Super Bowl I"
Source: reprinted with permission of AP Images

was officially the "AFL vs. NFL World Championship Game." But almost everyone including the media was calling it "the Super Bowl," and obviously the name has stuck. It became the game's official title before Super Bowl III, but the NFL insisted on the use of Roman numerals to add a sense of tradition and permanence.

This first championship game between the two professional leagues was also the first time either league had played its title game at a neutral site, which more than likely explains why the game was not a sell-out, even though tickets sold for just six to twelve dollars. All previous NFL and AFL league championships had been played in the home stadium of one of the two teams. The attendance at "Super

Bowl I" was 61,946, far short of the Los Angeles Coliseum capacity of over 100,000, so before the game Pete Rozelle had the public address announcer urge the scattered fans to move closer to the field and to the 50-yard line. He knew that would help make the game look more important on television.

CBS was charged with producing the game telecast and providing a feed to NBC's truck so that they could add their own commentators, graphics, and replays. The CBS production plan for this championship game was very similar to their regular season complement of seven primary coverage cameras, but they did add an extra hand-held camera in the tunnel to get shots of the teams coming onto the field, and they hard-wired cameras into each of the two locker rooms for post-game interviews and celebration shots. The coverage was minimal compared with the 40+ camera productions at Super Bowls in the twenty-first century.

Each network added talent to their ordinary game complement of one play-by-play announcer and one "color" commentator. CBS used Ray Scott as their main play-by-play announcer with Frank Gifford and veteran Jack Whitaker. Whitaker did most of the second half play-by-play and he was responsible for adding the "color," which meant keeping an eye on the bands, the celebrities, the crowd: in effect all of the colorful "non-football" angles. CBS added Pat Summerall to do sideline reporting and cover the post-game locker room. Summerall, like Gifford, was a former New York Giant, who by 1967 had already been working full-time for CBS for several years.

NBC assigned their number-one AFL commentary team of Curt Gowdy and Paul Christman, adding Charley Jones on the sidelines, Jim Simpson as their studio host, and George Ratterman for the post-game locker room. Gowdy remembered how strange it was to call the game off of a monitor in their booth, which was showing him and Christman the CBS live feed.He said, "We could have been in Cheyenne, Wyoming and done the game."

Accommodating NBC and sharing facilities with them was the most difficult part of Super Bowl I for CBS Sports executive producer Bill Fitts. He headed the CBS production teams for Super Bowls I, II, IV, VI, and VIII. Fitts remembers the tiny TV truck they used at the LA Coliseum, and having to make room for NBC's producer Lou Kusserow, who insisted on being in the CBS truck during the game so that he could coordinate what was being fed to his NBC production truck. Fitts said the truck was "a mad house, Kusserow was even louder than me!" CBS had anticipated the confusion, so in what was surely a snub for their innovative lead NFL director Tony Verna, they brought in Bob Daly, who was known for his level-headed and calm demeanor from CBS productions like *The Ed Sullivan Show*, to direct the telecast. And Bill Creasy, a CBS producer with ample experience at the highest level, was the game producer.

The CBS team had pride in their years of NFL production, and in the fact that the television ratings for their NFL games were so much higher at that point than for the AFL games on NBC. This pride came across to the NBC production team as a patronizing attitude that led to friction at Super Bowl I. Curt Gowdy remembered going to a production meeting at the CBS hotel in Beverly Hills and feeling like he had walked "into the enemy camp."

The network competition escalated into a few scuffles between CBS and NBC technicians at the broadcasts compound outside the stadium. NFL Films reported that the solution was to erect a ten-foot chain link fence between the two trucks. The forced cooperation between networks was unique to Super Bowl I, and was never again repeated. Starting with Super Bowl II the following year, CBS and NBC alternated coverage with CBS doing the game in the even-numbered years and NBC in the odd. This pattern continued until Super Bowl XX in January of 1985, when ABC's new NFL rights package bought them a place in the rotation.

One of the other elements that made the telecast of the first NFL vs. AFL confrontation different from previous title games was the pageantry planned for the pre-game. A flock of doves was to be released and two jet-pack pilots with "AFL" and "NFL" emblazoned on their respective chests would fly over the field and land at the 50-yard line, where they would then ceremonially shake hands to represent the joining of the two leagues.

On the Saturday before the game Bill Fitts insisted on rehearsing the doves and the jet-pack pilots. He said he had to see where they would fly so that his director would know how to follow them with the CBS cameras come Sunday. The owner of the doves did not want to rehearse: "They're not homing pigeons," he told Fitts. "They'll fly away and I'll have to get more doves." Fitts was adamant, so standing on the field he learned two things from his doves rehearsal: which direction the birds would fly, and that as soon as they are released, doves immediately poop. "I was covered in bird poop," he said. "I won't ever rehearse this again in my life!"

The jet-pack pilots also complained about rehearsing because it would force them to use precious fuel. But they too complied with the CBS producer showing him and Bob Daly in the truck the routes they would fly.

Neither CBS nor NBC saw their shared broadcast experience at the first Super Bowl as optimal, but both shows progressed without incident until halftime. The Packers led 17–7 at the break, and play was scheduled to resume exactly twenty minutes later. Over his years of producing games for CBS, Bill Fitts had come to know the NFL's head of officials Mark Duncan as "a hard-ass." Halftimes for regular season games were fifteen minutes, and Duncan did not like the idea of extending it to twenty minutes for the championship game. The halftime entertainment was to be provided by New Orleans jazz trumpeter Al Hirt and the Grambling College and University of Arizona marching bands.

Fitts recalls Duncan telling him before the game began: "Halftime is twenty minutes. Then we're kicking off. I don't care what your red-hat is doing." The red-hat is the stage manager on the sideline who is in contact with the TV truck to signal the referees when the telecast is back from commercial. They always wore red hats so it was easy for the referees to pick them out on the crowded sidelines.

Bill Fitts said he relayed Mark Duncan's warning to his NBC counterpart, Lou Kusserow. Come halftime, CBS got their required commercial breaks in early so they would have time to spare before the second half kickoff. But NBC still had one break to get in as the twenty-minute clock was counting down. "Lou, you better get your ass in commercial," Fitts remembers hollering at Kusserow.

With a minute and fifteen seconds left before the second half was scheduled to begin, NBC finally went to their last halftime break, which meant that the red-hat would have to hold the kick until after Mark Duncan's watch hit :00. But the official was true to his word, and he signaled the start of the second half while the NBC TV audience was still watching commercials, and Green Bay kicked off to the Chiefs. From his play-by-play position CBS's Jack Whitaker said he immediately saw flags thrown and heard whistles blowing, but he didn't know why. He turned to Frank Gifford, who shrugged his shoulders, not knowing what had happened either. The officials signaled the ball from the first kickoff dead and the Packers had to kick off a second time, and this time NBC was back from break.

The final skirmish in the Super Bowl I competition between CBS and NBC came after Green Bay had won 35–17. The winning coach, Vince Lombardi, was being interviewed by both Pat Summerall for CBS and George Ratterman of NBC, who had to share one microphone. As he asked a question, Ratterman put his hand on the mike that Summerall had been holding in front of Lombardi. From the CBS truck, the network's programming chief, Bill McPhail yelled at his producers, "Tell him to get that damn microphone back!" So as Lombardi was responding, Summerall could be seen slowly pulling the mike back from Ratterman's grasp.

The next morning the New York Times said of the first Super Bowl, "The contest was more ordinary than super." The Packers had proven they were the superior team, and they reinforced the generally held public opinion that the NFL in its fifth decade of play was a league of much stronger teams than the AFL, which had been in existence for only seven seasons.

The Nielsen Company reported that CBS won the ratings battle with a 22.6 rating, which represented a 43 percent share of all the televisions that were in use on that Sunday afternoon. NBC's rating was an 18.5 with a 36 percent share. Combining the ratings points means that 41.1 percent of all the homes in the United States had tuned in to watch the World Championship Game between the NFL and the AFL: a total of 75.5 million viewers.

NOT A SURE THING

Pete Rozelle was determined that Super Bowl II, to be played at the Orange Bowl in Miami, would be a sell-out. The league had more time to promote the game and they actually reduced ticket prices to increase the attendance. A total of 75,546 fans turned out on January 14, 1968, making the game the first $3 million dollar gate in the history of the sport. But what they saw was another dominant performance by the Green Bay Packers who led the Oakland Raiders 33–7, until Daryle Lamonica hit Bill Miller for a touchdown late in the fourth quarter to make the final score 33–14.

The back-to-back Packer championships underscored the common perception that the NFL and AFL were two unequal leagues. Most fans and media alike thought a victory by the NFL's Baltimore Colts over the New York Jets in Super Bowl III, also to be played at the Orange Bowl, was a foregone conclusion. The Colts were favored by as many as nineteen points the week of the game in January 1969.

Pete Rozelle was concerned about the long-term outlook and audience for the season-ending Super Bowl if the public began to see it as a predictable annual NFL beat-down of the AFL champions. So in his news conference the Friday before Super Bowl III, the commissioner announced that the league was considering changing the post-season playoff structure so that two NFL teams could meet in a Super Bowl after the 1970 season, when the merger would be complete and teams from both leagues were to start playing a unified schedule. The New York Times sports headline on Saturday morning, January 11, 1969, read: "Rozelle Indicates Tomorrow's Super Bowl Contest Could Be Next to Last."

Television viewers overwhelming expected an easy Colts victory, and the ratings actually dropped from Super Bowl II. Only 36 percent of American homes watched the Colts play the Jets, the lowest-rated Super Bowl in the history of the series. But after Joe Namath and the Jets stunned the Colts with a 16–7 victory for the AFL, all talk of changing the playoff structure was dropped.

Figure 4.3 Joe Namath (12) leads the New York Jets to victory over the Baltimore Colts in Super Bowl III at Miami's Orange Bowl
Source: reprinted with permission of Getty Images

Namath had guaranteed a Jets victory, but almost no one took him seriously. He was accepting the award as "Player of the Year" at the Miami Touchdown Club dinner the Thursday before the Super Bowl was to be played. While Namath was at the mike, a Colts supporter in the audience hollered out, "We're gonna kick your ass." Namath replied, "Wait a minute, let's hold on. You Baltimore guys have been talking all week, but I've got news for you, buddy. We're gonna win the game. I guarantee it." Namath said he made the comment out of anger, not arrogance, but it set off a media storm that set the stage for the Super Bowl that would have a more wide-ranging impact than any before or since.

The Jets' victory in Super Bowl III made the game the true climax for each football season. It would never again be looked upon as a dénouement that followed the more important league championship games, a virtual exhibition game between the big boys and their weaker step-brothers. The stigma of league inequality would finally be laid to rest the following year when the Kansas City Chiefs defeated the Minnesota Vikings in Super Bowl IV for a second consecutive AFL triumph. Advertising rates for the Super Bowl telecast took off after Super Bowl III, making it economically more important and a much larger factor in future television rights negotiations for NFL product. Television ratings bounced back for Super Bowl IV to 39.4, a 10 percent increase in a year, and from that point a steady rise continued unabated, making the Super Bowl the most-watched program on American television year after year: a ritual of TV viewing without equal in the United States.

The game itself, after just three years in existence, had been elevated in the minds of the public and the media to the lofty status of the World Series, the Kentucky Derby, and The Masters golf tournament as a premier event in the world of sports.

Joe Namath's triumph in Super Bowl III, making good on his guarantee, ushered in a new era of individual star power in team sports. He became the prototype for the modern television celebrity athlete. He combined success on the field of play with good looks, the latest fashions, a well-spoken easy delivery in the media, and speculation about his sex life, which would be elevated every time he escorted yet another beautiful woman to the trendiest clubs and restaurants in New York. Namath was part owner of a club called "Bachelors III" until the NFL forced him to sell his stake because it claimed the club had become a place frequented by known gamblers and others with unsavory backgrounds. Namath's star power translated into commercial endorsements and wealth approaching the level of television stars who had gained fame in other forms of entertainment, and it added to the collective power of all players who could rightly claim their share of the value they brought to team ownership. A shift in power from the owners to the players and their unions was underway.

"ARE YOU READY FOR SOME (PRIME TIME) FOOTBALL?"

On their run to Super Bowl III, the New York Jets played the Oakland Raiders at the Oakland Coliseum on Sunday November 17, 1968. The game had started at 1 p.m. Pacific Time, 4 p.m. Eastern on NBC, and it was running long. The program scheduled at 7 p.m. Eastern was the classic children's film Heidi, and NBC's broadcast operations supervisor in New York, Dick Cline, had no network guidelines that would have allowed him to let the game continue on air past 7 p.m. NBC's executive producer Scotty Connal was at his home in Connecticut watching the game, and trying to get through to broadcast operations in New York with instructions to stay with the game until its conclusion. But the switchboard there was receiving so many calls from viewers who either wanted the network to stick with the game or were asking what would happen to the Heidi telecast if the game did spill over, that Connal could not get through.

So at 7 p.m. sharp, after the Jets had taken a 32–29 lead on a field goal with 1:15 left on the game clock, NBC went to commercial and then switched to Heidi.

What viewers didn't see was Raiders quarterback Daryle Lamonica throw a touchdown pass to Charlie Smith, giving Oakland the lead with forty-two seconds left. The Jets then fumbled the ensuing kickoff. Raider Preston Ridlehuber fell on the ball in the end zone for the second Oakland touchdown in nine seconds. Final score: Oakland 43, New York 32. Dick Cline, who went on to have a distinguished career as a television sports director, said that a call from NBC president Julian Goodman did get through, but by that time it was too late to carry out his demand to, "Go back to the game."

The story made the front page of the *New York Times* of Monday morning, November 18, 1968. The headline was: "Jets Cut for 'Heidi'; TV Fans Complain." And on NBC's nightly news program *The Huntley Brinkley Report* that Monday evening, David Brinkley reported that "NBC apologized for the error, but by then Oakland had scored two touchdowns in the last minute, had beaten New York, the game was over. The fans who missed it could not be consoled."

What would go down in history as "the Heidi Game" had several valuable lessons that would have their impact in the years to come:

- Professional football on television was reaching and affecting so many millions of people that coverage on the front page of the nation's foremost newspaper was warranted. If a televised game had been similarly cut off five or ten years earlier, there almost certainly would not have been the same level of public outcry or national media attention.

- The appetite for the sport extended beyond Sunday afternoons into prime time where it could rival traditional entertainment shows.

- TV truck, network operations, and programming executives would forever after be connected by telephone hotlines so that last-minute programming changes could always be made.

THE BIRTH OF MONDAY NIGHT FOOTBALL

> I believe the single biggest moment in American sports TV was the coming of Monday Night Football. It was the coming out party for American Sport.
>
> (Dick Ebersol, president of NBC Sports, 1989–2011)

NFL Commissioner Pete Rozelle had seen prime time television as an opportunity for expansion in the early 1960s. So as an experiment the league scheduled its first Monday night game on September 28, 1964. The game between the Green Bay Packers and the Detroit Lions was not televised, but it drew a sell-out crowd of 59,203 to Tiger Stadium. Rozelle had shown that fans would embrace games on a weeknight. Now he had to find a network partner.

When it still had the AFL package, ABC had proposed doing a weekly Friday night football game to replace its *Gillette Friday Night Fights* package, which was not doing well in the ratings. The marketing manager at Ford, Lee Iacocca, who would later gain fame as the chief executive at Chrysler, had agreed to sponsor the new Friday night AFL series. But the NCAA got wind of the plan and spread the word that ABC was planning to put live football games on TV on Friday nights, which could cause some people to stay home and not support high school football games, traditionally played on Friday evenings. It wasn't long before Congress amended the Sports Broadcasting Act to nullify the antitrust exemption for any professional football played on a Friday night after 6 p.m. or at any time on a Saturday between the second Friday of September and the second Saturday of December on "any telecasting station located within seventy-five miles of the game site of any intercollegiate or interscholastic football contest." That effectively killed ABC's *Friday Night Football* idea.

In 1966, the NFL began a four-year trial with its broadcast partners: CBS televised one Monday night prime time game in 1966 and one in 1967, and NBC did the same with AFL matchups in 1968 and 1969. None of the games was a huge ratings success, but the league was not discouraged. The table was set for Monday Night Football to break new ground in American sports entertainment history.

Not long after the New York Jets victory in Super Bowl III, Commissioner Rozelle began a series of lunches in Manhattan with ABC Sports executive producer Roone Arledge to talk about NFL football in prime time on Mondays. Arledge did not yet have the green light from his bosses to cut a deal: ABC Chairman Leonard Goldenson reportedly was in favor of the plan, but his new network president Elton Rule did not like the idea of disrupting the entertainment schedule in prime time.

Rozelle liked Arledge's proposed approach to prime time football that would mix entertainment with football and thereby attract more women to the television audience, but it was always his intention to offer the Monday night series to his partners at CBS and NBC first. And Rozelle knew that ABC was a poor third in the prime time ratings race, which meant cross-promotion for this new series would reach far fewer people on ABC than on either of the other two networks.

A TV insiders' joke at the time was: "How do you end the Vietnam War? Put it on ABC and it'll be canceled in thirteen weeks."

The NFL had one other option that did not require a contract with CBS, NBC, or ABC: a syndication partnership with the Hughes Sports Network, which was bankrolled by eccentric billionaire Howard Hughes. Hughes would offer to sell the NFL package directly to any television stations who wanted to buy the programming. Word quickly reached ABC that up to one hundred of its affiliated stations, including powerful WPVI-TV in Philadelphia, were ready to drop their low-rated Monday night ABC shows and take the syndicated football games instead. This would have been a crippling blow to ABC. The network reacted swiftly out of fear that it would have to "go dark" on Monday evenings, and the board of directors approved spending $25.5 million for a three-year contract with the NFL.

But Pete Rozelle insisted on giving the right of first refusal to CBS and NBC. CBS was the ratings leader and had such a strong Monday lineup of shows, including *Here's Lucy* starring Lucille Ball, *Mayberry R.F.D.*, *The Doris Day Show*, and at 10 p.m. Eastern *The Carol Burnett Show*, that they decided to pass on Pete Rozelle's Monday Night Football offer.

NBC thought about taking it, but the network would have had to move its hit show *Rowan and Martin's Laugh-In* from Mondays to another night. And an even greater stumbling block for NBC, where the scars from the "Heidi Game" were still fresh, would be that if any Monday night NFL game ran long it would force them to push back the start time of *The Tonight Show starring Johnny Carson*. *The Tonight Show* was NBC's biggest moneymaker, and the programming department did not want to upset Johnny Carson, so they never raised the topic with him and turned down the NFL in prime time.

When the Commissioner and ABC resumed talks, Rozelle made it clear that the network would have to change its three-year offer to four years beginning with the 1970 season, in order to coincide with the new four-year deals that the league was negotiating with CBS and NBC for its Sunday games and four Super Bowls. ABC got the rights to *Monday Night Football* for $8.6 million dollars per year for a total of $34.4 million over the four-year term. CBS agreed to pay the NFL $18 million per year and NBC signed for $15 million to televise pre-season and regular season games, the playoffs, and four Pro Bowls. In addition CBS and NBC bought the rights to alternate televising the next four Super Bowls for a fee of $2.5 million per game. Together CBS and NBC would pay $142 million dollars for their four-year rights packages.

Commissioner Rozelle was able to go back to his owners with a smile on his face: the NFL would be seen live on each of America's three major television networks, the league would have a weekly prime time television presence for a minimum of four years, and each team would collect $1.6 million in TV rights per year for the life of the contracts.

The ink on the ABC contract was barely dry when Roone Arledge pitched one of his most revolutionary ideas to Pete Rozelle. Arledge wanted to use a three-man commentary booth for *Monday Night Football*, and his choice for "the third man" was former attorney and controversial ABC Sports reporter Howard Cosell, who had gained national prominence covering Muhammad Ali's fights and legal struggles. Arledge's argument was that Cosell would not let the audience ignore him; "he forced you to watch."

Knowing how obnoxious some people found Cosell, the commissioner's first response was, "Why not just dig up Attila the Hun?"

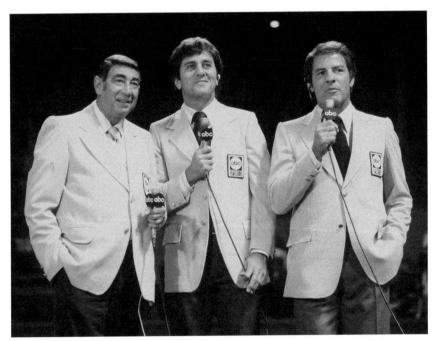

Figure 4.4 The ABC *Monday Night Football* announce team, from left, Howard Cosell, Don Meredith, and Frank Gifford
Source: reprinted with permission of ABC Television Group

ABC's first choice for the expert football analyst position was Frank Gifford, but he still had a year left on his contract with CBS that he intended to honor. Gifford did however recommend a friend for the job who he said "would really be great," recently retired Dallas Cowboys quarterback Don Meredith, who had quickly decided that life as a stockbroker was not for him. Arledge asked Gifford to have his friend give him a ring.

Meredith called ABC four days in a row leaving a message for Roone Arledge each day, but he got no response. His fifth message was that he was starting negotiations with CBS to work on that network's college football games. Arledge had a reputation for not returning phone calls promptly, but message number five got his attention and a lunch meeting was set up with assistance from Frank Gifford.

In his autobiography *Roone*, Arledge remembered that he had his apologies all prepared when Don Meredith showed up at Toots Shor's restaurant at the appointed hour. Meredith however spoke first: "The only reason I came is to tell you to your face what a horse's ass you are." Arledge's quick reply was, "And that, sir, is the kind of candor I want in an expert commentator."

The two men sat down and three hours later they had the details of an agreement written on a napkin. Arledge could not wait to see the chemistry develop between Meredith, the Southern gentleman football star, and the brash Eastern intellectual Howard Cosell. He paired these two opposite personalities with ABC college football play-by-play man Keith Jackson, and the *Monday Night Football* three-man booth was complete.

NFL *Monday Night Football* debuted on September 21, 1970, in Cleveland. The owner of the Browns at the time, Art Modell, said that many of his fellow owners were wary of taking the first Monday night game for fear that attendance would not be as strong as on Sunday afternoons. So Modell said, "Let me take a chance in Cleveland. Just give me the Jets," because of the New York television audience. The largest crowd ever to see a Browns' game before or since, a total of 85,703, poured into Cleveland Municipal Stadium to be part of history. It was the beginning of what would become a *Monday Night Football* phenomenon: the tenor of the home crowds changed to a carnival atmosphere. Fans festooned the stadiums with banners, many with references to Howard Cosell or "Dandy Don" Meredith, and more people dressed in wild costumes in hopes of being seen on national TV. Meredith called the weekly *Monday Night Football* scene "Mother Love's Traveling Freak Show."

The live game that viewers saw that opening Monday night in September of 1970 was unlike anything they had ever seen. ABC's open made you feel like you were inside the TV truck watching the countdown to airtime. Director Chet Forte was able to provide shots and camera angles that had never been used before. "I had ten, eleven cameras on *Monday Night Football*," he said. "They couldn't hide from me. If the players did something, I found it." It was all part of Roone Arledge's philosophy to "bring the viewer to the game," instead of bringing the game to the viewer.

The television audience that watched the Browns defeat the Jets 31–21 was much larger than ABC had projected. Thirty-three percent of the American viewing audience tuned in, giving ABC a ratings victory over the CBS and NBC entertainment lineups that those two networks had chosen to retain instead of taking a chance with NFL football in prime time.

During the season the stadiums continued to sell out and record numbers turned to ABC to be part of the party and to hear what Meredith and Cosell would say.

Their exchanges, with Meredith constantly ribbing Cosell or questioning his use of words Don had never heard before, became part of the "must-see" entertainment. Not everyone was an instant fan. ABC Chairman Leonard Goldenson got a call after the first game from Ford Motor Company chairman Henry Ford II, one of ABC's biggest sponsors, demanding that Cosell be taken off the show because "he's hogging all the time. He talks so much I can't enjoy the game." Arledge was called into Goldenson's office, but he convinced his boss to hold firm with Cosell, assuring him that, "It's only been one show. The audience needs to get to know him." Ford called back a few weeks later and said he'd grown to like the patter in the booth.

A *TV Guide* poll that first season found that Howard Cosell was both the "most-hated" and the "most-liked" sportscaster in the United States. The celebrity status of the TV talent was something completely new to American sports television. The game had always been "the thing" and the commentators were part of the furniture, never taking the spotlight for themselves. ABC changed that forever in 1970. The network also welcomed celebrities from the entertainment world and politics to join the fun in the booth, and in so doing add their fans and supporters to broaden ABC's audience for what had become more "show" than "game." Perhaps the most interesting pairing of celebrity visitors was during halftime of a Washington Redskins vs. Los Angeles Rams game on December 9, 1974, when John Lennon and outgoing California governor Ronald Reagan were in ABC's LA Coliseum booth at the same time. "Now there's a pair," said Arledge.

So many people chose to sit in front of their televisions on Mondays that attendance at movie theaters dropped significantly. Theater owners in parts of the country offered discounts or free snacks to entice customers. Many bowling leagues abandoned Monday nights and moved their games to later in the week. Process-servers got busy, knowing that most of the people they were seeking would be home on Monday nights.

In short order *Monday Night Football* had become the NFL's premier showcase and most valuable property. The league's Sunday games competed with each other for television audience, and millions of would-be viewers were attending the games. Other sports like basketball, hockey, and golf also claimed a piece of the Sunday afternoon TV real estate. On Monday nights however, there was no sports competition and the lights were on in only one stadium, so that fans who had been in their stadium seats on Sunday would be on their sofas at home on Mondays. And even if the matchup was between two teams you didn't follow, there were always Howard Cosell's halftime highlights of the best from the Sunday games, which became a major draw themselves. In this era before there was an ESPN, the best way to see all the highlights together was to watch *Monday Night Football*.

When Frank Gifford became available in 1971, Roone Arledge hired him to take over the play-by-play host role from Keith Jackson because he was looking for a "bigger personality" in the booth. Gifford would continue with the series for thirty-five years, setting up a succession of broadcast partners who would eventually replace Howard Cosell and Don Meredith as they moved on to other pursuits. Keith Jackson was given ABC's number-one college football on-air job, which moved Chris Schenkel from the top spot to the network's number two game each weekend.

In its thirty-six seasons on ABC, *Monday Night Football* became an institution. It changed Americans' expectations for all televised sport, creating what would become an insatiable appetite for more angles, more replays, more personality and entertainment, more drama and more fun. The shows made NFL football more conspicuous and more important, a powerful presence on weekends and prime time on all three of the nation's broadcast television networks. The huge audiences it attracted made NFL rights more valuable, and the commercials sold within the games more expensive.

And *Monday Night Football* brought people together through common experience: bleary eyes and yawns at the office or at school on Tuesday mornings, extra cups of coffee as you relived the latest comedy or controversy from Cosell and Meredith, and the sense of belonging with all your "rowdy friends" to the same weekly carnival that made you laugh, got your blood boiling, or had you jumping out of your seat to cheer an amazing touchdown run by Earl Campbell or pass from Dan Marino.

Television reviewer Jack Gould sensed a foreshadowing of what was to come in his *New York Times* column the morning after ABC televised that first Monday night game from Cleveland in September 1970. Gould wrote that this "innovation will be watched carefully by media students." He asked how would sports do up against the movies and situation comedies that were the staple of prime time? Would women surrender to their husbands the control of what the family watched on a weeknight, or would "the increasing prevalence of multiple-set households" divide families into separate rooms, creating a rift in the harmony of the one-set home? Jack Gould concluded that "should evening network sports give entertainment a serious challenge, last night could be remembered as marking one more change in the course of television." That it did.

As the economic realities of the television industry changed in the decades since its 1970 debut, *Monday Night Football* moved from ABC to co-owned ESPN in the fall of 2006. (We'll address this topic in depth in the chapter on the economics of sports television.) ESPN's contract agreement for the series guaranteed the NFL $1.1 billion per year for eight years. In thirty-six years the value of the rights to *Monday Night Football* had grown from $8.6 million per year to $1.1 billion, a 129-fold increase. The 2011 renewal of the ESPN–NFL contract added nine more years to the deal at a staggering $1.9 billion per year.

THE NFL TODAY

The pre-game and post-game studio shows that have become such a staple of sports television trace their origins back to 1956, when CBS started doing a preview of their Sunday games simply called *Football Preview*. Before 1956, any show relying on video clips and highlights would have been impossible because that was the year that videotape was introduced by the Ampex Corporation. *Football Preview* preceded the CBS telecast of each Sunday's game, varying between fifteen and thirty minutes in length. It became *Pro Football Kickoff* a year later, and in 1964, with a regular thirty-minute time slot, it was re-titled *The NFL Today*.

The purpose of any pre-game show is three-fold:

- Promote the upcoming game or event on your network so that more people will be enticed to watch.

- Present the story lines that are expected to unfold and the stars expected to control the contest so that, when viewers decide to watch, they will stay tuned longer. The greater the time spent viewing by each member of the television audience, the higher the overall program rating will be.

- Create additional advertising inventory for sponsors who have either a) already bought commercials in the game and want to increase the number of times their message is presented, or b) could not buy spots in the actual game because the existing inventory was sold out, or because the commercials within the games were too expensive. Commercials in the pre-game shows are invariably sold at a lower price than those that will air within the actual game or event.

These early NFL pre-game shows consisted primarily of the network football analysts setting up that day's matchups. They were not a showcase for personality or entertainment. Frank Gifford did add some star power to *The NFL Today* when he took over as its host on CBS from 1966 through the 1970 season, after which he made his move to ABC and *Monday Night Football*.

The sports studio show changed forever in 1975, when the new president of CBS Sports, Robert Wussler, along with producer Mike Pearl, totally re-built *The NFL Today*, adding personality, interviews, style, and fun. Wussler assigned Brent Musburger as the host, Phyllis George as co-host and primary interviewer, and former NFL player Irv Cross as the football expert. Acknowledging the huge public interest in gambling on NFL games, Wussler also hired Jimmy "The Greek" Snyder as the show's Las Vegas insider.

Musburger had been doing a Sunday post-game show in Chicago that brought in feeds from all the games around the country. He thrived on the fast pace of the show, quickly moving from one highlight to the next. His producer on that show, Bill Fitts, said, "Brent was like a kid in a candy store."

Phyllis George was Miss America 1971, and during her reign was the guest on talk shows all over the country, including at least three appearances on *The Tonight Show with Johnny Carson* on NBC. Her personality and ease on camera caught Wussler's eye, and when he brought her to CBS Sports for the first time he told staffers "let's make her a star."

Phyllis George added character and charm to the football studio show, and her ability to put interview subjects at ease got many to open up and show a personal side that had never been seen by television viewers before. Looking back on the success of *The NFL Today*, Mike Pearl said, "Nobody ever got players or coaches to respond in such a natural tone as she did."

In an interview that first season with Dallas Cowboys quarterback Roger Staubach, an Annapolis graduate and future Hall of Famer, Phyllis George said, "Roger you have an all-American image, you're kind of a straight guy. Do you enjoy it or is it a burden?" Staubach responded, "You interviewed Joe Namath. Everyone in the world compares me to Joe Namath. . . . he's a single bachelor swinging. . . . having all the fun and I'm married. . . . but you know I enjoy sex as much as Joe Namath, only I do it with one girl," referring to his wife Marianne. Phyllis George helped make the human side of athletes part of the story, adding depth and interest to the telecasts, and showing that, in the words of former NBC Sports president Dick Ebersol, "football was not just about men watching men."

When he joined CBS as a game analyst in 1971, Irv Cross became the first African-American sportscaster in the history of American television. Since the very first televised game in 1939, every sportscaster's face had been white. Cross had been a defensive back for nine seasons with the Philadelphia Eagles and Los Angeles Rams. His deep knowledge of the game and the ease with which he interacted and shared a laugh with his NFL Today co-hosts paved the way for African-American sportscasters ever since, many of whom Cross says still thank him for what he accomplished. In 2009, the Pro Football Hall of Fame honored Irv Cross with its Pete Rozelle Radio Television Award.

"We were CBS's *Mod Squad*," said Phyllis George, referring to a 1970s era TV cop show that featured a white male officer, a white female, and an African-American male. "And we had the Greek," she added.

Jimmy "The Greek" Snyder, born Demetrios Georgios Synodinos, was an oddsmaker who set the Las Vegas betting line for football games. Again CBS was breaking new ground because no one with professional gambling ties or expertise had ever been part of a network sports telecast. "The Greek" became a fixture for twelve years on *The NFL Today*, making his predictions and explaining how factors like team speed and the defensive line would affect a game's outcome. Snyder was fired by CBS in 1988, after he made racially offensive statements about the "breeding" of African-Americans during the days of slavery. The comments were in an interview with WRC-TV in Washington, DC, which was part of a report that aired on Martin Luther King Day that year.

By doing stories and interviews that went far beyond game highlights and "X's and O's" *The NFL Today* broadened the audience for professional football on television. Mike Pearl, who produced the show from 1975–80, described its mission: "I want to be able to have the audience laugh, or I want them to cry, or I want them to say 'gee whiz.'"

NFL FILMS: THE BEST SPORTS PROMOTION EVER

Ed Sabol married into the overcoat business and spent fifteen years working in the Philadelphia factory that his wife's family had founded. The business was successful, but Sabol later said, "It was like going to the dentist every day." In 1956, at the age of forty, Ed Sabol cashed in his share of the business. He owned a Bell and Howell 16 mm camera that he used to film his son Steve's football games as Steve grew up, along with vacations and family events. Filming and performing brought him joy, so he decided to turn his hobby into his vocation.

In 1962, Sabol started Blair Motion Pictures, Inc., named for his daughter. He did a vacation film, a stop-action film on the construction of a Howard Johnson's motel, and a few other small projects, but he loved shooting football. Another Philadelphia company, Tel-Ra Productions, had been doing the official film of each NFL championship game for several years. Their films were shot primarily from a high angle with virtually no close-ups, and they were edited in chronological order, giving them the look of a coach's scouting film with an announcer voice over added. He learned that Tel-Ra had paid $2500 for the film rights to the 1961 NFL championship game. Sabol thought he could do a better job, but his little company had never shot a pro football game before. So to get noticed he doubled the bid to $5000, and wrote out a check for the rights to the NFL championship game of 1962. Commissioner Pete Rozelle did take notice, inviting Sabol to a meeting in his New York office. At that meeting, Ed Sabol proposed shooting the game with eight cameras instead of Tel-Ra's four, using slow motion, Zoomar lenses for close-up shots, and adding dramatic music and a documentary-style narration. Rozelle took two days to make his decision, and when he awarded the contract to Blair Productions he told Sabol, "I just hope that we get a film out of this."

The Green Bay Packers won their second consecutive NFL title in the championship game against the New York Giants at Yankee Stadium on December 30, 1962. Six weeks later Ed Sabol's film was presented to the NFL, officials from the Giants, and to the press at Toots Shor's restaurant in Manhattan. Entitled *Pro Football's Longest Day*, it opened with shots comparing Green Bay, Wisconsin, population 62,888, with New York City, the largest metropolis in the country. Chris Schenkel's voice-over, written by Ed Sabol himself, led into on-camera introductions by Packers' quarterback Bart Starr and head coach Vince Lombardi, followed by the Giants star running back Frank Gifford.

When the screening was done, Pete Rozelle knew what he had gotten: "The best football film I've ever seen," he told Sabol.

Sabol's Blair Productions did the 1963 and 1964 championship games as well. As his relationship with the NFL developed and the league kept raising the price for its film rights, Ed Sabol suggested that the league take the company in-house to use as a promotional vehicle, not just for title games, but for every team's highlight films. He made the proposal to Commissioner Rozelle who in turn won the approval of the owners to buy Blair Productions for $280,000, a pricetag of $20,000 for each of the league's fourteen teams. They put Ed Sabol on the NFL payroll and renamed his company NFL Films.

NFL Films would become the story-teller and the myth-maker of pro football, selling the drama, the beauty, and the fun of the game, leaving most of the negative aspects out. It was the perfect marketing tool to portray, as one NFL Films cinematographer put it, "reality as we wish it was." Close-ups of grimacing faces, troubled eyes, and bloody hands along with powerful hits in slow motion all became trademarks, adding intensity and making the game feel larger than life.

Steve Sabol joined his father in the business after having played football at Colorado College. Steve was an Art History major who said his middling grades proved that he "watched lots of movies." He developed the NFL Films shooting philosophy of "trees, moles and weasels." They wanted to see the action from up high (treetop level), from the ground as if the camera were popping out of a mole hole, and from everywhere a "weasel" could sneak into: behind the benches, outside the stadium, in the stands, or in the locker rooms.

Blair Productions had rented their films out to clubs and organizations to recoup their expenses. But Pete Rozelle's goal for NFL Films was to get the films on television to increase the popularity of the league and its players.

In 1965, the job of syndicating NFL Films programs to television stations nationwide was entrusted to Inez Aimee, who had syndication experience with several entertainment shows including *Sheriff of Cochise* and a submarine drama called *Silent Service*. She set up a small office in New York, and immediately started calling her TV station contacts to sell the *NFL Game of the Week* series.

The plan was for NFL Films to send two camera operators to every NFL game every weekend, one shooting high angle and the other from the sidelines. They would then produce a weekly half-hour dramatic highlights show for each team's market. The raw film was processed overnight on Sundays and Mondays while the producers and camera operators were asleep in NFL Films' back room. As their film came out of the processor they would be awakened so they could start writing, editing, and producing the films. Each *NFL Game of the Week* episode had to be finished by Wednesdays for overnight shipping to each syndicated station.

There were thousands of feet of film to screen through because Ed Sabol insisted that each game be shot in slow motion. That meant each photographer used double the amount of film that would have been needed to shoot a game in real time. But the dramatic look of game action, faces, and tight shots of hands, feet, or the ball spiraling toward you set NFL Films apart from television coverage

Figure 4.5 Ed Sabol, on right, with son Steve Sabol in the early years of NFL Films
Source: © NFL Films

and made each film memorable. The films took on the sound of epic movies with the addition of John Facenda's "voice of God" narrations. Sabol offered Facenda the chance to do the voice-overs after he saw and, more importantly, heard him anchoring the news on the local CBS television station in Philadelphia, WCAU TV.

Inez Aimee's first call was to WTMJ, the CBS TV affiliate in Milwaukee where an old friend, Billy Flynn, was the station manager. CBS was televising the NFL games on Sundays, and Green Bay was in the Milwaukee television market. Aimee thought it was a natural place to start.

She wasn't prepared for Flynn's response: "You want me to pay money for the film of a game I've already seen, that we probably already aired, and I already know the final score?" NFL Films had not sent out any samples of their work, so Inez Aimee said it took several persuasive calls to make that first sale. When she did get some demo reels to send out, primarily to CBS stations, NFL *Game of the Week* started clearing in more markets. Within five years it was seen nationwide along with other NFL Films anthology shows such as *This is Pro Football,* which focused position by position on the best players in the game, and *Football Follies,* which was filled with bloopers and blunders. Every NFL Films production delivered the powerful promotional message that NFL football was filled with fun, thrilling moments, dramatic story lines, hard-working heroes, and was entertaining for women as well as men.

When ESPN debuted in September 1979, NFL Films found a national network platform for its programming. The fledgling network with thousands of hours to fill aired virtually everything that NFL Films could produce, and to this day still airs all thirty-two NFL team year-in-review highlight shows.

Ed Sabol was honored with induction into the Pro Football Hall of Fame in 2011. Generations have grown up watching the shows produced by his NFL Films team, winners of over one hundred Emmy Awards for their outstanding quality. They are films about the NFL produced by the NFL and distributed worldwide, making them the most successful sports marketing and promotion campaign of all time. Despite attempts on numerous occasions, none of the other leagues has ever come close to duplicating the formula.

THE NFL AND TV: MADE FOR EACH OTHER

The union of the National Football League and American television came together so perfectly, it is as if the sport itself had been created for TV, or that TV technology was created to cover the NFL. The NFL was organized in the 1920s, long before anyone even owned a television set, but the AFL was conceived by Lamar Hunt on the premise that football was perfect for television. He could not have been more correct.

Professional football games are spectacles with short bursts of amazingly athletic and often violent action that you can see and, very importantly, hear better on your television at home than you could from almost any seat at the stadium. The plays leave just enough breathing room in between for each to be admired, analyzed in instant replay, and appreciated. Each game is filled with the compelling stories of men young and old who come from different backgrounds, and teams with different histories and personalities competing for high stakes and the adoration of millions. The games fit into a finite period of time, and the story of each game, when it is complete, can be told in a set of edited highlights with hard-driving music added to enhance the dramatic effect.

The punctuated action of football allows the television production team to incorporate the full range of technology at their fingertips: replays from multiple camera views, analysis tools to focus on different position players and track their movements, and pre-recorded or live interview segments. The opportunity for the frequent use of technological enhancements between plays has served to promote the development of even more new and visually exciting television equipment and techniques.

The continuous action sports such as soccer and hockey that don't have regular and automatic pauses are not nearly as television-friendly. By the time there is a break in the action, a replay that may have seemed important right after it happened may no longer be relevant. The same is true to a lesser extent of basketball, where play can continue for a number of minutes if there is no time-out or foul called. Baseball has a pause after every pitch is thrown, but the television producer may have to wait an inning or more for the kind of exciting action that would warrant the use of replays and analysis from multiple angles that the producer of a football telecast has after almost every play.

Every sport has its great stories and interesting people, but none has these in combination with the powerful visual action and internal game pacing that have made the NFL's partnership with television so successful. That perfect marriage, which we saw consummated between 1965 and 1975, has set the standard for all sports television programming development and audience measurement, as well as production innovation. Upcoming chapters in this text will specifically address TV sports programming, production, and ratings.

SUMMARY

National television exposure on two networks in the early 1960s was a major factor in the rise of professional football to become America's favorite sport. The success of the new American Football League, both on television and with charismatic stars like Joe Namath, made a merger with the NFL the only viable economic option for team owners in both leagues, who would otherwise be faced with escalating costs to sign the best players. The merger of the NFL and AFL was announced in the summer of 1966, following negotiations between AFL founder and Kansas City Chiefs owner Lamar Hunt, and Dallas Cowboys general manager Tex Schramm. That announcement included plans for the first Super Bowl to be played in January of 1967.

Congressional approval was needed for the antitrust exemption that was contained in the Sports Broadcasting Act of 1961 to be extended to also cover the merger of two leagues and their joint negotiations for television rights. NFL Commissioner Pete Rozelle needed the help of House Majority Leader Wade Boggs of Louisiana, who ushered the amendment through Congress with the understanding that, in exchange, the NFL would put its next expansion franchise in his home state. The New Orleans Saints were established and began play in the fall of 1967.

The first meeting of the NFL and AFL champions was January 15, 1967, at the Los Angeles Coliseum in a game that was called "the AFL–NFL World Championship" between the Green Bay Packers and Kansas City Chiefs. The league did not officially adopt the title "Super Bowl" until 1969. CBS and NBC both televised that first championship game, the only time it has aired simultaneously on two networks. This created a number of problems and tensions between the two broadcasters.

The most significant Super Bowl ever played was Super Bowl III, between the heavily-favored Baltimore Colts and the New York Jets. The two previous Super Bowls had been easy victories for the NFL representative, the Green Bay Packers. The Jets 16–7 upset win at Miami's Orange Bowl dispelled the notion that the NFL and AFL were two unequal partners, and any plans to change the format of the game to allow two NFL teams to meet were scrapped.

ABC's Monday Night Football changed television sports when it debuted in 1970. It doubled the number of cameras used at each game, and added entertainment, personality, and star quality to the telecasts. MNF became a prime time sensation, increasing the NFL's national exposure, broadening the audience to include more women, and boosting league revenues.

The NFL Today on CBS, which "premiered with its cast of Brent Musburger, Phyllis George, Irv Cross, and Jimmy "the Greek" Snyder in 1975, had the same kind of dramatic impact on studio shows that previewed and promoted upcoming games. Mixing features, interviews, betting lines, and entertainment, *The NFL Today* became the model for networks to this day for the expansion of their sports programming to go beyond just game coverage.

The NFL created a hugely successful promotional vehicle when it hired Ed Sabol and established NFL Films in the 1960s. The documentaries and highlights shows that were produced and syndicated nationwide accentuated the drama, stars, and fun of professional football, making NFL Films the league's story-teller and myth-maker.

DISCUSSION TOPICS/ASSIGNMENTS

1   Do a report on the extent of television coverage in the 1960s for any sport other than professional football. How does it compare with the number of hours and broadcast media commitments to those sports now?

2   Find a sport that had more prominent television coverage in the 1960s than it does today and study the reasons for its decline.

3   Chart the increase in television sports rights payments from 1970 until the present in each of the following sports. Compare the growth rates with the size of the television audience for each sport: professional football, college football, major league baseball, and professional basketball.

4   Research the career of former NFL Commissioner Alvin "Pete" Rozelle and write about the five most important innovations he made that impacted television distribution and media coverage of NFL product.

5   Compare any of the pre-game shows currently on the air with *The NFL Today* from 1975. Find the areas of commonality, and discuss the changes that have occurred in the interim. Then answer the question, "How effective is the current program at enticing me to watch the game, and, if I watch, am I staying tuned longer to follow the story lines and stars presented in the pre-game show?"

6   Watch *Pro Football's Longest Day*, the NFL Films documentary on the 1962 NFL Championship game. It is available at NFL.com. How does the style and content compare with the current network coverage of NFL games?

5 THE ESPN ERA

If you're a fan, IF you're a fan, what you'll see in the next minutes, hours and days to follow may convince you you've gone to sports heaven.

(The first words spoken on ESPN, September 7, 1979, delivered by Lee Leonard)

Table 5.1 Chapter 5: The Rundown

- ESPN "keys to victory."
  - Cable television is born.
  - Communications satellites make twenty-four-hour cable networks possible.
  - More teams plus more games equals more sports content.
- The founding of ESPN.
- Getty Oil buys control.
- The ESPN premiere, September 7, 1979.
- "Narrow-casting" targets specific audience demographics.
- ESPN's rapid growth and change including telecasts of NCAA Men's Basketball Tournament games and the NFL Draft.
- The dual-revenue stream from advertisers and cable affiliates makes ESPN a power in sports television.
- ESPN is sold to ABC Inc., and sets course to become "the Worldwide Leader in Sports."
- ESPN reaches over 50 percent of American TV homes in 1987, *A Story Book Year*.
- How ESPN has changed everything in sports television and impacted all sports media.

It's unlikely that very many people heard those words live at 7 p.m. Eastern Time on Friday night September 7, 1979, when ESPN debuted as the first "total sports network." Less than 5 million homes in the United States could receive ESPN's signal. Even fewer could have imagined the force that ESPN would become in the American sports industry. The creation of an all-sports cable television network in 1979 required a set of specific conditions to exist concurrently, as well as considerable creativity, courage, and a sizeable investment of capital. Borrowing an albeit over-used term from sports broadcasting, let's call these conditions our "keys to victory" for ESPN.

KEY #1: CABLE TELEVISION

John and Margaret Walson owned a hardware store in Mahanoy City, Pennsylvania, called Service Electric. In 1948, the Walsons had some new General Electric television sets on the shelf, but nobody was buying. The reason: Mahanoy City is ninety-eight miles northwest of Philadelphia where the nearest TV stations were located, so reception in town was poor to non-existent. If you lived in Mahanoy City, you couldn't justify buying a television if you couldn't see any shows.

John Walson figured out a simple remedy that he was sure would help him sell sets. He put an antenna on top of an old utility pole on the highest neighboring hill to pick up the TV signals from Philadelphia, and amplified and routed them to his Service Electric store using a coaxial cable. When customers came into the store they could see and hear television programming, and if they bought a set the Walsons would offer to hook them up to their cable for an installation fee of one hundred dollars, plus two dollars per month. *The first cable bill anyone ever paid in the US was two dollars.* Service Electric started selling a lot more TV sets and cable television was born as community antenna television (CATV). (Service Electric is still the cable operator in that part of Pennsylvania, with nearly 300,000 customers at last count.)

In the 1950s, 60s and 70s, CATV spread to communities across the country that found themselves in the same geographic situation as Mahanoy City: too far away from television stations even for an antenna mounted on the roof of one's home to improve the signal reception. By 1979, the year of ESPN's birth, a total of 14.8 million American homes were wired for cable, a national penetration rate of just 20 percent.

As it grew the cable industry was strictly a hardware business, not a programming business. Cable was a means for people to receive programs produced exclusively by broadcast networks and stations until November of 1972, when Home Box Office (HBO) began distributing movies and some live sporting events without commercial interruption. The programming was delivered via microwave to cable systems for a monthly fee. Coincidentally, the very first HBO subscribers were 365 customers of Service Electric Cable in the Wilkes-Barre, Pennsylvania, area. Within a year, HBO was sending its microwave feed to fourteen cable systems that had sold the service to 8000 paying subscribers.

KEY #2: COMMUNICATIONS SATELLITES

The live transmission of television signals via satellite, which had been possible across the oceans since Syncom 3 and Early Bird were launched in the mid-1960s, would not become a reality for domestic TV distribution until Western Union sent Westar 1 into orbit in 1974, and RCA sent up SATCOM 1 in December of 1975. SATCOM 1 was America's first commercial communications satellite that could be used by broadcast and cable networks to distribute programming to their affiliates across the country. The efficiency and advantage of satellite transmission became quickly apparent. Before 1975, all television transmission was either by dedicated AT&T lines that could accommodate color video and two channels of audio, or by microwave, which required hundreds of simultaneous feeds from an origination point to individual terrestrial antennas and repeating stations. One satellite transmission, on the other hand, could reach an infinite number of receivers with just one feed. HBO was the first cable programmer to lease one of the SATCOM 1 transponders, thereby expanding its reach to every cable system in the continental United States.

Figure 5.1 The Earth is ringed by a veritable necklace of satellites in geo-synchronous orbit 22,300 miles above the equator. It is called the "Clarke Belt" in honor of author Arthur C. Clarke, who first envisioned communications using satellites in a letter to the editor of *Wireless World* magazine in 1945
Source: courtesy *Tele-Satellite Magazine*

Ted Turner began using SATCOM 1 in 1977 to send his WTCG Channel 17 in Atlanta to cable systems, making it the nation's first "super-station." A large portion of Turner's programming was Atlanta Braves baseball games. He owned the team and didn't have to pay himself any rights fees.

With these small steps, cable television had begun the transition from a hardware business into a programming business. It was a "video supermarket," according to HBO vice-president Jim Heyworth, which he told the *New York Times* in the summer of 1979 was "now faced with the challenge of determining how best to fill its vacant shelves."

KEY #3: MORE SPORTS CONTENT

As the United States population grew from 179 million in 1960 to 226.5 million in 1980, and as television and all forms of communication expanded during those two decades, reaching into every community large and small, the number of sports teams, stadiums and events, and therefore the number of games and fans expanded as well. With 8760 hours to fill each year, ESPN would need plenty of sports content.

Major League Baseball had sixteen teams in 1960, eight in the American League and eight in the National League. By 1980, there were twenty-six teams: fourteen in the American League and twelve in the National. The baseball regular season increased from 154 games to 162 games in the early 1960s, and the League Championship playoff series was added in 1969. Before that the team with the best regular season record in the American League met the team with the best record in the National League in the World Series, and that was the only post-season playoff series.

In 1960, the NFL had only twelve teams with a twelve-game regular season. The AFL started play that year with eight teams, and they each played fourteen games. The two professional football leagues had a total of twenty teams in the US, and each league played exactly one post-season game: their respective league championships. Twenty years later the combined NFL of 1980 had eight more teams for a total of twenty-eight, and each played sixteen regular season games. By 1980, the number of post-season playoff games had risen from just one to nine, starting with two wildcard games—one in the National Football Conference and one in the American Football Conference—and ending with the Super Bowl.

The NBA and NHL each grew dramatically between 1960 and 1980. The NBA grew from just eight teams in 1960 to a total of twenty-three in 1980. No NBA team was based west of the St Louis Hawks or south of the Cincinnati Royals in 1960, but the league had reached across the country by 1980. The NHL only had six teams in 1960, none farther west than the Chicago Blackhawks and none south of the New York Rangers. In the ensuing twenty years the league had grown to twenty-one teams coast to coast.

College football and basketball were also experiencing growth spurts. From 1960 to 1980, college football expanded from ten regular season games and only nine post-season bowl games to a regular season schedule of twelve games per team and fifteen bowls. (In the "ESPN-era" since 1980, the number of college football bowl games has mushroomed: thirty-five were scheduled for the 2011–12 post-season.) There were also twenty-five more universities playing at the top level of college football, then called Division 1-A: the 114 teams in Division 1-A in 1960 had grown to a total of 139 in 1980.

Only twenty-five teams made the post-season NCAA Men's College Basketball Tournament in 1960, and the top schools were playing regular seasons of twenty-four games each. The tournament expanded from forty to forty-eight teams from 1979 to 1980, and the regular season had grown to a thirty-game schedule for most universities.

More teams playing more games represented a dramatic expansion of live sports content. But the time dedicated to sports telecasts on the three major broadcast networks in 1980 had remained virtually unchanged over the same period of time. Sports was scheduled in four to six hour blocks on Saturdays and Sundays. More games available for the same small number of hours allowed each network to be very selective, but as a result a larger percentage of each sport's games were left un-televised. That would begin to change as ESPN, with its voracious appetite for sports content, became a player in sports television.

THE ESP NETWORK

ESPN may have never been founded if Bill Rasmussen, the forty-five-year-old communications director for the New England Whalers hockey team, hadn't been fired. Rasmussen had been sports director and then news director at a TV station in Springfield, Massachusetts, before he joined the Whalers, and he had years of advertising and promotion experience before that, along with an MBA degree from Rutgers. But as of May 27, 1978, he was unemployed.

Part of Rasmussen's job with the Whalers had been to produce a weekly promotional hockey highlights show that was hand-delivered to nine different cable systems in Connecticut for them to air at their discretion. When faced with deciding what he wanted to do with the rest of his life, Rasmussen began thinking about putting together a package of Connecticut college sports events and New England Whalers games to distribute via a network to those nine cable systems and any others who would be interested. At that time the Whalers did not have a local television agreement to air any of their games in Connecticut.

With the help of a friend at United Cable Television of Plainville, CT, Bill Rasmussen invited every cable operator in the state to a meeting on June 26, 1978, at which he planned to present his idea and assess potential interest. About half the state's cable operators showed up, and they made it clear that Rasmussen would have plenty of obstacles if he decided to move forward. For one thing, the cable systems did not have a common source for receiving signals. The national programming they got came directly to them as separate feeds from their multi-system operators (United Cable, Cox Communications, etc.) via microwave, and they used their own antennas to receive programming from the local Connecticut TV stations.

Rasmussen remembers Jim Dovey, the vice president of United Cable of Plainville, telling him at the June 26 meeting, "You really ought to investigate

Figure 5.2 ESPN founder Bill Rasmussen
Source: courtesy ESPN

Add to that the necessity at the same time to find and secure a building site for the offices, control rooms, and studios that would be needed for the launch of a television network. These challenges would make a daunting "to do list" for even the most seasoned television professionals, not to mention a few self-described "little guys from Connecticut." But Bill Rasmussen set out to solve each problem, starting with the NCAA.

CHALLENGE #1: PROGRAMMING

Rasmussen contacted University of Connecticut athletic director John Toner, who was an influential member of the NCAA Council, a body that served very much like a board of directors for the organization. Toner was able to connect Rasmussen with the man who had been the executive director of the NCAA since 1951, Walter Byers.

Beginning in October of 1978, Rasmussen made a number of trips to NCAA headquarters in Shawnee Mission, Kansas, to present his plan for televising hundreds of hours of collegiate competitions that had never before been shown on national television. Walter Byers wielded a great deal of power in college athletics and was known as a man set in his ways, who was difficult to approach and even harder to win over. He was the only executive director the NCAA had ever had. But Bill Rasmussen said that what caught Byers' attention was the fact that the ESP Network was offering to provide the first-ever nationwide television coverage for more than thirty NCAA national championships in sports from volleyball to lacrosse, plus all the early round games from the NCAA men's basketball tournament.

On Valentine's Day, February 14, 1979, the NCAA agreed to enter into a contract with ESPN. Rasmussen returned to Shawnee Mission, Kansas, on March 9 to sign the document in which ESPN agreed to pay the NCAA for exclusive rights to televise

Figure 5.3 ESP Network construction site in Bristol, Connecticut, in the summer of 1979. A Bristol councilman had warned that the powerful transmission waves from satellite dishes would kill birds in flight. No dead birds were reported.

Source: courtesy ESPN

a specified set of events, either live or on tape delay, which in the network's first year alone would total 455.5 hours. When you see the huge popularity that "March Madness" now enjoys, it is hard to believe that, before March of 1980, the early rounds of the NCAA tournament had never been on national television. (That first NCAA contract with ESPN was dated March 1, 1979, but the actual signing date was March 9, 1979.)

CHALLENGE #2: FINANCING

Even the best of ideas can never become reality without some seed money to help it grow. Bill Rasmussen's flights and hotel rooms as he flew around the country making his presentations had to be paid for, or he never could have spread the word. Not sure where to turn first for financial backing, he reached out to the real estate management firm that handled the complex where he and his son Scott had condominiums in Farmington, Connecticut. He knew that KS. Sweet Associates, based outside Philadelphia, in King of Prussia, Pennsylvania, handled capital for more than real estate investments, and he was hoping they could give him some advice. What Rasmussen eventually got from KS. Sweet was a commitment of $75,000, which grew to a $200,000 loan by the time they had found a major investor for the project.

The Getty Oil Company had invested some of its vast profits in a diverse set of holdings from an insurance company to real estate holdings that included pistachio farms in California, to communications. In December of 1978, the partners at KS. Sweet put Rasmussen in touch with Stuart Evey, the vice president of Getty's Real Estate and Forest Products Division, which oversaw all the company's non-oil investments. The division would soon be re-named as Getty Diversified Operations. Rasmussen flew to Los Angeles two weeks before Christmas, 1978, to meet Evey at Getty's main offices, make his presentation, and then ask for $10 million dollars that would be split evenly between equity and long-term debt.

Stuart Evey thought the television network proposal was worthy of further evaluation, and he liked the idea of getting into the entertainment business. But as a clear example of how interdependent the challenges facing Rasmussen were, Getty waited until eight days after the NCAA agreement was reached to commit any

Figure 5.4 Stuart Evey invested Getty Oil capital in the ESPN start-up
Source: courtesy StuartEvey.com

Figure 5.5 ESPN's first president, Chet Simmons, 1928–2010
Source: courtesy ESPN

funding to ESPN. The oil company paid off the $200,000 loan from K. S. Sweet and bought an option for 85 percent of the new network. Rasmussen had gotten the investment he needed, but he had effectively lost control of his creation.

One of the first steps Stuart Evey took was to begin searching for an ESPN president with a strong background in television network sports. Rasmussen's title would become Chairman of the Board, and, in July 1979, Chester R. "Chet" Simmons was lured away from his job as president of NBC Sports to join ESPN. Simmons had helped Ed Scherick found Sports Programs, Inc. in 1957, the precursor of ABC Sports. He worked with Roone Arledge at ABC Sports until 1964, when he joined NBC Sports, becoming its president in 1977.

CHALLENGE #3: THE CABLE SYSTEMS

Also in the first few months of 1979, Bill Rasmussen started traveling the country to meet with the leaders of the MSOs, from whom he needed commitments to subscribe to the new sports network and distribute its programming to their share of the 14 million Americans homes that had been wired for cable. Part of his pitch was that he was in negotiations to bring plenty of never-before televised college sports programming to his new network. Rasmussen admitted that his strategy was to take the potential positives from each of his concurrent efforts with the NCAA, cable operators, and investors, and use them to help convince whichever group he was meeting with next.

When his proposal for a fee of one cent per day was rejected by every MSO he visited, Bill Rasmussen had to find a viable alternative. Once Getty's financial backing was secured, ESPN's strategy to build its subscriber base quickly was to apply part of its marketing budget to *pay the cable systems* to put the new network in their channel lineups. Imagine how persuasive this was for cable operators: an all-sports network offers to give you the service AND they will pay you a few cents per month for every subscriber you have. Plus ESPN allocated 30 percent of their total advertising inventory for the local cable systems to sell. That would allow the operators to sell commercials within network games and events to local advertisers, and keep 100 percent of any charges they would collect from those commercial sales. At this early juncture in the history of cable television, however, only about 10 percent of cable systems were actually selling local ads. In the years since, local ad sales have become an important part of the revenue stream for every cable system.

Less than two weeks after signing the programming deal with the NCAA, Bill Rasmussen had his first cable affiliate: Gene Schneider, the president of United Cable Television, which had its national headquarters in Denver, agreed to add ESPN to its station lineup. This was most satisfying for Rasmussen considering the important role the United Cable system in Plainville, Connecticut, had played in helping him when his ideas for a cable sports television package were just forming. This first cable affiliate agreement came on the same day, March 21, 1979, that the Bristol, Connecticut Redevelopment Authority gave ESPN its official approval to start building on a one-acre parcel of reclaimed landfill on Route 229, across from a metal salvage yard, and next door to a greasy-spoon restaurant called "Hamps."

Over the course of the next few months, and after an enthusiastic response in May of 1979 at the National Cable Television Association's annual Cable Show in Las Vegas, ESPN had signed up enough cable partners to reach an estimated 4 million homes by the date of its premiere in September 1979.

Launching ESPN in the 21st century would have been a much more difficult proposition: the hundreds of choices now available on cable television make channel space extremely precious, and the competition for slots is fierce and expensive. But, in 1979, with a sparse lineup usually composed of about a dozen stations: the local NBC, CBS, and ABC affiliates, a few "super-stations" like WOR, WPIX, and WNEW from New York, WTCG Atlanta, or WGN from Chicago, plus perhaps HBO, cable systems had plenty of empty channels.

CHALLENGE #4: ADVERTISING

Bill Rasmussen's cross-country odyssey continued, taking him to St Louis, where he convinced one of the largest advertisers in broadcast sports, Anheuser-Busch, to become ESPN's charter sponsor. In May of 1979, A-B agreed to pay $1,380,000 for one-eighth of all ESPN's commercial inventory through the end of 1980. At that time it was the largest advertising contract in cable television history. The agreement gave A-B "exclusivity," meaning that no other beer could be advertised on the new network. And, if ESPN wanted to televise a sporting event that was sponsored or underwritten by a rival brewery, the network would need to get permission to exercise one of its small allotment of exceptions to the "A-B exclusivity." A year after ESPN went on the air, Anheuser-Busch renewed the contract for five more years at a significantly higher price: $25 million.

Other national advertisers that bought time on ESPN before it went live included Pontiac, Hertz, Sony, the *Wall Street Journal*, and, not surprisingly, Getty Oil.

THE PREMIERE

On September 7, 1979, ESPN's building wasn't finished, the tape machines that would play out the network's recorded opening had not yet arrived (they got to Bristol at 2 p.m. that afternoon), the studio was still under construction, the control room for the first shows was in a rented TV truck parked outside, and the company's new president was saying he knew they should have postponed the launch until January 1, 1980. But at 7 p.m. that Friday evening ESPN would start sending its programming to a little over 600 individual cable systems, and a new era in sports television would begin.

Producing the premiere was a man with a very steady hand, Bill Creasy, who had been hired to be ESPN's first vice president for programming. Creasy had produced the football game in which instant replay was used for the first time in history: the Army–Navy game on December 7, 1963. He was the producer in the CBS truck for the very first Super Bowl in 1967. He had years of experience under every imaginable condition in studios and at live remotes. Bill Creasy was handling the first day's chaos as well as anyone could: dealing with technical problems, adjusting his show format, and taping segments with Bill Rasmussen, Chet Simmons, and Stuart Evey to be ready for ESPN's first show, which was a half-hour *SportsCenter* with Lee Leonard and George Grande. Conspicuous on the studio wall behind the anchor desk was the logo of the NCAA, testament to how important it had been and would continue to be in the success of ESPN.

That first *SportsCenter* was followed by a half-hour *NCAA Preview* show to set up the fall 1979 college football season, and at 8 p.m. the network's first live event: a game from the World Series of Professional Slow-Pitch Softball in Lannon, Wisconsin, outside Milwaukee. The matchup was between two teams called the "Kentucky Bourbons" and the "Milwaukee Schlitz," which caused a minor uproar in Bristol where they didn't want the first day of their advertising contract with Budweiser to be their last. In 1979, Budweiser was the top-selling brand of beer in the US, and Schlitz was a strong rival in second place.

The director on site, Kent Samul, came up with a simple solution: "We'll just call the teams 'Kentucky' and 'Milwaukee' during the show," he said. And that's how play by play announcer Joe Boyle and analyst Jim Price, a former catcher for the Detroit Tigers, referred to them for the entire telecast. One of Chet Simmons' first moves when he became president had been to hire NBC veteran commentator Jim Simpson to give ESPN credibility as it got started, but the honor of calling the first live game in the network's history went to Boyle and Price.

On the phone to Samul the entire game was ESPN's new executive producer, Allan B. "Scotty" Connal, another veteran hired away from NBC. Kent Samul remembers it being a high-scoring game with runs coming too fast for the graphics generator in the television truck to keep up. Updating the score was a painstaking process that required the operator to change functions, type in each character, then store each new graphic separately. "I need the score," Connal was shouting over the phone. "I do too Scotty," Samul replied. Into 2011, Kent Samul had directed live or taped events for ESPN in every year of the network's history.

Humble beginnings to be sure, but the "Total Sports Network" was on its way. For the first year, programming was scheduled from 6 p.m. to 4 a.m. on weekdays and twenty-four hours per day on the weekends. ESPN did not have sports twenty-four hours a day, seven days a week until September 1, 1980. Columnist Red Smith had foreseen that momentous day with comic fear, in the *New York Times* of December 3, 1979. Sports on television every hour of every day, he said would represent "the ghastliest threat to the social fabric of America since the invention of the automobile."

NARROW-CASTING

What ESPN did represent was a radical change from traditional broadcasting to "narrow-casting." Instead of building a schedule of programs that would appeal to the general viewing public, which was what CBS, NBC, and ABC were doing to attract the largest possible audiences, ESPN's mission was to target a narrower segment of the audience and win their loyalty.

The target audience was men, especially young men who hadn't made lifetime choices as to which cars they would drive, or beers they would drink. Delivering a small, homogeneous male audience meant that advertisers like beers, car-makers, automotive products, razors, and shaving gels, could spend fewer dollars per commercial and reach an audience made up of a larger percentage of their potential buyers. There was no need for them to spend far more money per commercial for advertising time in broadcast network prime time comedies or dramas, if half or more of the mass heterogeneous audience would be women who had no interest in buying their products.

Another important advantage of "narrow-casting" to a targeted audience is that a network's promotional messages become that much more valuable. A captive audience of sports fans is far more likely to watch more sports than an audience that is a mix of all demographics, so promoting tomorrow's college basketball game to the fans watching tonight's game is going to be an effective use of time. The same holds true for promoting an upcoming tennis telecast to the upscale audience watching golf. Research shows that the same audience demographics will tune in to watch both.

The trend toward "narrow-casting" was joined when CNN went on the air June 1, 1980, and other cable networks followed. CNN could target educated, higher-income viewers who wanted more news more often than they could get on the broadcast networks, and they could offer this specific audience to advertisers who knew these people were their potential customers.

Today the American television audience on any given evening is fragmented across a myriad of special interests and program types, and, as a result, the sum of the viewers watching "narrow-casting" networks is greater than the number of viewers watching the four broad-appeal networks combined.

ESPN'S RAPID GROWTH AND CHANGE

Getty Oil's Stu Evey and his appointed president Chet Simmons quickly decided that they needed to leave the Rasmussens behind. At a Sunday breakfast two days after the launch, Bill Rasmussen recalled Evey telling him, "Chet's in charge. You stay out of his way." By October 1, Scott Rasmussen was out of the picture, having been offered a 75 percent pay cut. Bill Rasmussen was out of the decision-making mix at ESPN within a year after its premiere, and he sold his shares in 1984.

A migration of old pros from NBC Sports in New York was making the move 120 miles northeast to Bristol, Connecticut, and they were taking over. Among them was Bill Fitts, the man who had been executive producer for Super Bowl I on CBS, who at the beginning of 1980 was hired to lead ESPN's remote and studio production. He had moved to NBC after Robert Wussler took over the sports division at CBS, and had recently been working on a variety of independent productions.

It was the end of January, 1980, and Fitts had been at ESPN only a few days when Chet Simmons returned from Pasadena and Super Bowl XIV with an exciting announcement: "We're gonna do the NFL Draft in April." In Pasadena, Simmons had run into Val Pinchbeck, the NFL's senior vice president for broadcasting, and asked him if there was anything the new "Total Sports Network" could do with the NFL. Pinchbeck told Simmons that the NFL was concerned that it disappeared from the public eye during the off-season, and perhaps the annual NFL Draft would be a way to get the league back into the TV spotlight in April.

Fitts' response to his new boss was, "Chet are you crazy? Have you been to a draft? There's nothing to see. There's nobody there, just a few people on phones." Fitts remembers Simmons telling him, "Bill, it's the NFL Draft. . . . N-F-L. We've gotta do it to get the NFL on our air." So before he even learned his way around the brand new building, Bill Fitts had called on his old NFL researcher, Frank Ross, and gotten a couple production assistants to help him start calling the major college football programs in the country to ask for film or videotape of their respective draft prospects.

When draft day arrived on April 29, 1980, The NFL Draft became a televised event for the first time, and Bill Fitts recalls having video of all but two players who were selected in the first two rounds. Each year since, the interest in the draft has grown, along with the length and scope of the telecast. It marked the beginning of a programming vision that ESPN would expand in years to come: create events like the X Games or Espy Awards, and inaugurate coverage of existing events that had never before been considered as "sports television content." These include the player drafts in the NBA and Major League Baseball, the Baseball Hall of Fame induction ceremonies, the Scripps National Spelling Bee, and the NCAA Tournament Selection Show.

While one small team was at work collecting video for the NFL Draft, Bill Fitts was faced with how to produce the NCAA championships, the acquisition of which had played such a pivotal role in the founding of the network. In its first March of Champions, ESPN would televise twenty championships from all three NCAA divisions and twenty-three early-round games from the men's basketball tournament. The NCAA hired the production trucks and crews for each of the basketball games in order to syndicate the telecasts to TV stations in the local markets that followed specific teams. What Fitts had to do was take the signals from each game into Bristol and integrate them using a 25-year-old studio host fresh from his job as sports director at Suburban Cablevision in East Orange, New Jersey, Bob Ley. He paired Ley with the former coach of the University of Detroit men's basketball team and the Detroit Pistons, Dick Vitale.

For the first time in sports television history, viewers could watch multiple games at the same time on the same channel. ESPN began what would become the very common practice of cutting from one game to another as tight contests developed or blow-outs made other outcomes apparent. Bill Fitts was orchestrating all the switches from a small production control room, hoping to avoid having Bob Ley throw to a game where play was stopping for a time-out or a commercial break. But ESPN had no communications with any of the NCAA trucks, so a lot of the decisions were simply "best guesses." The following year the NCAA was encouraged enough

Figure 5.6 Dick Vitale and Bob Ley on ESPN's College Basketball set. They were in the studio wrapping around ESPN's first coverage of the NCAA Men's Basketball Tournament in 1980
Source: courtesy ESPN

by the success of the shows that they allowed ESPN to put a phone and an associate director in each game's truck to better coordinate the tournament coverage.

THE DUAL-REVENUE STREAM

Word was starting to spread that there was a new channel on cable television that did nothing but sports all day and all night. By May 31, 1981, less than two years after its launch, the number of homes that could receive ESPN hit 10 million, and, in October of 1983, it became the largest cable network in the United States when the total reached 27.5 million homes.

Chet Simmons left ESPN after three years at the helm to become the first commissioner of the new United States Football League (USFL). He was succeeded in June of 1982, by J. William Grimes, who came to the network with a background in sales, unlike his predecessor who was a production executive. Grimes had been general sales manager then executive vice president of the CBS Radio division.

Just before Simmons left and Grimes arrived, Getty Diversified had commissioned McKinsey & Company consultants to do a study of ESPN's projected future. Getty's investment had gone from $10 million to $25 million in three years, but the network was not yet profitable, with its only source of revenue coming from the commercial advertising it sold. McKinsey's lead consultant on the project, Roger Werner, projected that it could take five years and $120 million more to make ESPN profitable without changing the business plan. Werner recommended that the network should stop paying cable systems and instead start charging them a monthly fee in order for ESPN to generate a second consistent stream of revenue. Part of the argument was simple human nature: if you have to pay for something, you attach a greater value to it. And Werner said ESPN should be viewed as a valuable property, not as a give-away.

Bill Grimes was a strong proponent of the plan, and just a few months into his tenure ESPN started charging its affiliated cable systems six cents per home per month. Some cable systems, who were upset that the check they had been receiving from ESPN had just become a bill, dropped the sports network from their lineup of stations. But the vast majority of cable operators had seen how important it was for them to have ESPN as a prime selling point that could convince new subscribers to scrap their old antennas and sign up for cable. And many of the systems that dropped ESPN when the network started charging had to deal with irate customers, some of whom actually picketed outside cable offices demanding that they get their ESPN back.

Grimes said that there was also some resistance within ESPN among executives who thought charging a monthly fee was the wrong move. They thought that the network would lose subscribers because cable operators who had been getting paid to carry the ESPN would never pay for it. The difference of opinion cost a few people their jobs. Roger Werner got a new job though. Grimes hired him away from McKinsey & Company and installed him as vice president of finance, administration, and planning. When Bill Grimes left ESPN in 1988, Roger Werner became the network's third president.

The six cent charge per home per month was adding $20 million per year to ESPN's bottom line when the network became cable's largest at the end of 1983. The fee increased to ten cents by 1985, and as ESPN added programming like NFL games, Major League Baseball, and the NBA, it in turn charged its cable affiliates more each month for what had become a more valuable service.

In February 2011, ESPN's subscriber base surpassed 100 million American homes and the monthly fee had risen to an average of $4.69 per home. Multiply $4.69 by 100 million homes and you get $469 million in subscriber fees paid to ESPN each month. Multiply that by twelve months in a year to get $5.628 billion in annual revenue before the network sells even one commercial. Add the billions of dollars in advertising and sponsorship that ESPN does sell each year, and it's easy to see why the dual stream of revenue from advertising and cable fees has become the formula for increasing income in the television industry. It's what brought *Monday Night Football* from ABC to ESPN in 2006, but more on that later.

The dual-revenue stream has now become an economic imperative for virtually every network, not just cable networks. To survive in a very competitive television marketplace, networks need more than just the money they earn from advertising. The traditional broadcast networks have all put a price on the value of their program lineups that they now charge cable operators as part of their "re-transmission consent" agreements. In the past, networks like CBS, NBC, ABC, and FOX rarely if ever charged cable systems for their programming: the networks wanted the broadest distribution possible and that meant their stations needed to be re-transmitted via cable. Now the networks look at their programs and say, "If ESPN can charge more than four dollars per month per home, our shows must be worth at least a fraction of that." We will get deeper into the programming and economics of sports on television in later chapters.

THE WORLDWIDE LEADER IN SPORTS

ESPN went from being owned by an oil company to being owned by a broadcast communications company in 1984, and the resulting changes and improvements set the network, then less than five years old, on a course to become "the Worldwide Leader in Sports." On January 4, 1984, ABC exercised an option that it had held since August of 1982, and bought 15 percent of ESPN from Getty for an estimated $25 million. Less than a week later, Getty merged with Texaco, so for a few months every ESPN employee was a Texaco employee. But that didn't last long.

In May 1984, Texaco agreed to sell the remaining 85 percent of ESPN to ABC Video Enterprises, a unit of ABC Inc., for $202 million. That brought the full purchase price for the network and its facilities to $227 million. Thirteen percent of that went to Bill Rasmussen and his family in return for his remaining shares. Later in the year ABC Video Enterprises raised $60 million in cash by selling a 20 percent stake in ESPN to Nabisco Brands. (In 1988, this portion of the company was sold to the Hearst Corporation.) ESPN finally turned a profit in the fourth quarter of 1984, with a steady flow of monthly fees coming in from what had become a subscriber base of 34 million homes. If Texaco had held off on selling the network for even nine more months, the selling price would certainly have gone well above $227 million.

The combination of ABC and Nabisco put ESPN's ownership in the hands of television professionals: Nabisco had invested in Ohlmeyer Communications Company (OCC), and it chose to be represented on ESPN's board of directors by Don Ohlmeyer, OCC's founder, and his partner John Martin, both veterans of broadcast network sports. One of the first impressions the new owners had after visiting ESPN's Bristol, Connecticut, operations was, "How do they do so much with so little?" Herb Granath, the president of ABC Video Enterprises, and the team of Ohlmeyer and Martin set about making changes and allocating additional funds so that ESPN could do even more.

For example, *SportsCenter* had relied heavily on daily highlights that were edited from live games that were down-linked from satellites and recorded day and night in a small screening room with only eight videotape decks. Any other video stories came from a set of stringer reporters and video photographers who were paid a few hundred dollars each to shoot interviews and features, and then ship the tapes with any scripts or notes to Bristol via overnight couriers for editing the next day. It wasn't long after Don Ohlmeyer saw this operation in action that money became available to start doing live satellite reports. Full-time reporters in the field soon replaced most of the stringers, and more travel dollars were freed up for *SportsCenter* anchors like Chris Berman, Bob Ley, and Tom Mees to get out from behind the desk and start covering events from site.

Equipment was upgraded, work space was expanded, and over the next year ESPN started buying the rights to more high-profile sporting events and leagues: a prime time package of live college football games, Atlantic Coast Conference (ACC) college basketball, the National Hockey League, the Nabisco Masters tennis tournament, and the 1987 America's Cup yacht racing from Fremantle, Australia. A chronological listing of every ESPN programming acquisition can be viewed at ESPNCorp.com.

A STORY BOOK YEAR

As a gift for every employee at the end of 1987, ESPN published a thin, hard-bound "story book," which opened with, "Once upon a time in the land of Bristol a dream was born. A dream of sports. All the time. ESPN they called it and for seven years the dream grew. And in the eighth year, many magical things happened."

The magic began in January with live coverage of the America's Cup races between Dennis Conner's *Stars and Stripes*, representing the United States, and *Kookaburra*

III, the yacht that was defending the cup for Australia, the first time in 132 years that the defender was not the US. ESPN received national attention for bringing live coverage of sailors frantically trimming their jibs and scurrying across the decks of racing yachts in the Indian Ocean to viewers sitting at home in America during the wee hours of the morning. The America's Cup wasn't a ratings success, but it proved that ESPN could produce compelling live television from one of the most distant spots on the globe, which elevated the network's standing with the public and within the television industry.

Every NFL game that had ever been televised beginning in 1939 had been on broadcast, over-the-air television until 1987. On March 15, the NFL reached a three-year agreement with ESPN to put thirteen games for each of the next three seasons on cable television. America's number-one television sport would add credibility and send millions of fans to ESPN. The company "story book" called the NFL acquisition "ESPN's greatest moment." The first NFL telecast on ESPN was an August 16, 1987, pre-season game: the Chicago Bears playing the Miami Dolphins at the brand new Joe Robbie Stadium (now Sun Life Stadium). It immediately became the most-watched program to date on ESPN, gaining a 10.8 rating. Double-digit ratings on any cable network were unheard of in 1987.

But perhaps the most important event of 1987, and possibly in ESPN's first eight years, occurred quietly on July 23, 1987. On that date ESPN became the first cable network to achieve 50 percent penetration in the United States. It could be seen in 43.7 million homes, more than half the television homes in the nation. From a curiosity in 1979, delivered via cable technology that wasn't even available

Figure 5.7 ESPN headquarters on the network's 25th anniversary, September 7, 2004
Source: courtesy ESPN

in 80 percent of American homes at that time, ESPN had become a national television force in less than eight years.

The implications were enormous. ESPN's advertising sales force could sell commercials that would go to televisions in a majority of American households. Clients who had previously not been interested in advertising on a minor network that couldn't even be seen on most televisions, began buying time and targeting the sports audience on cable. Leagues and events that wanted national television coverage became interested in talking with ESPN because the network had a national audience. In January, 1989, a year and a half after hitting the magic 50 percent penetration mark, ESPN signed a four-year deal with Major League Baseball to televise 175 baseball games each year.

ESPN's *A Story Book Year* concluded with, "1987, a dream come true." Dreams far beyond what Bill and Scott Rasmussen envisioned had become reality. The network had become part of America's sports media establishment, competing with the traditional broadcast networks for advertisers, audience, and the rights to events. It has grown in power, penetration, and public perception every year since 1987, adding the ESPN Radio Network in 1992, ESPN2 in 1993, and four more domestic television networks since. ESPN International debuted in 1989, with limited programs fed to Latin America. It's now a multi-language service seen in 200 countries. ESPN.com was launched in 1995, which quickly became one of the most-visited sports sites on the internet. The delivery of live and taped programming was expanded to broadband internet in 2005 with ESPN360, which is now called ESPN3.

ESPN became part of the Walt Disney Company in 1996, when Disney paid $19 billion dollars for Capital Cities/ABC, the media conglomerate that had been formed in 1985 by the acquisition of ABC Inc. by Capital Cities Communications. All parties who were either part of the merger or reporting on it for the business press agreed that one of the most important properties in the deal was ESPN because of its profitability, its valuable rights deals with major professional leagues and events, and its multi-dimensional reach in the United States and internationally.

ESPN CHANGED EVERYTHING

The proliferation of ESPN and its success on multiple distribution platforms has had such an impact on the sports media that it's not an overstatement to say "ESPN changed everything." Consider its effect on the following:

- *How people receive sports.* Sports television is no longer like the restaurant you go to on the weekends, but instead it's the kitchen. It's accessible in your home every hour of every day. And it's immediate. Games, scores, and highlights are always available. There's no waiting until the local TV news comes on or the newspaper arrives in the morning. This twenty-four-hour accessibility, be it on television, ESPN Radio, or the internet has changed sports from a special commodity to something far more pervasive and, as a result, commonplace.

- *How we consume major sporting events.* Consider the largest of annual sporting events, the Super Bowl. Before the ESPN era there was a pre-game show followed by the Super Bowl, and then a post-game locker room trophy presentation, all on the same day. Now hundreds of hours of programming with dozens of commentators, reporters, and analysts fill the two weeks between the NFL league championship games and the Super Bowl. Those hours were never available on the broadcast network carrying the game. On cable television they were available in abundance, and "shoulder programming" was born: the shows on either side of major events that set the story lines, promote and predict beforehand, and then analyze the results and put them into perspective in the hours and days after the final buzzer sounds.

- *We have become a nation of highlights watchers.* The average length of time that viewers watch televised sporting events is only a fraction of the total length of any game. For example, the average time spent viewing a *Monday Night Football* game is approximately one hour. That's less than a third of the entire game telecast, and for all other sports the percentage is even smaller. Americans with their shortened attention spans move on to other things or head for bed. If you know that you can watch a complete highlights package that gives you the story, the stars, and the outcome of every game, and you can watch it on *SportsCenter* morning, noon, or night, or online whenever you choose, there is less reason to watch a game from beginning to end.

- *ESPN has made sports bigger.* Thousands more hours of sports programming were produced each year from events that had never been televised and from established events that previously had limited exposure. Before ESPN, only the final two weekends of the NCAA Men's Basketball Tournament were televised nationally. Now viewers can watch every game that's played from every arena. *The Masters* golf tournament was televised on Saturday and Sunday afternoons only. Now all four rounds are available on television, and several major events now have television coverage on every day of competition, from every hole. Or in the case of the tennis grand slams like Wimbledon, matches every day for two weeks from every TV court are available on multiple channels, including live streaming on the internet. The events and their sponsors get exponentially more exposure, and players who don't make it to the championship final can still win fans and endorsement money because they will be seen on television. Nothing and no one goes unnoticed.

- *Sports, leagues, conferences, and events have all grown in stature.* It is hard to believe, but the NCAA used to limit the number of college football games that could be televised on any single Saturday, and they limited the number of TV appearances that individual colleges could make during a season. Now that the top teams in every conference are on television every week, and not just on Saturdays, fans nationwide can cheer for or against Oregon, Oklahoma, Alabama, or Notre Dame. The Big Ten, for example, is no longer just a Midwest regional entity, but it is a national presence with its own television network. Cable television has put the spotlight on the smaller "mid-major" conferences that were unknown outside their home areas before, and on lower-profile sports as well like lacrosse and volleyball.

- *Rights fees have increased.* The dollars that ESPN can bring to bear in negotiating for the rights and the additional hours of coverage that it can devote to attractive sports properties has increased the competition for high-profile series and events, and raised the stakes. The leagues and organizers like the International Olympic Committee that can guarantee a huge audience for their events reap the rewards, which are measured in the billions.

- *Broadcast network sports strategies have changed.* Several sports have migrated to cable, either to ESPN, regional sports networks, or league-owned sport-specific networks. That means that CBS, NBC, ABC, and FOX have all consolidated their sports portfolios to 500 hours per year or less. Each of these networks has become more selective, choosing sports as a signature that helps define who they are as a company. NBC is identified with the Olympics and *Sunday Night NFL,* CBS with *March Madness* and *The Masters,* ABC, whose sports division has been absorbed by co-owned ESPN, has the NBA and college football as its sports signatures, and for FOX it is the NFL. Not only did ESPN take over ABC Sports, it also effectively killed *ABC Wide World of Sports.* Events from across the country and around the world no longer worked as a weekly anthology when ESPN was covering more than fifty different sports: the *Acapulco Cliff Diving* that had been a fixture on *Wide World* became its own stand-alone show on ESPN.

- *Sports TV production standards and budgets changed.* The sheer volume of studio shows and games that ESPN was producing required the network to carefully control its spending on talent, production staff, technical equipment, and travel. For years virtually everyone flying for ESPN, including the commentators, got a coach ticket bought at least fourteen days in advance. A good portion of the technical crew for any game was hired locally, holding costs down even further. ESPN proved that they could produce a successful telecast without spending extravagantly. Quantity did not kill quality, but it did force every network that was producing sports television to re-assess how much they were spending per game.

TV ON A SHOESTRING

In 1991, I did my first "surround programming" from the Kentucky Derby as an ESPN coordinating producer, working with our production packager, Winner Communications from Tulsa. We produced the Kentucky Oaks race as a one-hour show on the Friday before the Derby, and then on Derby day we were live for the four hours of racing before ABC's coverage began. We had one remote truck at Churchill Downs. ABC had four, plus two portable office trailers. Our production office was in the laundry room of the Kentucky Derby Museum, where I remember going over show formats with producer Tom Dawson, director Doug Wren, and host Chris Lincoln, our papers spread across the tops of clothes dryers that were running.

The ABC talent and producers arrived at the track from the big downtown Louisville hotels in separate limousines. We drove rental cars in from our aging motel across the river in Indiana. ESPN did five hours of respectable, not great, television that weekend, more than double ABC's hours, and I was told that our budget was smaller than ABC's hotel bill for the event.

ESPN show budgets have increased considerably in the years since, but working economically is still important at a network where thousands of shows have to be produced every year.

- *Local sports television changed its focus.* When all the national sports news and highlights were available on *SportsCenter* supported by the comments and analysis of prominent ex-players and coaches, local TV stations had to shift more of their emphasis to what their viewers could not get from ESPN: local high school and college teams and players. No longer were viewers tuning in to the local news program at 6 p.m. to catch highlights from the previous night's games. More than likely they had already seen the highlights packages at least once on *SportsCenter* or on the internet. The beneficiaries of this shift were the high schools and local colleges who got more attention and, with it, more promotion on local stations.

- *How newspapers and magazines cover sports.* The traditional "game story" in the local newspaper is headed for extinction because, by the time the paper is published, almost every sports fan knows the results and statistics. Print reporters and editors have to go deeper into sports stories to give readers the "how" and "why" behind what's happening and find entertaining sidebars. Personality profiles on players and coaches get more space. Investigative reporting that takes a period of weeks or months to develop remains a strength that newspapers and magazines have over the broadcast media, which has to concentrate on filling hours and hours of air time day after day. The success of these investigative reporters however has fueled a "brain-drain" from magazines and newspapers, with ESPN and other networks and websites hiring away the best and brightest.

- *Sports talk radio grew.* More people who saw more sports every day became more informed, and, in many cases, more opinionated. Sports radio in markets large and small across the country has provided a place for them to share their opinions. It is safe to say that, if there were no ESPN, and fans couldn't see the vast amount and variety of sports available on cable television and other platforms, there would only be sports radio stations in those few cities that are home to multiple major league franchises.

- *The sports celebrity phenomenon.* Athletes and coaches, who are seen on television more often than most governors, senators, or even the president, have become household names whose lives are the subject of interrogation and interpretation by curious fans. To be sure there were sports celebrities like Babe Ruth, Willie Mays, Joe Namath, and Wilt Chamberlain before the ESPN era, but the public only saw them in limited doses, and their girlfriends or after-hours habits were not common knowledge. Would Duke's "Coach K" be nationally recognized if his regular season basketball games weren't seen on cable and broadcast television for months on end? Would anyone care who NBA star Lamar Odom's wife was? Life under the spotlight twenty-four hours a day has made celebrities out of people who would have been unknowns in the years before sports coverage expanded.

- *The attitude of sports.* Local sports anchors across the country often appear as if they are all auditioning for a job on *SportsCenter*. You see a cocky irreverence, a showiness, and far too often the search for the next catch phrase like Stuart Scott's "boo-yah." And the attitudes of the athletes themselves have evolved, with far more appearing to be self-centered self-promoters who know that, if they go for the impossible dunk and make it, they'll wind up making the *SportsCenter* highlights and maybe even swing a commercial endorsement deal. Did anyone ever see a football player do an "end-zone dance" before 1979?

- *Cross-promotional synergy.* The power of ESPN is greater than the sum of its parts, because each of those parts is promoting the others. Shows on ESPN, ESPN2, and ESPNU all promote each other, they promote Spanish-language shows on ESPNdeportes, coverage on ESPN Radio or online at ESPN3.com and ESPN.com, and articles in *ESPN The Magazine*. And the online services, radio hosts, and magazine all promote the programs and personalities on ESPN's television networks. The emphasis on cross-promotion increased after ESPN became part of Disney. The promotion of so many Disney properties across all of ESPN's platforms has, for some observers, turned "synergy" into a distasteful word.

- *New and previously unseen events arrived on TV.* This would be an exhaustive list, but start with the NFL Draft, the X Games, the *Scripps National Spelling Bee*, the College Baseball World Series, the *Espy*'s, and the twenty new college football bowl games that have been created since 1980. The network has also turned multiple, unrelated games into week-long series like "Rivalry Week" in college football and basketball. When there are 8760 hours to fill on each network each year, the appetite for content is voracious. So if there's a competition with a story line, ESPN is likely to give it a look.

- *The evolution of women's sports.* ESPN televises every game of the NCAA Women's College Basketball Tournament. Not a single game was aired before the network was established. Women's softball, volleyball, gymnastics, track and field, swimming, and more have all found their way into the ESPN program schedule, which means the fan base for each has the potential for expansion, and young women who love sports find role models to emulate and, perhaps one day, to surpass.

- *Our expectations.* More than anything else, ESPN has changed what sports fans expect to see on *television.* We expect that every game that our favorite baseball, football, or basketball team plays will be televised. We expect to see every highlight from every game, not just those played by the league leaders or the top-ten ranked college teams, but from EVERY game. We expect to hear experts break down the important factors that will affect each game's outcome, and we expect that interviews, analysis, and debate will follow. We expect to get personal information about our favorite players, to see them laugh and cry and interact with each other on the field and off. And we expect coverage of controversies, arrests, labor strife, and all the scandalous dirt about any player or coach who steps one foot over the line.

SUMMARY

The founding of ESPN in 1979 was the result of a set of forces and conditions that came together over the course of more than thirty years. Cable television was born in 1948 in eastern Pennsylvania as community antenna television (CATV). Its sole purpose at the time was to bring the signals from distant television stations to homes that weren't close enough to large cities to get TV reception. By 1979, 20 percent of American homes had been wired for cable. Commercial communications satellites were launched in the 1970s, making it possible to feed television programming twenty-four hours a day and have it received anywhere in the United States. And the expansion of professional leagues and of college sports meant that there were more games and events that could become content for a new television network.

A visionary named Bill Rasmussen, who had no national television experience, developed the concept of a twenty-four-hours sports network after losing his job as communications director for the NHL hockey team in Hartford, Connecticut. He set his sights on the NCAA as the source for the programming he would need to make the network attractive. He secured carriage of the network on cable systems across the country, advertising revenue in the form of a long-term exclusive contract with Anheuser-Busch, and capital investment first from the firm that owned his condominium property and then from the Getty Oil Company. And Rasmussen accomplished all of these objectives simultaneously over the course of several months.

ESPN's "narrow-casting" model targets a demographic segment of the total television audience (sports fans, primarily male aged 12–49+) and provides them with content specific to their interests. Advertisers can reach a high concentration of the customers who will buy their products through narrow-casting, an economical alternative to buying more expensive commercials in broad-interest entertainment shows that reach larger, diverse audiences of men and women, young and old. One of the most important milestones in the history of the network came in 1987 when its penetration first exceeded 50 percent of American homes, which made ESPN a more attractive advertising option for national sponsors.

The availability of thousands of hours per year allowed ESPN to create new events for television and produce events that had never before been televised like the annual NFL Draft. "Shoulder" or "surround" programming became a specialty, with preview and sport-specific analysis shows leading up to and following big events like the Super Bowl, which ESPN has never televised.

The dual-revenue stream from advertising and from subscription fees paid by cable and all television delivery systems has fueled ESPN's success, making it possible for the network to compete for any television sports rights package and pay billions of dollars for the ones it most desires. This template has changed the television industry. It's one of the many ways in which ESPN has changed how sports are covered in the United States, and the expectations of every sports fan.

ESPN may not have changed "everything" since 1979, but virtually nothing in sports television has remained untouched by its power and influence. The network has gone from an unlikely underdog to a behemoth that some critics see as a threat to the simple values and diverse nature of sport that they cherish most. They fear that ESPN's overwhelming presence and power have homogenized and "synergized" sports television into a sponsored "product" for the single goal of making huge profits.

But at ESPN there remains an enthusiasm for sports that thrives on competition: the excitement of the games and events that the network covers, and the challenge to beat the traditional broadcast networks and all comers, to win the most-coveted rights packages, produce the most comprehensive and compelling telecasts, be awarded the most Sports Emmys, and prove every day that "the little guys from Connecticut" are second to none.

DISCUSSION TOPICS/ASSIGNMENTS

1   Compare ESPN's early development and rate of growth with that of any of the following cable networks: CNN, TBS, USA Network. Look at the networks' first five years. How effective were they as "narrow-casters" in attracting and building their target audiences?

2   Select one of the major sports in the United States and chart its expansion from its earliest incorporation. How did the creation of new franchises, the movement of teams, and the growth in audience mirror the growth and geographic shift of the US population and the increased penetration of sports television? In class,

compare sports to determine which ones lagged, kept pace with, or anticipated and exploited these trends.

3 Research how the dual-revenue stream has changed the competitive picture in the television Industry. What has each of the broadcast networks done using re-transmission consent agreements and other strategies to increase their revenue stream beyond just advertising?

4 Take any one of the ways in which "ESPN changed everything" and expand upon it in a short report. How would you assess the impact on the sports industry, the media, social or cultural change, and/or on yourself and what you watch on television?

5 Each student should over the course of a week make a log of which sporting events he or she has watched, and specifically note the time they tuned in and when they tuned out. Compile the "time spent viewing" figures and compare sport with sport, by gender, and by time of day. To what other activities or programs did they migrate?

6 PROGRAMMING SPORTS ON TELEVISION

Know your audience.
(Aristotle)

Table 6.1 Chapter 6: The Rundown

- The television programmer as cultural interpreter.
- The programming marketplace.
- Live sports is "DVR-proof."
- The three primary sources of sports programming.
- Guidelines for sports programs.
- Programming: what's the job?
- Competition and "cannibalization."
- Counter-programming.
- New shows: from concept to TV premiere.
- Multi-platform programming.
- "Shoulder" programming.
- The disintermediation of sports television.
- Pressuring the programmers.

The means of communication have changed dramatically in the centuries since Aristotle, but the elements of effective communication are remarkably unchanged. To attract viewers and deliver messages that will hold their interest, Aristotle's lesson still holds true: you have to know your audience. You need to know who they are, which includes the demographics of age, gender, education, ethnic background, and income level. Where do they live, where did they come from, what do they like, what moves or entertains them, how much time do they have for leisure activities, at what time of day or night are they watching and on which devices? The more answers that a television programmer has to these questions, the more likely that person will be to organize a schedule of events and shows that will attract viewership.

Television programmers are cultural interpreters who analyze the information that they gather and put it in the context of prevailing and evolving social preferences and trends. Then it is their job to make decisions as to which programs should be planned, acquired, and created that will appeal to the audience that they have targeted whenever, wherever, and however those viewers are available. The quality of those decisions will determine the success or failure of the network or channel. Misreading viewer preferences and appetites, or failing to see cultural trends, will result in smaller audiences, less advertiser interest, and lower revenues. The importance of the programmer for television networks cannot be understated.

THE PROGRAMMING MARKETPLACE

Sports has proven to be an important and lucrative programming strategy in an era when the proliferation and use of digital video recorders (DVRs) continues to increase. Live sports events are a perishable commodity: if you know the final score or result, the relevancy of the product to you is greatly reduced. As a result, well over 90 percent of all sports viewing occurs live as it happens. By comparison, the percentage of entertainment programming that is viewed as it airs has continued to decline as more and more people record their favorite shows onto the home DVR for "time-shifted" viewing later. The significant difference is that, when you watch sports live, you can't fast-forward through the commercials like you can on a DVR. Advertisers know that there is a far better chance their messages will be seen in sports programming because the genre is virtually "DVR-proof."

The sports television marketplace is driven by profit and loss, just like any other business. The programming department will estimate how much each individual program or series will generate in advertising and sponsorship revenue, and add the value of the promotion that can be presented in the shows to drive audience to the network's other properties. On the opposite side of the ledger are all the costs associated with acquiring, producing, and delivering the programs. These would include rights fees, talent and production costs, travel and location expenses, any staging or sets required, marketing fees and sales commissions, plus the satellite transmission or program shipment.

If the revenue offsets the cost of the programming by a margin large enough to generate a profit, it is likely that the network will find time for it in the air schedule. However, not all programs need to have a bottom line that's in the black. The importance of some programming like the Olympic Games, the Super Bowl, or the FIFA World Cup exceeds the value of the actual dollars returned. The prestige and the promotional value that these properties hold for a network, along with the opportunities presented at each for hosting major clients and advertisers, can outweigh the deficit on the "profit and loss" (P&L) statement. The programming department needs to judge how many series or events that don't show a profit it can afford to televise over the course of a year and still make money. Regardless of the prestige and other benefits accrued from televising premiere events, the goal of a network is to make money, not to lose it.

PROGRAMMING SOURCES

There are three basic sources for programming available to every network or television station that has decided to make sports part or all of its schedule.

1   Rights contracts. The television network or station pays a contracted amount of money to the organizer/owner of the event(s) for the exclusive rights to televise a set number of games or shows over a specified period of time. For example, the International Olympic Committee is the organizer of the Olympic Games. The Augusta National Golf Club is the owner and organizer of The

Masters golf tournament. Negotiating for broadcast and media distribution rights with these organizers and content owners is how the networks acquire most of the major sports properties that appeal to the largest audiences: the NFL, the Olympics, the NBA, Major League Baseball, college football and basketball, NASCAR, and the NHL. They also use rights contracts to acquire many other sports series and events that don't reach mass audiences.

A case in point: in the spring of 2011, Comcast NBC signed a new ten-year rights contract with the NHL, agreeing to pay the NHL $2 billion for the exclusive television rights to one hundred regular season games and every Stanley Cup playoff game in each of the ten years. The number of years, games, and dollars are all specified. To prevent their value from being diluted, most rights contracts now extend the exclusivity to include all digital media, not just television, so that fans do not have the option to watch proprietary NHL content anywhere but on a Comcast NBC channel, website, or mobile application.

2   Clients or partners. Unlike rights contracts, which are fairly uniform in structure and content, programming deals with clients or partners can vary widely based upon individual situations. These deals can cover a sizeable portion of a network's sports programming depending upon how much money it wants to spend and how it chooses to do business. Here are a few variations:

a   Partnerships. Before NBC signed its new ten-year contract with the NHL, the network had a programming contract that paid no rights fee to the league. Instead the NHL and NBC entered into a partnership that pooled the profits from advertising and league sponsorships, and then divided those dollars according to an agreed-upon formula. Prior to this partnership contract with NBC, the NHL was collecting approximately $120 million per year in rights from ESPN. But when the league canceled its 2004–05 season in a disagreement with players over a salary cap, the property dropped in value, and the NHL found that a revenue-sharing partnership without a rights fee was the best way to get its games back in front of a national television audience.

b   Time-buys. The owner or organizer of an event or series of events can choose a network that fits its targeted audience goals, and offer to buy as many hours as it needs to present its programs or events either live or in a recorded and/or edited format. This type of arrangement can be very desirable for networks or individual stations, because they are guaranteed a profit that is not contingent upon their sale of a single commercial.

Responsibility for the sale of all the advertising as well as the production of a time-buy telecast(s) falls to the event organizer. Networks that sell programming time maintain a set of guidelines covering what type of advertising is allowed within and how the shows should be produced. These will almost always include:

–   The number of minutes per hour that must be allotted for commercials.

- The number of program segments per hour. (Example: a show broken into eight segments will have seven internal commercial breaks, each of a pre-determined length.)

- The type of content and language that the network will allow. Most sports programming is "G" rated so that it attracts young and old viewers alike.

- Power of approval over all the talent who will appear in the program and what they will be allowed to wear. Viewers don't distinguish between client-supplied programs and shows produced by the network itself, so the professionalism of the commentators must meet network standards. And any talent apparel that has visible advertising or political logos or messaging is usually prohibited.

- Products or services that are not allowed to advertise in the program or sponsor any segments or features within. Most networks maintain a ban on ads for firearms or other weapons, gambling services, and controversial political advocacy as well as commercials that promote any competing network.

- Production elements that affect the final look of the program. These include the style of graphics and any animations to be used, what music can be licensed or played in the program, microphone flags that identify the network and/or event, how the finished program will be transmitted or delivered to the network, and which legal entity is entitled to the copyright.

The Ironman Triathlon is an example of a "time-buy." Timex, the maker of Ironman wristwatches, organizes the annual competition and buys time to televise the edited show on NBC. Timex can use all of the advertising time for its own products or sell commercials to other approved advertisers. The company then has to hire an independent production firm that provides all of the personnel and technical equipment necessary to record and edit the video and audio, putting it all together into a finished package that NBC will accept and air.

A time-buy does guarantee the network or station a profit, but when an event organizer or its naming sponsor assumes responsibility for producing and selling the program, the level of control the network has over the finished product that goes on the air can't help but be reduced. The vigilance of the network's assigned programming and production watchdogs will determine to a great degree whether the show that is delivered meets the specified standards and therefore looks to the viewer just like any other show that the network produces itself.

c   Barter agreements. An organizer or advertiser can agree to produce a program at its own cost and provide it to the network free of charge. In exchange, the organizer or advertiser retains a specified amount of the commercial time available in the program. The sale of those commercials is intended to offset the production costs. The network does not receive a cash payment as it would for a time-buy, but it does get free programming in which it can sell a good percentage of the advertising and keep all those dollars. The same issues of control over the final product that a network has with time-buys also exist with any bartered programs.

d   Cash barter. This is a variation that blends the "time-buy" and "barter" models. A certain amount of cash changes hands, and the network divides the total commercial time with the organizer or advertiser. But the amounts and ratios are subject to negotiation, as is the responsibility for which entity pays all or part of the production costs.

3   Owned programming. This is any event or series that is created or owned by the network or station for which no rights fees need to be paid. ESPN created the X Games and annually stages summer and winter competitions. The network pays to build all the ramps and jumps, enters lease agreements with venues, pays for the transportation and housing of all the athletes, and covers the cost of their services, plus all of the management, marketing, security, and every other function required to put on an event for the public. But ESPN never has to negotiate with a league or organizer for rights fees.

SportsCenter and all other sports newscasts on any network or television station are another example of owned programming. The network enters into reciprocal agreements with other sports programmers allowing them to use highlights from each other's events. Beyond that no rights deals need to be drawn, and the cost of production is more than offset by the amount of money the network can collect from the sale of advertising and sponsorships in the owned program.

Each of the league-owned networks such as NFL Network, MLB Network, and NBA TV, as well as the regional sports networks that are owned in whole or in part by teams, exist because of their owned programming. The NFL does not pay rights to televise its own games or highlights, but the league could make more money if it chose to sell the rights to those games to other networks. The New England Sports Network (NESN) televises over 140 Boston Red Sox games and most of the Boston Bruins games without paying a dime for rights because the Red Sox own 80 percent of the network and the Bruins own the other 20 percent.

PROGRAMMING: WHAT'S THE JOB?

The programming department has to be at the center of any television network: its programmers must interact with almost every other department and with the network's most important partners, which are its content providers and advertisers. Every program acquisition has to be made with an understanding of how each show or series will fit into the network's air schedule and overall strategy for attracting and building its target audience. Reaching an agreement for the rights to televise a series of events or for the production of any new programming can be a laborious process mired in details large and small, but the signing of a contract is not where the programming department's work ends. The implementation of the agreement, the maintenance of the relationship with each partner league, organizer, or producer, and the development of new shows or specials to expand the franchise for maximum value are also important parts of the programmer's responsibilities.

The basics of the job do not vary much from network to network. What does vary is the scope of the job. The traditional broadcast networks, NBC, CBS, and FOX, each televise 500 hours of sports or less per year. For them, "sports is a picture window," aptly described by Mike Aresco, the executive vice president of programming at CBS Sports. It shows off a set of prestigious acquisitions that help define the network. To program those 500 hours each year on CBS, Aresco's staff numbers less than ten.

The programming department at ESPN has over 220 full-time staffers. They perform the same set of tasks and go through the same processes that Aresco's team at CBS does, but they program 8760 hours per year on ESPN, another 8760 hours each on ESPN2, ESPNews, ESPNU, ESPN Classic, ESPNdeportes, and Mobile ESPN, plus ABC's few hundred hours of sports per year. That's over 50,000 hours of sports programming before you add any of the events that are on ESPN's online, non-linear network, ESPN3.

Each network that has shows scheduled one after the other over a twenty-four-hour broadcast day is "linear." Shows lead into and follow one another, requiring the programming executives to consider how best to transition audiences from one to the next, aligning their schedules for maximum viewership and a minimum of abrupt changes of course. An online network such as ESPN3 with multiple events and shows all available simultaneously is not programmed in a "linear" fashion, but rather as a non-linear menu of choices that will appeal to a variety of targeted audiences at specific times of the day or week.

THE COMPETITION FOR YOUR "EYEBALLS"

Regardless of the total hours programmed, linear or non-linear, the programmer needs to keep an eye on the competition. To John Wildhack, ESPN's executive vice president for programming for eighteen years, "the competition is every other leisure pursuit, the movies, every cable and broadcast network, the internet. In short, anything people do in their free time that is not spent with one of the ESPN networks."

ESPN has created its own competition by offering six different networks to US domestic cable subscribers. "Cannibalization" is the term the programming executives there use to describe the effect that scheduling an attractive event or show on ESPN2 or ESPNU will have on the size of the sports viewing audience that is watching what's on ESPN or ABC at the same hour. What they have found however is that the *cumulative audience* across all of ESPN's networks is greater than the audience they could attract with a single offering on just one network. Comcast has the same strategy with its NBC Sports group, which now includes the NBC Sports Network (formerly Versus), the Golf Channel, and Universal Sports.

Consider the analogy of car dealers on a suburban strip of road. You probably have one of these "auto rows" in your community or nearby. If every dealership has a separate, competing owner, the profits from the total number of cars sold will be divided up into little pieces. But if one dealer owns three or four of the car lots, its revenues are multiplied because it is getting business from a larger percentage of the car-buying public. The total number of cars sold on auto row can remain unchanged, but the dealer with more real estate will make more money. ESPN sees the same advantage in owning more of the real estate on your cable box even if their networks do "cannibalize" each other.

The networks compete with each other for ratings when they go head to head with sports programming, and when the most coveted television rights properties come up for renewal. Most rights contracts give the current rights holder the opportunity to negotiate first for renewal and, should that fail, the first right to match or beat a competing offer. It's called "FNFR," first negotiation, first refusal. Choosing which events and series to bid for that will add value, viewers, and generate revenue for the network is the most important decision that a sports television programmer faces. Just as critical is deciding how much to bid in order to win the rights package being sought and not put the network into the red.

When a competing network wins a premium sports property, the programmer's job becomes *counter-programming*. When NBC schedules Olympic programming, which traditionally attracts more female viewers than male (the ratio is usually 55 percent female to 45 percent male), the competing networks will counter-program with shows proven to draw large percentages of men like NBA games, sports news and talk shows like *Pardon the Interruption*, *NFL Total Access*, or sports documentaries. When *Monday Night Football* was still on ABC, ESPN had success counter-programming with figure skating events to draw the women who were not NFL fans.

The real fight is for your time. People have far more choices today as to how they spend their time. The hours that someone is on Facebook, which didn't exist before 2004, can represent hours that are not spent watching sports on television. However, as more individuals go online while simultaneously watching television, and as more internet-enabled television sets find their way into American homes, the challenge for TV sports programmers will be to develop programming that takes advantage of this trend, exploits the interactivity, and rewards the "co-viewing" audience with more layers of sports content and entertainment on multiple platforms.

FROM CONCEPT TO TV PREMIERE

To demonstrate how the responsibilities of a sports television programmer work, let's assume that you have an idea for a new series that you want to pitch to one or more of the networks that televise sports. You prepare a proposal that includes how many games or events would take place, over what period of time, at which venues (indoors or out), airing live or recorded and edited, and any sponsor support you may or may not have. The programming department is your first point of contact, and from there it coordinates with the sixteen other departments listed below, whose efforts will intersect and overlap over the course of months or years to take you from your original concept to the television premiere.

Legal Department

Before a programmer can even look at your proposal, it goes to the network's legal department. An attorney will send you a "hold harmless" letter that you must sign stating that, if the network is already working on a similar concept or series created by someone else, you cannot sue for theft of intellectual property.

If you sign the letter and the programming department decides to move forward with the project, the legal department will get involved again when contracts need to be drafted, copyrights checked, talent and producers hired, music licensed, and any other part of the agreement needs to be formalized.

Audience Research

The network needs to know how your new series will appeal to the television audience. Will it draw young viewers or older ones, men or women or both? Are you ahead of the cultural wave, or seriously behind it? Researchers will study demographics, compare the performance of any other similar shows, and in many cases organize focus groups to provide feedback on what people like or don't like about the proposed new series. When the research comes back, the programmer takes on the mantle of the "cultural interpreter" to judge whether your idea can capture the attention of enough viewers in the network's targeted demographic to make it attractive to the advertisers who want to reach those viewers.

Advertising Sales

It is vitally important for the programmers to know if there would be advertiser interest in your series. The sales executives who interact with advertising agencies and major sponsors on a constant basis will use the audience research projections to assess what the market may be for any series that targets a specific audience and then identify potential advertisers. If their report back to the programming department says that there just aren't enough sponsors interested in the product, your proposal is unlikely to move forward to the next step. If there is significant interest, the advertising sales department will start work on a presentation deck and may ask to have a short demonstration video or pilot for the new series produced, which can be shown to agencies and potential advertisers.

Production

The programming department needs to know how much it will cost to produce the new series and compare that with the potential advertising revenue the shows would generate. The network's head of production will usually assign a coordinating producer to study the proposal and build a production plan and a budget. The production plan would at a minimum include:

- The number of cameras required to cover the event.

- The recording devices needed for replays and the playback of any edited elements.

- The devices needed to add scoring and all graphics to the presentation.

- Any studio, sets, or commentary booths needed.

- Music and animations to be composed and created for the shows.

- And, most importantly, how many talent, production, and technical personnel will be needed for each program.

The production department is also responsible for producing any demonstration video or pilot needed by the advertising and marketing departments. To build the production plan and budget, representatives from the programming and production departments must work closely with two other groups: operations and program finance.

Operations

The operations department puts together the technical complement for every televised program or series. An operations manager or producer will organize a site survey visit with his or her counterpart in the production department to each of the venues where your series of events will be staged. Operations will determine:

- Camera positions and the amount of cable needed to connect each one with the television production truck, if the stadium or arena has not been pre-cabled for television.

- The truck, studio, or production facility best suited to successfully produce each event.

- Equipment, space, and any construction required for studios, sets, and commentary positions.

- Lighting needs.

- The satellite or fiber transmission, phone lines, and communications equipment that are needed to connect the producers with the network and feed the program back for air.

- The number of "set days" required at each venue in order to prepare for a live telecast. A large percentage of live sports programs actually have NO set days. The truck and crew arrive in the morning, set up for the evening's telecast, and then, at the conclusion of the game, they break it all down and head for the next event.

- The number of technicians needed for each production, and how many can be hired locally. The cost of production can be reduced by hiring camera operators and other skilled technicians who are based within driving distance of an event. It's expensive to travel and house the thirty to forty people you need for a college basketball telecast or the 150 plus who work on every *Monday Night Football* game. However, the higher the rights fees and the more revenue that a series generates for the network, the more accomplished specialists will be sent to each event and the fewer local hires will be part of the crew.

Program Finance

Once the production and operations people have their plan for the series in place, they will share the details with a financial analyst whose job it is to calculate the total cost of every element, show by show. The bottom-line figure for the series then goes into the profit and loss statement. If the projected cost of production is too high relative to the projected revenue the series can produce, cuts may need to be made in the size of the crew and the technical complement of equipment. If a bare-bones production plan still costs too much to yield a profit, the new series will likely be shelved in favor of some other proposal that will make the network more money.

If your proposed series survives the financial analysis stage, a decision will then be made by the programming department based on the profit projections to either fund the entire production and thereby keep all the advertising revenue, or offer you a barter or time-buy deal. Either of the latter would force you to go out and find your own sponsor support and funding.

Assuming your project moves forward with one of these funding models, the following departments then get involved:

Marketing will assign a team to build a plan and a budget for marketing the new series, which may include campaigns online, on radio and television, and in publications.

Promotions will begin work on possible campaigns that can be used on the network itself and on whatever other platforms the marketing department deems are necessary to inform people in the target audience of the new programming.

Affiliate marketing spreads the word to the network's affiliated stations or cable systems to enlist their support and get promotional assistance. The success of any affiliate is directly related to the ability of the programs provided by networks to attract large audiences. If a sizeable number of affiliates don't think the proposed new series will appeal to their viewers, the questions they raise can cause a network to reassess the wisdom of making programming changes.

Network facilities is charged with hiring the satellite uplinks or fiber links needed for transmission, as well as the transmission time itself. No networks own their own satellites or fiber communications systems, so enough time needs to be booked for every show to test the video and audio transmission before the event, to feed the event or game itself including time for any possible overtime period, and then to transmit any post-game interviews, analysis, or highlights feeds that the network may need.

Technical operations is responsible for the network's home base technical equipment and facilities as well as all technical personnel. Production control rooms may need to be assigned and staffed to receive a live event transmission and integrate any studio components like halftime shows or score updates. At the very least, technicians need to monitor all program transmissions for technical quality control, and each show has to be recorded for network archives or possible re-broadcast at a later date.

Creative services will start working on designs for the look and feel of the new shows. This includes the style of graphics to be incorporated, the animations or edited video needed for the show open and all transitional elements that identify segments ("Player of the Game," "Star-Watch," etc.), and the music package. Most networks pay composers to create the themes and musical beds that you associate with each series. The music is then owned by the network so that no additional licensing fees need to be paid every time the composition is played on air. The use of any music that is not a "work made for hire" owned by the network, such as popular music or highlight beds packaged by commercial music libraries, will result in the network being charged a licensing fee.

Program integration is the arm of the programming department that coordinates the flow of the broadcast day, from live event to taped program to studio show, and every combination thereof. Guidelines and conditions need to be established and distributed well ahead of time to plan for how the network reacts when a live event runs long, ends early, or is delayed by inclement weather or technical difficulties. (Clear guidelines in the hands of all parties at site and at network control would have averted NBC's "Heidi game" fiasco in 1968 that we discussed in Chapter 4.)

Commercial operations builds each day's commercial log, which lists every commercial for every break in every show. This group is responsible for the execution of the agreements that the network makes with advertisers and program producers for a specific number of commercial spots in a show, any sponsored features within the show (for examples, "The Toyota Halftime Report" or the "AFLAC Trivia Question"), and all billboards ("Today's show is brought to you by . . .").

Information technology will work with the producers and operations managers to provide all the electronic scoring and data displays needed for sports events and shows. Your proposed new series may have a completely different set of statistics to track that will help explain the competition and develop story lines. Or technicians at each site may need to connect an interface to the arena or stadium's official scorekeeper so that the game score and stats like yardage gained, balls and strikes, unforced errors, laps led, or world-record pace can be instantly accessed and super-imposed on screen.

The work of the programming executive initiates and coordinates all of these functions. The work of hundreds of specially trained professionals and a significant set of varied resources are all part of the many-layered process of creating new television programming. To maximize the audience that will be reached by the new series and thereby maximize its chances for success, the programmer must take steps to ensure the broadest possible multi-platform distribution. So the network's digital media department needs to be part of the development process.

Highlights and previews for each new show, as well as all past episodes, can be made available on the internet for viewing on home computers, eReaders, tablets, and smart phones. Score alerts can be sent to mobile phones. Your original music package can be made available on iTunes. Stories, player profiles, and interviews can be published in sport-specific magazines and distributed to bloggers and specialty websites that cover your sport. Players, managers, and commentators can all be available for appearances on the radio and podcasts.

For television networks that create entertainment content, "all of these new platforms represent huge opportunities," said Disney chairman Robert Iger in an interview with the *Wall Street Journal*. "When you have opportunities to distribute the things you create in more ways and more places with more flexibility, that is viewed by us as something that's very, very positive," he explained.

SHOULDER PROGRAMMING

Building a successful programming franchise out of any sport or series requires tremendous effort, the coordination of multiple, parallel, and intersecting tasks, a multi-platform vision, and one more thing: the creation of "shoulder programming." If the primary program like *Monday Night Football* is the head, all the programs that surround it with previews before and analysis after are the shoulders. The game telecast starts at 8:30 p.m. Eastern Time each week, but ESPN starts its shoulder programming five hours earlier with *NFL Live* at 3:30 p.m. Eastern Time. Coverage continues for hours after the game on *SportsCenter*, ESPNews, ESPN Radio, and ESPN.com. And ESPN sells advertising in every one of these shoulder programs on every one of its platforms to sponsors who want to connect with *Monday Night Football* fans. The combination of all these revenue streams is a big part of what made it possible for ESPN to take over the Monday Night NFL franchise from ABC, which could not commit hours of shoulder programming before and after games.

For the thirty-six years that ABC had the franchise, it could only sell commercials in one three-and-a-half hour game. ESPN has greatly expanded that window with its shoulder programming and multiple platforms, making it no mystery as to why television's most successful sports series, *Monday Night Football*, migrated from ABC to ESPN in 2006.

PRESSURING THE PROGRAMMERS

There is an understanding that networks cover news and that their analysts have to criticize and foster debate, but there is sensitivity to what is said and by whom. A league or any other event organizer that is the target of criticism in shows aired by its broadcast partner can bring pressure to bear in ways both subtle and overt. The network's programming department can feel that pressure when it has to negotiate with its league partner for the best games or favorable start times. It may discover that the best matchups are finding their way onto other rights-holders' air schedules, or are being held onto by the league as content for its owned network. Under that pressure networks must weigh their options carefully: do they maintain a hands-off policy and give their reporters and analysts complete freedom, or do they come down on the side of protecting their partnership and tighten the leash on critical news coverage and analysis? It is a tricky balance with the programmers at the fulcrum.

ESPN surrendered to the pressure of its partners at the NFL when the network canceled its *Playmakers* series in 2004, after just one season. At the time, ESPN was airing NFL games on Sunday nights and was making plans for its *Monday Night Football* bid. *Playmakers* was a dramatic series about a fictional professional football team that focused on controversial topics like drugs and sex. It got many good reviews and had attracted a respectable, not huge, audience. But complaints from then NFL Commissioner Paul Tagliabue to Disney's chief executive at the time, Michael Eisner, helped hasten its cancellation. *Playmakers* was not a sports news or analysis program, but without saying the words "National Football League" it did put professional football in a harsh and at times unsavory light. The lesson to be deduced: never under-estimate the power of a partnership between a network and a league when billions of dollars are at stake.

ESPN did not lose its share of the sports television audience when it canceled *Playmakers*. Nor did its programming department feel the need to replace it with another dramatic series. That's because the events and shows that filled that empty slot in the schedule contained the "drama of athletic competition," and the compelling, unscripted stories that attract fans. A scripted dramatic series can never approach the spontaneity that is at the heart of live sports programming or offer its unique story twists and turns. As long as games and players continue to be exciting, teams remain the object of lifelong love, hope, or scorn, and, as long as live competition arouses passion, millions of people will continue to make the conscious choice to spend their leisure time watching sports on television.

SUMMARY

The job of programming a network is to acquire content and develop shows that will attract the targeted audience in significant numbers in order to generate profits. To do so, the television programmer must constantly play the role of cultural interpreter: tracking popular trends, social preferences, and demographic data, to make sure that any new content being developed stays abreast of changing interests, appetites, platforms, and devices.

One of the major advantages that sports has over all other types of television programming is that almost everyone watches the games and matches live as they happen. That makes them "DVR-proof," unlike scripted entertainment shows that can be recorded to a DVR for "time-shifted" viewing at a later time. The likelihood therefore that a viewer will watch the commercial messages in sports is far greater than for any other programming, which makes sports on television a more valuable commodity.

Programmers have a multitude of options available to them for the acquisition of shows. These include 1) television rights contracts negotiated with leagues and organizers for a set number of shows over a set period of time for a fixed amount of dollars, 2) partnerships between networks, organizers, and sponsors that either share the costs of production and the profits from advertising, or allow the purchase of blocks of time on a network during which the organizer airs a show or event that it has produced independently, and 3) original shows that the network develops and owns for which it pays no rights fees but is responsible for all production costs. On sports networks many of these owned shows take the form of "shoulder programming" that expand successful franchises by filling the days and hours leading up to events with features and analysis, and following them with interviews, highlights, and more analysis.

The programming department is at the center of any network, taking initiatives that set in motion the functions of almost every other department. It is responsible for scheduling all shows, maintaining the network's standards and guidelines, and counter-programming against competing networks. The advent of broadband video content delivery on the internet has changed programming from a linear process of assembling a chronological schedule of shows to the non-linear aggregating of several shows and live events that are available to viewers simultaneously.

DISCUSSION TOPICS/ASSIGNMENTS

1   Identify a trend in sports or in contemporary culture, and then create a proposal for a program or series that would capitalize on that trend. Your proposal could be an extension or variation of current sports programming, or something completely new. Select your target audience for the programming and support your ideas with research on the viewing habits and behavior of potential audience members.

2   Find published information on the rights fees paid by two broadcast networks for at least two sports programming properties each. Then compare the dollars spent on these properties per year and per hour of program product to the audience ratings figures for the shows. Which network is getting better value for its rights payments? What other factors add to or subtract from the value?

3   Take your favorite sports series or event and develop a "counter-programming" plan that could successfully draw viewers away from that series to a competing sports network. What demographics would you target for your competing programs? How would you schedule the shows?

4   Contact a media professional at any network or local television station who works for one of the departments listed in the "From Concept to TV Premiere" segment of this chapter. Ask him or her how their responsibilities intersect with other departments. What kind of research or input from others do they need to make decisions that affect their jobs? Where do they see themselves in the overall process of creating, producing, or maintaining sports programs?

5   Monitor your own sports viewing habits for one week. Do you "co-view" television and internet sites? Discuss how the subjects on the two screens intersect or are divergent. What web content makes your sports viewing experience more enjoyable or interesting? How many different sites do you visit during your viewing session? Are you most active on the internet during commercials or during the show?

7 PRODUCING SPORTS ON TELEVISION

Sports is human life in microcosm.
(Howard Cosell)

Table 7.1 Chapter 7: The Rundown

- Telling sports stories.
- What's at stake in each competition?
- Showing viewers the exquisite intricacies.
- The unpredictable nature of sport.
- The "knowns" and "unknowns."
- Engaging and serving the audience.
- The TV sports toolbox.
- TV sports production roles.
- When the game is over, the show isn't.

Every life is filled with stories. Stories of success and failure, of challenges and obstacles, of goals achieved or never met, of renewal and redemption, work done well or never well enough, of people who play by the rules and those who either push the limits or don't play fair. In each life there are beginnings, middles, and ends. There is celebration and despair. And the optimist in us hopes that each life is enriched by love and at least one passion to pursue.

When lives intersect, where passions and goals come into confrontation you have drama, suspense, and more stories. To produce sports on television is to research and study all the potential stories that could play out in each contest, then use every tool of sight and sound at your command to present these stories from beginning to end in a manner so entertaining and informative that your audience will eagerly anticipate your next show.

TELLING STORIES

Every game, match, or event has many stories, big and small. It is the responsibility of the producers as journalists to uncover and report them. For example, a producer may be assigned to a boxing show whose headliners are unknown outside their home regions. Simply presenting each fighter's record and the basic "Tale of the Tape" information like height, weight, and reach is not going to attract or hold an audience. But by spending the time to do some research on each fighter, the producer may find that "Boxer A" works full time in a warehouse, makes breakfast every morning for his three children before they head for school, and trains on nights and weekends because he just doesn't make enough money in the fight game to support his family.

Now you have a story, and you have given your viewers a reason to root for this hard-working man. His name may not be famous, but the audience can relate to him as a human being. Anyone who has struggled to make ends meet, who has worked overtime to pursue his or her dream can identify with "Boxer A." What happens to him, whether he succeeds or fails, now means something to the viewer.

People as social beings are always interested in other people. It's part of what defines us as human. What else could explain our fan culture where stars become household names overnight and celebrity TV shows and magazines have millions of avid followers? Our interest in each other is what makes us want to know about the lives of our favorite players, what they did when they were growing up, how they got to the highest levels of their sport, and how they cope with the competition and the pressure in their professional and personal lives.

The individual sports like boxing, tennis, and golf, as well as all the team sports, are over-flowing with wonderful stories of people pursuing goals they started dreaming about when they were children, of challenges and obstacles met and overcome, of rookies with unlimited potential and veterans struggling to keep their jobs or sharing their expertise with the younger generation that will replace them.

And yet the majority of sports telecasts live only in the moment. Their focus is that day's performance, so they will tell you or show you a graphic with details like: a running back has 86 yards rushing, a batter is 1-for-3 with one RBI, or the point guard has made five assists and has scored nine points. Only the very best producers and commentators go deeper to bring players to life, to humanize them and make them more interesting. Adding a simple parenthetical phrase or a lower-third graphic that gives the viewer just a little more biographical information can make a viewer care about an athlete who would otherwise be just another guy with a number on his back.

Tell me that a player's hometown is in my home state and suddenly I care about how well he or she does on the field that day, and during the ensuing season. Tell me that the player graduated from my alma mater, and I'm a fan for life. Give me a quick note about personal triumph like "this is his first game back after two months of physical rehabilitation," or "she's the youngest of five girls who always had to beat her older sisters on the basketball court," and I automatically want that person to succeed. Take the time to pre-record or do live interviews that will bring the athletes to life. If they share an insight into their success or just a smile, everyone watching has just gotten to know that player better, through his or her words, the tone of voice, facial expressions, and how they communicate with their eyes. If you make the audience care about the performers and the outcome, you will keep them watching and coming back for more.

WHAT'S AT STAKE?

Every live sports event is a struggle that plays out before your eyes with the ending held in suspense. It is the producer's responsibility to tell the viewer *why it matters*, why you should spend your time watching this event instead of doing something else. The key is to identify what's at stake, what stories and matchups to watch for within the game, and how the team and individual players will be affected by the event and its outcome. To properly set up these stories, the opening of each show needs to clearly and succinctly define:

- The rivalries and history of the featured matchup or event.

- What victory or defeat will mean—a move up or down in the rankings, a spot in the playoffs, an NCAA bid, a rematch with an old rival or a new contender in the next round, the continuation of a streak, a new beginning, or a final chapter.

- The games within the game—the veteran offensive line vs. the defensive line that has two rookies and two second-year players, the confrontation between two all-star basketball centers in the paint, the scoring prowess of a soccer player against the league's leading goalkeeper.

- What the viewer will enjoy seeing—great power, precision, footwork, ball control, colorful showmanship. The best athletes in the world performing at the highest level, making moves the average person can only admire, never duplicate.

- What will change as a result of this competition. The impact on individuals, on team lineups and strategies, the tenure of a coach or manager, league standings, playoff chances, even the impact on communities and countries.

- The venue as the site of past glory or defeat, as home-field advantage or as antagonistic nemesis.

Television viewers armed with their TV remotes are a transient lot. So, even when all these stories have been properly introduced at the beginning of the show, regular resets are needed to help viewers who tuned in late to catch up. Returning from commercial breaks or during segments these resets serve as status reports. How are the stories defined at the outset playing out? Has the offensive onslaught that was anticipated turned into a defensive struggle, and, if so, why? Is the player who needed a stellar performance to keep his or her starting spot getting it done or falling short? If a loss means an early exit from the playoffs, what needs to be done to "seize victory from the jaws of defeat?" Adding quick story lines along with the score at regular intervals during each game or match gives meaning to the event and engages viewers who just tuned in as well as those who have been watching from the outset.

Producers who respect the sports they cover and share their passion with fans will always strive to show viewers something that *they may not see on their own* in order to heighten their enjoyment of the play:

- A tendency to be exploited, a move that telegraphs what's coming next, slight shifts in momentum.

- The *exquisite intricacies* of a sport played at its highest level, like the change of speeds an all-pro receiver makes when he changes direction, the slightly dropped shoulder that changes the angle of a boxer's next punch, or the deep knee bend that puts added power and speed into a tennis champion's serve.

It is not enough to tell the viewer *what* has happened. What's important is *why* and *how* plays, players, and teams succeed or fail. Once made aware of the factors that separate success from failure and the nuances and intangibles that distinguish good performances from great, the viewers will start to pay attention to more of what's happening before their eyes, not just the "down and distance" or "inning and score."

During the course of a long season it is easy for production teams to fall into a rhythm with every new show looking and sounding just like the one from last night or last weekend. To avoid this numbing repetition the best advice is to never settle for the comfortable routine. Always look for new stories and angles to explore, and innovative ways to tell them. The best producers are inquisitive and creative, not just at the beginning of the season, but leading up to and during every game or match.

THE UNPREDICTABILITY OF SPORT

The compelling nature of sport is its unpredictability. The heavy favorite doesn't always win, so you have to watch to see what happens. Ask the Baltimore Colts who lost to the underdog New York Jets in Super Bowl III. Ask Mike Tyson who appeared invincible as world heavyweight champion until he was knocked out in 1990 by James "Buster" Douglas, a journeyman fighter with four losses on his record. You never know what's going to happen, so the producer needs to prepare for every possible eventuality.

The team assigned to cover any sporting event starts out with a set of *knowns*, which provide story lines and production possibilities. In most cases these include:

1 The venue. The arena or stadium, indoors or out, in which the event will take place. Research will reveal any noteworthy events that have taken place there in the past, or if this is the first time it has hosted this sport or contest.

2 The competitors. The teams or combatants facing each other. Stories to develop include the backgrounds and histories of each team and player, and when they have met before. In the individual sports like golf or tennis, however, the big star could miss the cut or lose in the early rounds, putting lesser-known players into the spotlight. So that requires even more research, covering dozens of contenders.

3 What's at stake? What will the outcome of this contest mean? Does the winning team move into first place or clinch a playoff berth? Will a winning streak or losing streak be broken? Is a starting player in jeopardy of losing his or her position if they don't perform well? Is this the first opportunity for a rookie and how will he or she deal with the pressure?

4 The rules. How the sport is played, what's legal, and what will be penalized.

5 The start time. When the event is scheduled to begin and how much time you have from the time you go on the air until the first ball or the start of each race or contest.

6 The scheduled length of the show. The total number of hours that are allotted for the event, along with instructions for what to do if the contest ends early or runs long.

7 Your personnel. You know who is assigned to your team in every role: producers and directors, play-by-play hosts and analysts, technicians, production assistants, statisticians, runners, and everyone in between.

8 Scheduled travel times. When the teams, players, your crew, and your production truck are scheduled to arrive. If the team or players are arriving from a great distance or from having just played an important or overtime game, there is another story to pursue.

9 The weather forecast. This affects all outdoor events, but is especially critical for golf tournaments, auto races, horse races, or tennis matches. The producer will want to know which competitors do best in the weather conditions expected: which horses run better on a sloppy track, which football teams have better records in freezing temperatures. And the threat of bad weather can also force changes in travel plans for the competitors and television crew members alike, all of which can affect the TV production.

10 Camera and microphone positions. In a site survey prior to the event, the producer, director, and operations manager will have scouted the venue to select the best places for cameras and microphones to provide the viewers with defining views of every critical action and the sounds of the game. Providing the TV audiences with video and sounds of everything that affects the outcome of a sporting event is the best way to tell its stories.

11 The content and length of pre-produced elements. Packaged teases and animations, features, interview segments, edited video from previous games or matchups, graphics panels with biographical or statistical information. These are all built to add context and interest to the telecast.

12 Total commercial time and number of breaks. How many times the show is required to take breaks in action and how long each break must be.

13 Sponsored features. The elements that must play in each show with sponsor identification and how each is to be executed. For example, "The Play of the Game presented by _____," or "The _____ Sky-Cam." Money has been paid to the network or station in advance, so these features must be incorporated into the show.

14 Promotional elements. The visuals and scripts for each upcoming program that must be promoted during the event, when these need to run (first half/second half/pre-game or post-game), and how often during the show.

15 The next show. On linear networks, the crew at each live event knows what program they precede. There are also guidelines explaining how that may change if an event runs very short or very long.

These are the givens, the beginnings from which the producer works forward. Research and materials need to be gathered and prepared on deadline in order to be ready for what is required and expected. But just as much or more work goes into preparing for the unexpected, the unknowns:

1 Venue problems. The production team should know how to deal with technical, mechanical, or access problems at the venue. What do you do if the lights go out or the backboard breaks? How do you fill time if the game or match is delayed while problems are fixed? Do you have pre-recorded packages or a replay of the last game or match ready to go?

2 Who will emerge as the star? A player coming off the bench could be the hero, which means that the producer needs to have information and stats about every player who could possibly get into the contest, not just the starters. Graphics need to be built ahead of time for each player with details on his or her scoring average, batting average, best past performance, career highlights, and more.

3 The story of the game. The producer works with the entire broadcast team to anticipate *every* possible outcome. The contest could be an offensive exhibition or a defensive struggle, a ten-stroke victory or a "nail-biter" that goes down to the final playoff putt. If the underdog wins, how does that affect the standings, the coach and players, the losers? Each scenario requires preparation so that the audience continues to get information and entertainment regardless of who is winning or losing or what the margin of victory may be.

4 Rules violations. Dealing with a common penalty is easy, but information and expertise need to be ready if a rare penalty is called or if an official's call is challenged. The last thing any network wants is for its commentators or shows to appear confused or uninformed.

5 The actual start time. A game may be scheduled to start at five minutes after the hour, but, if one of the two tennis players decides he or she needs to run to the bathroom, the start time is going to change. The pre-game pyrotechnics may leave behind too much smoke to start the game, so the producer has to be prepared to fill extra time before kick-off or first tip. And everyone on the crew needs to know in advance what to do if plans suddenly change.

6 The actual length of the show. When baseball games go into extra innings, football games go into overtime, golf tournaments end in playoffs, or tennis matches go past 6–6 in the fifth set, every production team needs to know how to continue. Do satellite or fiber transmission times need to be extended? How many more commercials will run? Do promos get repeated or are new ones added? How do you arrange bathroom breaks for crew members who haven't left their posts in three or four hours?

7 Personnel substitutions. Illness, family emergencies, canceled flights, or bad weather can prevent assigned crew members from making it to the venue. The producer needs to have options ready and available so that a local free-lancer or back-up commentator can be brought on in time for the show.

8 The weather. Even if the forecast was for sunny, cloudless skies, a thunderstorm or stray shower could affect an event staged outdoors. (I once had an indoor event that was delayed by rain: the roof leaked.)

9 Technical problems. One or more cameras could go down, so the best directors know how to cover an event with only one or two cameras functioning. Microphones stop working without notice, so spare microphones need to be at the ready with enough audio personnel to respond and repair. Recorded interviews may not play back, so notes on what the player or coach said should be ready so that important storylines are not abandoned just because of technical problems.

10 Impact on the next show. If the live event on the air runs well under its expected time, the network may require the production team to do post-game interviews and analysis segments, or it may call for an early throw to the next event for "bonus coverage." The producers of both shows need to be ready. Or, if the first show runs past its scheduled "off-time," the talent there may be required to start updating the audience on the progress of the game that is being pre-empted, or toss to short updates from the next venue. Planning for these possibilities will make the on-air execution seamless. Sitting at home watching television, it's painfully obvious to everyone when this kind of planning hasn't taken place.

ENGAGING AND SERVING THE AUDIENCE

All production decisions should be made on behalf of the viewer.

It's a simple statement, but when applied it can make the difference between success and failure for any televised event or series. The viewer is the ultimate boss in sports television, not a room full of executives with impressive-sounding titles. Serve the viewers, give them entertainment and information, stories about people and teams that do extraordinary things. Add replays and analysis that will increase their enjoyment and improve their understanding of the sport's "exquisite intricacies." Do it without squeezing in over-commercialized sponsorship messages that distract from the story or take time away from game coverage. Do all these things and your show will be rewarded with strong audience ratings and loyal fans who watch for longer periods of time. If a producer makes a decision because he or she thinks the audience will like it, not because he or she thinks the boss will like it, it will be the right decision more often than not. If viewers like the show, the higher audience ratings will translate into more advertising or subscription revenue, and then the boss will love the results.

THE TV SPORTS TOOLBOX

All television programs, including all sports programs, are a product of just four things:

- Time.

- Resources.

- People.

- Information.

If you have lots of lead time before your show, you can plan and develop new strategies, search for the best talent and give them ample training. A large budget will provide all the resources you need to produce the best possible show. That includes extra cameras and microphones in unique places, innovative technology to provide new, eye-catching ways of analyzing action, and additional editing facilities to improve the overall look of shows and how the stories are presented. Every telecast is made better by creative, hard-working, resourceful people. And every telecast is composed of information: team and individual records and histories, rivalries, biographies, anecdotes, scoring data and statistics.

If you are short on time and resources, don't have enough people or people who are smart and creative, and your information is incomplete or inaccurate, your show will suffer. However, making the most with what you are given, and never settling for something you can't be proud of, is the formula for success at any level.

Regardless of how large or small the budget, and whether there was a month to prepare or just a day, each sports event producer has a toolbox in which he or she will find everything needed to craft a compelling television product. Using each of these tools expertly will engage and serve viewers.

- *Live pictures* that are wide enough to show how plays develop, then tight enough to see dramatic moves and faces filled with emotion. Pictures tell us about the people, their families, the place, tradition, and community. As contests progress toward their conclusion, each play becomes more important and the pressure on each player builds, so camera shots should gradually move in tighter. Close-ups capture tension and human drama, and they show viewers how each performer is handling the pressure or reveling in the moment.

- *Replays* show how and why something happened, and provide the viewer with the best views of every game-changing play. Replays document the big moments from all the best angles. They can show the "games within the game" and the one-on-one matchups that good analysts use to educate the viewer to explain what worked, what didn't, and why. Replays can show us how trends develop within each contest and provide insight into what may happen next. And they communicate human emotion in the reactions of victor and vanquished alike.

- *Commentary* leads the viewer through each event, setting up the story lines and what's at stake, and then describing how that changes and evolves. We will look at the role and responsibility of television sports commentators in the next chapter on sports talent, but it is the producer's job to define each commentator's assignment, what type of information each should focus on, and when each is expected to speak or be silent.

- *Audio* from the arena, the court, or the field of play communicates in ways for which words will always fall short. You don't need an announcer to tell you that "this place is rocking" if the producer and director have deployed enough microphones to catch the excitement and intensity of a sell-out crowd. The viewer can instantly sense by audio alone the importance of any event. If a winning serve or return is met with only a smattering of applause, it won't matter who the players are and whether the picture is framed so you can see how many people are in the stands or not. The television audience knows that this tennis match doesn't matter.

The sounds of players colliding, of pucks hitting goal posts, of foot against soccer ball, of coaches exhorting or consoling players, all add to the viewer's comprehension of what is happening and why it has meaning.

- *Music* adds feeling, identity, and drama to sports television. It would be hard to imagine *Monday Night Football* without the theme music that has been an audio cue for the series for decades. It's a signature that identifies the show from the beginning and welcomes you back from a commercial break, conjuring memories of exciting, enjoyable games from the past. Music underscores the action of edited highlights or the emotions of an edited profile, but it can distract attention from live action.

The use of popular music is strictly regulated by licensing agencies and the artists themselves, so very often the music you hear repeatedly on television has been purchased from composers as "works made for hire" in order that they may be broadcast an infinite number of times without the network paying a fee each time.

- *Interviews*, either done live or pre-recorded and edited for insertion into the telecast, can be used to advance story lines and explain what's behind certain actions or reactions. Human beings are experts at reading what people really mean by what's in their voices and on their faces when they respond to questions. By choosing which questions to pose, which answers to use, and when to show an interview subject's face or cut to video of what's being discussed, the producer adds interest and another layer of information to the overall presentation.

- *Graphics* that are superimposed on the screen provide information about the competitors and help draw comparisons that give the viewer more to think about and a broader perspective. Well-researched graphics advance story lines, connect us with individual athletes, and add dimension to telecasts.

- *Scoring data* frames the action. The introduction of a constant score box during the ABC and ESPN telecasts of the 1994 World Cup of soccer changed the way Americans watch sport. No matter when viewers tune in, immediately knowing the score and how much time is left puts every action into perspective. A pitch thrown with a tie score in the bottom of the ninth inning can look just like a pitch thrown in the first, but it has far more meaning because of the timing and the score. A serve at 4–5 in the fifth set is far more important than a serve by the same player at 4–5 in the first. As data interface technology has improved and expanded, more instantaneous data is now available to add context to every pitch, pass, punch, or putt you may see.

- *Technological innovations* are developed and refined each year to enhance live television sports. From a simple "Telestrator" that allows the analyst to circle the player to watch in a replay, to computerized systems that track the speed and trajectory of a ball or allow the producer to rotate the field of play, technology can help improve a viewer's understanding of the action. The key decision to be made by the producer and director however is whether the addition of new technology actually represents an advancement and not a distraction that diverts attention away from the real story and in so doing wastes valuable air time. The bigger the production budget, the more technology can be applied to a telecast, but adding "bells and whistles" doesn't always translate into better audience ratings.

The best sports telecasts combine commentary and astute analysis with great pictures (live and in replay), audio from the field of play and participants, graphics that add context and information, and enhancements of sight and sound that add to the stories and entertainment value of the coverage. The telecast can be compared to a symphony filled with passion and excitement in which every instrument has its vital part, and the timing is critical. An orchestra only has one leader and one baton. For a sports telecast there are two. The producer and director work together to cue each instrument, get the most out of each section and blend them all together into a cohesive art form that communicates a multitude of messages to the intellects and emotions of each individual in the audience.

Figure 7.1 Inside NBC's *Sunday Night Football* production truck. Producer Fred Gaudelli is right next to director Drew Esocoff and technical director Geoff Butler.
Source: courtesy NBC *Sunday Night Football*

WHO DOES WHAT?

Every sports television production in the United States, from the local cable production of a high school football game to the Super Bowl, requires a core of professionals working in concert. The bigger the show the more people with a wider variety of specialties are added to the crew, but every sports telecast needs these basic jobs filled.

Producer

The producer is responsible for the content and the quality of the program. You can think of a producer as the "coach" of a team. He or she is the creative planner and administrative leader of the production crew, providing direction and guidance for all assigned personnel. The producer establishes the game plan, which includes a detailed rundown of which elements will be presented in what order and how the show open and every successive segment should be structured. He or she then assigns duties based upon the story lines that need to be developed and the elements that need to be built such as pre-produced interviews or highlight packages from past games.

The decisions that a producer makes will affect the perception of everyone in the viewing audience, which could be thousands or millions of people. The stories, words, and pictures chosen to document an event will define how it is perceived, and how every participant is perceived. The stories, words, and pictures that the producer chooses to omit are almost as important. If information is left out that could explain why a team or player failed to perform up to expectations, or why they exceeded expectations, the factors that go into molding the public's perception will be incomplete or, worse, inaccurate. The producer is responsible to each and every viewer to make the best choices that will tell the full, unbiased story of that event.

During a live event the producer is the primary story-teller, leading the commentators to explain key points, selecting replays that will emphasize or analyze why and how plays succeeded or failed, and choosing when to insert graphics and all other pre-produced elements such as interview excerpts. These will add to the viewer's understanding of what just happened, what it means as the game or season progresses, and who the players are who made it happen.

The producer is also accountable for the show's budget. When problems arise he or she must make decisions based upon what is needed and what it will cost. For sports that have seasons running several months, additional expenditures one week can usually be offset by savings over the next few weeks. Budgets for one-time-only events tend to be less flexible.

Director

The director is responsible for the visual coverage and the look of a televised event. You can think of the director as the "quarterback" who is executing the producer's game plan. The director plans where cameras should be placed to capture every action from the best angles. Then he or she leads a meeting of all camera operators to present the coverage plan and explain what is expected in every situation. For example, each operator needs to know what to shoot when the football moves inside the near 20-yard line or the 20-yard line at the opposite end of the field. The director has specific assignments for each camera after a touchdown is scored: which cameras shoot the player who scored, the jubilant crowd, each of the coaches, or the defensive player who was beaten on the play, and how wide or tight their shots should be.

The director is the leader of the technical crew and as such works with the operations manager to set the production schedule leading up to the game and trouble-shoot any operational issues that arise. The director takes the producer's rundown for the show and oversees the pre-production of all packaged elements, mixing video with natural sound, narration, music, graphics, and visual effects.

During the telecast the director instructs every camera operator as to the framing and/or movement of every shot, and then makes instantaneous decisions as to which cameras to take live to air. At the prompting of the producer, the director also calls for every replay and every graphic or packaged element. The director's voice alone is what leads the technical director to manipulate the switcher, pushing the right button for every visual input and effect.

Technical Director

The technical director connects the director's vision and creativity with the technology that puts video on television. It's as if the technical director was playing the piano by listening to the composer tell him which keys to press, one after the other for hours on end. The technical director must know the capabilities of the switcher at which he or she sits in the television truck or control room, and have memorized the location of every input on every bank of switches. There are only eighty-eight keys on a piano. Most television switchers have many more than that.

Operations Manager

The operations manager is responsible for the survey of each sports venue, for the entire technical operation, and for the hiring, direction, safety, and payment of the technical staff. A survey is done at each venue to identify camera and microphone positions, the location of the mobile television truck(s), transmission facilities, and temporary office trailers. In many cases the survey requires an advance visit to the venue by the director and the producer along with the operations manager to plan the logistics of the production. The survey must also determine the length of cable runs needed, provide for crew accommodations, meals, and parking, find safe areas of refuge in case of a fire or other emergency, and locate or plan for the installation restroom facilities.

Once on site, the operations manager coordinates the set-up, installation, and testing of all technical facilities, solving problems and responding to the specific needs of each show as they arise. He or she works with the director and producer to schedule every technician's start time so that all the tasks needed to prepare for the live telecast can be completed in time for a quick rehearsal before the show goes on the air. The ops manager also coordinates the credentialing process with the home team or organizer so that each crew member can gain access to the areas of the stadium, park, or arena where their job function requires them to be.

Associate Producer

The "AP" tells the story of the contest through graphics displays. He or she takes direction from the producer on which stories to pursue. Then, using research and discussions with the analyst(s) assigned to that game, they support those stories with statistical, historical, and biographical graphics that can be built ahead of time in preparation for the live telecast. The best APs use their knowledge of the sport and their research to add new story lines that complement the work of the producer.

The graphics build for many events starts days before they are scheduled to occur. The sophisticated software and hardware that make multi-color, three-dimensional moving graphics possible can be interfaced with data stored on laptops or that come directly from official scorers at events. So the associate producer can be typing sets of graphics while he or she is on the plane bound for the event, or in the hotel room the night before.

During a telecast the AP is constantly offering graphics that are pertinent to the game situation at hand for the producer's consideration. Statistics are checked and updated using the scoring interface, and as new stories develop new panels may have to be built with the graphics machine operator to compare one player or team to another, or the current game or quarter to one in the past. Having prepared panels for every player and virtually every eventuality, it is rare that even 20 percent of the graphics that are built and stored ever get inserted on air.

Additional associate producers work with talent on interviews, edit and produce features and teases, and build the video elements that give each sports series its "look." Most producers were promoted from associate producer because they demonstrated strength as story-tellers, the ability to see a game as having multiple layers and factors at work, and the skills to smoothly coordinate the efforts of several people in pressure-packed situations.

Assistant Director

The primary job responsibilities for an "AD" cover the video elements used within each telecast and the timing of every segment. It is possible for one person on a smaller production to handle all of these tasks, but very often the job is divided into two distinct roles: video AD and control AD

The video assistant director works with camera crews to record interviews with coaches and players plus get shots of practice sessions, the host city, or campus. Then the AD works with editors and technicians to produce show opens, teases, bumps, and packages integrating the video shot at site with clips from previous games, animated elements, graphics, and music. (A "bump" is the short video piece used to roll into a commercial break, or which is played coming directly back from a commercial.) Directors regularly put the AD in charge of pre-production in the truck while they hold their camera meetings or do other planning or trouble-shooting inside the venue.

During the live telecast this AD is usually in the video area of the truck helping the producer identify replay sequences, cuing the best interview excerpts or pre-produced packages to use at a particular juncture, and editing new "bumps" to music using fresh video from the game.

The control AD is the link between the remote TV truck and the network or television station's broadcast operations control room. Leading up to and during a live telecast the control AD keeps that communications link open, counting down to the scheduled start time of the show, counting the director into and out of pre-recorded elements that are rolled into the show, and counting into and back from commercials. The control AD also has the list of all sponsored features and promos that must get into each live show. He or she works with the producer on the placement of these elements, helping to make sure that nothing that was paid for by a sponsor or was mandated by the network fails to get into the telecast.

Larger productions with upwards of fifteen cameras will regularly add a third AD as an "iso producer." This AD serves as a second set of eyes for the producer, watching for which cameras feeding into which isolated replay devices captured the most defining looks of any particular play. The "iso producer" will quickly judge which replays should air in what order and deliver that sequence via headset to the producer. Also important in this role is the assignment and re-assignment of which cameras are being recorded at any one time based upon game situations. When action moves to one end of a football field, for example, the cameras at that end all have to feed into replay devices. That may cause cameras at the other end of the field to no longer be recorded. When possession changes and the ball starts heading back the other way, replay assignments will change accordingly.

The directors of sports television usually come from the ranks of the assistant directors or technical directors. These two groups learn how all the pieces of the director's job fit together and how that job interacts with the producer, the operations manager, and everyone else in the truck or control room.

Production Assistant

Every sports television production needs at least one strong, reliable "PA." The production assistants provide the building blocks needed by the producer at each event. PAs are assigned to screen through video to find great shots for teases or other edited features and show elements. These shots are then "clipped" to assemble a tape or disk of highlights for use by associate producers, assistant directors, and video editors. PAs are assigned to do research and dig for facts that will assist the AP in building graphics panels for each event. PAs can be assigned to get logos and sponsorship information from the Commercial Services department and have them packaged with scenic shots as the "brought to you by . . ." billboards.

Many production assistants do not travel with the remote production teams. Instead they serve as a conduit for materials from the network or television station to the traveling crew. Their responsibility is to support the production in every way possible, and the best PAs are those who think beyond the tasks they are assigned and volunteer ideas and additional video or research material that they think will enhance the quality of the shows. When it's time to fill an opening for an associate producer or assistant director, the PAs who have shown creativity and initiative will be the first to get promoted.

Coordinating or Executive Producer

This is the person who sets the overall goals for each series or set of shows. He or she is the creative and administrative lead who creates, plans, and designs new series and programs, or updates and revitalizes continuing shows that need to attract larger audiences. The coordinating or executive producer hires and/or assigns all producers, directors, APs, ADs, PAs, and talent. And the best ones provide their team members with continual feedback, constructive criticism, coaching, and ideas for innovation and improvement.

Coordinating producers interface with the programming and legal departments to ensure that what the network has agreed to in its contract with a league or event organizer can be done and will be executed. They work with the sales and marketing departments to protect the integrity of the on-air product while at the same time implementing sponsorships that produce revenue for the company. Working with the accounting and program finance departments they put together the annual budgets for each of their shows and series, and then allocate the money based upon a set of priorities that includes how large an audience will be reached and how complex or difficult each individual production will be. The coordinating producer must see each show or series as the product of a network, not simply as the work of one team of people in one department. To complete the sports analogy, think of the coordinating or executive producer as the team's "general manager."

THE GAME IS OVER

When the game is over, the job of the production team is not done. In fact, the precious few seconds or minutes between the end of play and the end of the show are crucial. Ending strong is just as important as starting strong. Every story line that was set up at the top of the telecast should have been wrapped up by the time the event ends. As predictions came true or were turned upside down, the producer and commentators should have been explaining why.

A show should never raise a question that it doesn't answer. If it tells you that the team now has the second best record in the month of June, that begs the question, "who has the best record?" If at the top of the show a star was introduced as "number three on his university's all-time rebounding list," has he now moved up to number two? The viewer deserves a finished product, so the best producers don't leave any loose ends.

It's vital for the successful sports telecast to put the result in perspective. What does the victory mean? What doors open as a result? Will the next fight be for the world title? Is the next match against an old rival or the defending champion? Is the team one step closer to the playoffs or to leveling their record at .500? What individual achievements did we see that may put an athlete into a whole new realm of recognition? And what does the defeat mean for those who lost? Is a successful season now out of reach? Will the starting lineup change, or is the coach or manager now in jeopardy of being fired?

In whatever the television sports production team does, it should never shortchange the viewer. The person who spent an hour or two or three of valuable time watching an event should always come away feeling that it was time well spent, that they were treated with respect, that they were entertained and informed. If they enjoyed the experience they'll always come back for more.

SUMMARY

Producing sports on television is first and foremost telling stories as they happen about people and teams, their successes and failures, and how they react to each. The best way to get viewers interested in an event that is about to happen is to tell them about the competitors, the rivalry, what's at stake in the contest that's about to occur, and why it's important. During the action, the television production team uses all of its cameras, microphones, technical equipment, and collective expertise to analyze what is happening, show why plays succeeded or failed, point out the "exquisite intricacies" of the sport, entertaining and informing the fans who are watching.

Every television show is the product of 1) the time available to plan leading up to the event, 2) the extent of the resources that the budget will allow that can be applied to the production, 3) the people assigned to or hired for the project, their creativity, knowledge, and resourcefulness, and 4) the information that is gathered and presented that adds meaning to each contest.

Games and matches that are televised live are unpredictable, which creates drama and suspense, and forces everyone on a TV crew to prepare as much or more for the unknown factors of the event as they do for what is known. The crew is led by the producer, who can be compared to the coach of the team, and the director, who is like the quarterback who executes the game plan. When they are at their best they will involve each crew member and every resource at their disposal to produce sports programs that show fans how and why things happened, tell them about the people who are making the plays, answer every question that arises, put the results into context, and leave their viewers happy that they spent their time watching and anticipating the next game.

DISCUSSION TOPICS/ASSIGNMENTS

1   Interview any member of a sports production team and ask what they do for the fan watching at home. How much preparation goes into each telecast? How do they interact with the other members of the team?

2   Check the upcoming sports schedule and select any event. Then make a list of the specific "knowns" and "unknowns" for this event. If you were the producer, what would you do to prepare for each?

3   Watch a sports telecast and make notes on what story lines were presented in the first two segments of the show. Put these in one column on the left of your document. Then in the right-hand column make notes on how each story line was followed or wrapped up.

4   Discuss what each class member considers to be the best sports story of the year. How did television tell the story? What made it memorable? Can you remember who the commentators were? Does it matter which network it was on?

5   Do a critical comparison of two telecasts of the same sport on different networks. How did each use the following elements to tell the stories of the event, and which network did the better job in each category?

   a   Live video.
   b   Replays.
   c   Audio: natural sound and music.
   d   Commentary.
   e   Interviews and features.
   f   Graphics.
   g   Scoring data.
   h   Technological enhancements.

8 THE EVOLUTION OF SPORTS COMMENTATORS

The job of the commentator is to amplify, clarify, punctuate and enjoy.

(Keith Jackson)

Table 8.1 Chapter 8: The Rundown

- The sports commentator's job.
- The elements of play-by-play.
- What analysts do.
- Evolving talent roles: from reporter to provocateur.
- The pioneers who broke color and gender barriers.
- What it takes to become a sports commentator.

For more than 30 years Keith Jackson was one of the pre-eminent sportscasters in America. He was the voice of ABC Sports' college football coverage, the first play-by-play host of ABC's *Monday Night Football*, and he is in the American Sportscasters Association Hall of Fame. His eloquent one-line job description quoted above can be used to define the role of every lead commentator who has ever broadcast sports on television or radio since the 1920s.

As the broadcast media have grown, however, the number of different on-air talent roles has multiplied. What has not changed is the responsibility to serve the audience, but the different sports talent jobs and their purpose in each telecast vary widely. No sports commentator regardless of his or her assignment will ever go wrong following Keith Jackson's blueprint.

THE SPORTS COMMENTATOR'S JOB

Amplify

Sportscasters amplify each event or story by providing details that will expand the viewer's understanding of what's happening. They amplify through the addition of background and statistical information, critical analysis of the competitors, the history of rivalries and venues, the strategies being used in each play, series of plays, or game, and an educated assessment of the quality of each player's performance. Sportscasters' sense of the stories in play and the drama within each sporting event, coupled with their explanations of what is at stake for each athlete and team, add to the telecast and make it more meaningful.

Figure 8.1 Keith Jackson
Source: reprinted with permission of Getty Images

The most literal definition of "amplify" is "to make louder." Television commentators do need to add volume and excitement to their voices when their faces can't be seen by the audience at home. In an on-camera show open, the talent can communicate using the excitement in their eyes, their facial expressions, and gestures, in addition to their words. When they start to call the game off-camera, the visual part of their communication goes away. To compensate for the loss, commentators do need to amplify their voices and excitement levels so that they don't sound uninterested.

Delivering details and storylines that amplify and enhance a sports broadcast set the television commentator apart from the public address announcer, whose basic job is to tell the spectators in a venue who is coming to bat at a baseball game, what's the down and distance in football, and who just scored regardless of the sport.

Clarify

The sports commentator is a guide who tells the viewer *what* is happening, *who* is responsible, *how* it happened, *when*, and *why*. Anyone whose job it is to answer these questions is a journalist, plain and simple. For the journalists who commentate on live television, their stories are spoken, not written. *Their work is simultaneously produced and consumed*, so the level of care they must take in what they say, how it's phrased, and their tone has to be higher than for any journalist who has the advantage of an editor or a producer who reviews and improves written or recorded stories that will be watched or read some time after they are produced.

To be able to competently clarify, the commentator must have a deep knowledge of the sport, its teams and/or participants, its history, and rules. It all starts with curiosity. Asking plenty of questions in the days before an event and doing the research to find answers will prepare the commentator for the role of "clarifier." The best sports talent are those who do their homework. For example, ESPN's Mike Tirico says the preparation required to do the play-by-play for one three-and-a-half-hour *Monday Night Football* game takes him a full seventy hours each week of the season.

Punctuate

Think of how different it would be to read a book that had no punctuation marks. No commas or periods for pauses that separate one thought or topic from the next. No exclamation points to add emphasis. No underlining to add importance, or question marks to raise an inquiry or doubt. Sports commentators add the punctuation marks to televised events by changing pace, inflection, tone, and volume. They communicate the importance and the drama of individual plays and then weave them into the story of an entire quarter, half, period, or game. They build suspense as contests move toward conclusion, analyzing how every component of the event affects the impending result.

Some of the best punctuation in sportscasts comes when the commentators stop talking to allow the power of the pictures and the sounds of the event to tell that part of the story. When a hard-fought championship is decided the viewer wants to hear the athletes' cries of exultation and the roar of the crowd, not a continuing narration that forces the sounds of the event into the background. Knowing when to "lay out" and when it's appropriate to speak again, to put what has just occurred into perspective, comes with understanding the tremendous impact that punctuation has on television sports.

Enjoy

This may be the one factor that separates the good commentators from the very best. In every profession, every walk of life, there are obvious distinctions between those who truly enjoy their jobs and those who are just going through the motions wishing they were somewhere else. The same is true in sports commentary. The audience can tell which talent have a passion for telling stories and reporting on events. You can tell if they love their sport and respect the skills, determination, and sacrifices being made by each participant on the field of play or on the sideline. The pleasure and excitement of these commentators is contagious. Their enjoyment becomes the viewer's enjoyment in a very personal form of one-to-one communication.

Consider the commentator who gets paid to attend sporting events, who has perhaps the best seat in the house, has access to the most in-depth research and accurate information, but who does not sound as if he or she is enjoying the experience. They may be amplifying, clarifying, and punctuating, but if they aren't communicating enjoyment they aren't doing the job as it should be done.

Pat Summerall, whose career as a sports commentator spanned five decades, made the point best by quoting one of his mentors, Hall of Fame sportscaster Jack Buck, who said, "Hey we're not broadcasting from Westminster Abbey. You can have a sense of humor. This is still a game. You can still have fun doing it."

PLAY-BY-PLAY

In the infancy of televised sport, play-by-play was the only commentary function. Bill Stern, Red Barber, and every other commentator who worked games in the early days of the medium worked alone. There was no analyst to rely upon to supply the how and why of each game, or personal stories and anecdotes about the players. There were no instant replays to dissect plays or demonstrate skills. There were no sideline reporters or studios filled with hosts and former players and coaches to add perspective and new story lines. One voice telling the audience what was happening and who was making it happen was deemed sufficient by the television stations and networks that covered sports.

The play-by-play role in the 21st century at its core is still the job that the early sportscasters did, but it has become far more complex with the expanding scope of coverage and production, and the accelerating rate of technical innovation. The key elements of the job are:

- Describe the event. Tell the stories that are developing and being resolved. And do so with authority, the authority that comes from being prepared, having command of all your resources, and being ready to react regardless of what happens.

- Put the event in context. Explain what's at stake, why the event is important, what impact its result will have on individuals and teams, cities, and universities.

- Frame the action. Set up each situation by supplying the answers to who, what, and when. It doesn't take a lot of words to convey this information, because there is no need to tell people what they can already see on their television screens. Framing the action does not mean that the television play-by-play commentator should try to verbalize every action. (Example: "The pitch!" or "he's running right.") That's radio, not television.

  Framing the action also requires frequent "resets" that tell viewers who may be just tuning in what the matchup is, the score, the venue, what's at stake, and who the voices are that they will hear.

- Identify trends as they develop. Connect or contrast current actions to those from earlier in the contest or the season, or from a player's or team's past.

- Expand and amplify. Give the viewer pertinent statistics, background information, and anecdotes that add meaning and interest to an event.

- Set up and draw information out of the analyst. Encourage critical assessments, comparisons, and opinions. Compare those with alternative opinions from coaches, managers, or other analysts of the sport.

- Provide opinion. As an educated observer of the sport and its stars, the play-by-play person is entitled to his or her own opinion. But these need to be stated as personal observations or assessments. Words spoken by the lead commentator for a television network or station can too easily be misinterpreted as representing the official position of that corporate entity.

- *Direct traffic.* Play-by-play announcers very often describe themselves as "traffic cops." They control the flow from the show open to live action to sponsored elements and commercial breaks, to promos to multiple talent in various locations, to the close of the show with the final score and a seamless toss to the show that's coming up next.

- *Humanize the athletes.* Introduce the audience to the individuals on the screen. Tell their stories of success, failure, and inspiration. This makes the viewers care about what happens in the event and to these people. And pronounce their names correctly!

- *Be courteous and respectful.* Keep your cool and your composure in dealing with analysts, interview subjects, and officials. This is especially important when talking with or about anyone who disagrees with the play-by-play person's or the network's point of view, or who has opinions or ideas that don't conform to mainstream thought.

- *Report breaking news.* If news happens at the event, if a player is traded, a manager is suspended, an accident or other disturbance occurs, the play-by-play voice automatically becomes the news anchor's voice. An excellent example is how Al Michaels adapted his reporting when an earthquake shook San Francisco on October 17, 1989, while he was on the air for ABC Sports covering the World Series at Candlestick Park.

- *See the big picture.* Put the current game into perspective as it relates to other results and news in the league or sport as a whole. Weigh the relevance of other sports news of the day.

In an interview with NFL Films, Al Michaels described his job doing play-by-play as helping people understand what is happening on the field or on the court, putting all the facts and statistics into "a contextual framework." The editing process, he said, is critical:

> What's important? There's so much information out there. You want to go into a game fully armed. I think we all do. But let the game play out, and then go with the game. We may have as broadcasters the greatest story in the world about the number-seven defensive back, but how does that play out if he doesn't get into the game or is not a relevant part of the game? Well, what we try to do is go in and say, "look we know this." If this guy all of a sudden has a big night or is involved in a big play, we can come in, personalize it, and make it more interesting to the average viewer.

ANALYSIS

The role of the analyst evolved in the 1950s, starting out as a "color" commentator. The original assignment for this second announcer on a big-event telecast was to talk about the pageantry surrounding the competition and the halftime bands. During the game they were called upon to add "color" to the lead commentator's call of the action. After the game they were usually dispatched to handle locker room interviews. Even after "color" commentators started adding their analysis of the play to telecasts, most were still required to leave the announce booth with a couple minutes left on the clock so that they could be at field level to do the post-game interviews.

The introduction of instant replay in 1963 forever changed the analyst's job. When an expert in the sport, a former player or athlete, could use a replay to explain plays and the intricacies involved in an athlete's or team's performance, the networks quickly lost interest in the traditional "color" commentary and halftime bands.

The key elements of the analyst's job are to:

Explain How and Why

This is most often done using instant replays. How did a play work? What are the moving parts? Why was the play chosen at this point of the game? Why did it succeed or fail? How does one athlete's level of performance set him or her apart from another?

Anticipate Change

Use current facts, trends, and statistics plus past histories and tendencies to project what the viewer can expect to see unfold in the upcoming contest, half, or closing minutes. This is far more than just predicting who will win. It adds the how and why to the equation. And, during a telecast when that anticipated change doesn't occur, the analyst can use the new evidence at hand to explain what happened and why.

The responsibility to anticipate change also requires the analyst to help the director and producer make their coverage plans. Sharing information about how teams will deploy their players, how certain players match up against their defenders, or how specific moves by individual athletes improve their performance, will help the director determine which cameras to use in which situations. And it helps the producer decide which players or units to isolate for replays that will add to the story of how the game is won or lost.

Explain Change

To detect a change in momentum or a developing trend is reporting, but to describe what caused the change is analysis. The best analysts can quickly spot tendencies as they develop during an event. For example, "with third down and less than four yards to go, they have handed the ball to running back 'A' nine out of ten times." Then showing the audience how the defense adjusts to this tendency will make the game more interesting to watch.

Prescribe Change

When players or teams fall short of their goals, it is up to the analyst to describe to the viewer what needs to change for failure to become success. The analyst's vision should take in not just what is happening on the field or court, but what isn't happening. His or her knowledge of all the pieces that must fit together for championships to be won should be used to prescribe the work or changes required for athletes and/or teams to achieve and maintain success.

Add Depth and Texture

Information and anecdotes about players, teams, venues, and rivalries that is not readily available to the average fan make television sports broadcasts more interesting. Analysts glean this information from their interviews with players and coaches, from attending practices, from professional researchers, and from simply walking on the field or through the stadium.

When John Madden was doing analysis on NFL telecasts, he would take a yellow legal-size pad to each team's practice leading up to a game and fill it with notes and observations. It didn't matter if he had seen one or both of the teams earlier in the season, he would always see something new that would add depth and texture to the game telecast. And he shared that insight with his producer and director to help them plan and prepare.

Make Distinctions

The trained eye of the expert analyst can distinguish the differences that set the very best athletes apart from their teammates and opponents. They can show us how player or team attributes, strengths, and weaknesses separate perennial winners from also-rans.

I have referred to the subtleties that distinguish the very best performances as the "exquisite intricacies" of sport. In many sports broadcasts you are watching the best in the world at what they do. When the analyst can dissect a performance and make the viewer aware of the subtleties that set one player or team above the rest, you will start to watch for these "exquisite intricacies." Learning which specifics to watch for makes the viewing experience more meaningful and enjoyable.

Compare and Contrast

Analysts have the advantage of attending practices and screening through video clips from virtually every game or match played by the competitors leading up to a live broadcast. They have observed past performances, past seasons, different combinations of personnel, and different opponents. On the air, the analyst can therefore compare what he or she is seeing with how the player or team handled the same situation in the past against the same or different opponents, or at an earlier juncture in the very same game being televised.

Analysts can point out what is working from what they saw in practice, and what is falling apart. They can show the viewer the contrast between different coaches' strategies, the actions and reactions of different players on the same or opposing teams, even how differently competitors deal with pressure, victory, and defeat.

Athletes or coaches who leave the game after retirement or injury to become television analysts can suddenly find themselves on "the other side," playing for a different team. Their television job now includes criticizing former teammates and colleagues who may feel betrayed and react emotionally. Players and coaches who had friendships or professional relationships with the analyst in the past often feel entitled to some protection from criticism, or at least to a little slack. When current competitors hear someone who they consider to be a friend or colleague point out their failings to millions of television viewers, they can get very upset. Several have refused to do any future interviews with the critical analyst who they now consider a "traitor."

The job of the analyst in many ways is to represent the viewers. Ask and answer the questions that viewers want to know about the contest and its players, show them how the game is executed, and, specifically, what it takes to win. To do that well, analysts must make the break from past ties and honestly evaluate every player and coach they see. Those who take it easy on friends and overlook flaws that impact the competition they are charged with covering will almost always be forced by demanding producers to make early exits from the broadcast booth.

Former athletes who have made successful careers as television analysts draw comparisons between their current jobs and their playing days. The intense preparation for each event is similar: watching game recordings, studying past performances and tendencies, meeting with players and coaches, and planning strategies with a team of professionals. The build-up to game day can have the same kind of adrenaline rush that the analyst felt when his or her uniform was not a business suit. When the analyst has that kind of excitement and love for the game, it comes through on TV.

EVOLVING TALENT ROLES

As the coverage of sports in the United States has expanded over the last half of the 20th century and the beginning of the 21st, so has the need for commentators with a wide variety of skills. When local television stations started doing newscasts in the late 1940s and early 1950s, the *sports anchor* job was born. Generations of sports anchors have reported the scores, voiced over highlights, and interviewed players and coaches. The job has evolved over the years, but it is basically the same from the smallest television market to the *SportsCenter* set in Bristol, Connecticut.

Sideline reporters made their debut in the 1960s when producers in search of stories, and frustrated by the limitations of their only commentators being sequestered in a small booth high above the action, extended their reach down to field level. Limitations are still imposed by leagues and organizers who want reporters and microphones to keep their distance from active competitors, but the information that can be gathered close to the action adds dimension and supplies answers when the unexpected occurs.

There is a distinction between the skill sets of sideline reporters in live telecasts and *sports reporters* who cover stories that are separate from live game coverage. For most of the latter, their "beat" is defined either by sport or by region, and their reports are seen on daily, weekly, or other regularly scheduled sports news and magazine shows, and/or online. Sideline reporters need to be experts at "self-editing" to keep their comments and interviews short in order that they not take time away from the live play. Sports reporters for any telecasts or platforms other than live games need to be excellent interviewers, writers, and editors. They too will do their share of live reports, but most are stand-ups that lead into or follow their produced and edited packages, which don't have the time constraints that are imposed by live games.

A television sports role similar to reporter, but with its own specific characteristics, is the *columnist*. These strong reporters deliver their own informed opinions along with their first-person coverage of news stories, individuals, and controversies. In their earliest incarnation they were referred to as *essayists*, and their job descriptions were built on the work of pioneers such as Jack Whitaker, Heywood Hale Broun, Howard Cosell, and Frank Deford, whose writing and observation skills were superb. ESPN's successful series *Pardon the Interruption* is predicated on the insights and opinions of two columnists, Tony Kornheiser and Michael Wilbon. The line across which their separate opinions either converge or collide is what makes the show compelling and draws an audience.

The role of *host* has evolved to become completely separate from the play-by-play commentator. When NBC televised Super Bowl III in 1969, Curt Gowdy hosted the show and did the play-by-play. That was the norm well into the 1970s. But as pre-game, halftime, and post-game shows were added and expanded to satisfy fans' growing appetite for sports, as well as provide more commercial opportunities for networks to earn additional revenue, studio hosts and on-site event hosts were added to the list of sports talent job descriptions.

The pre-game host, whether in a studio or at the site of the event, helps introduce viewers to the players and coaches who will be participating. Longer interviews that reveal what's going on inside a competitor's life could never fit into a live game where the only breaks in action are a few seconds between plays or a few minutes between periods. The host can take a broader approach than the play-by-play commentator, who is focused on the game at hand. The host's role is to look at the game as part of something larger: the league, the impact of other games or of this game on others, and issues within the sport itself. The host can also provide any number of tangential stories on related topics that deserve to be told, but would not be appropriate in the flow of live play-by-play.

Another vital skill for a host is to make the disorganized seem organized. Pre-game shows tend to be formatted well ahead of time with a rundown not unlike a news show that lists all the elements in order, their sources, and how long each is expected to run. But halftime and post-game shows with multiple games ending at different times, with some highlights being ready and others still waiting for the half to end or a final result to come in, can feel like a railroad station with several trains all converging at one intersection. The ability to remain calm and smoothly transition from one unscripted item to the next is the hallmark of a strong studio host.

One of the most important things that hosts do is set the table for their *studio analysts*, which is another category of sports television talent that has evolved over the past few decades. It is a hybrid of the game analyst position, but with more latitude and time to tell a story than the analyst in the booth, whose comments must be confined to a short sentence or two between plays. The lineage of modern studio analysts goes back to the debut of *The NFL Today* on CBS in 1975. Brent Musburger was host to studio regulars Irv Cross, Phyllis George, and Jimmy "The Greek" Snyder. Irv Cross had been a player, a coach, and a game analyst when he brought that experience to the CBS studio. Phyllis George specialized in interviews and features, and Snyder's narrow focus was the effect of personnel changes and game decisions on the betting line.

The number of specialties has multiplied in the years since 1975, and nothing would indicate that this diversification will end until the sports themselves stop evolving. *Studio specialists* can make a living as league "insiders" tapping their long-established networks of confidential contacts. They can focus on coaching tactics, game officiating and rules, player injuries, player selection drafts, fantasy games, legal and governmental issues, game day weather conditions, or topics of style and culture.

Sports television has been a place for *provocateurs* since the first time Howard Cosell needled Muhammad Ali or railed against "Dandy Don" Meredith and the "jockocracy" of athletes-turned-analysts that he claimed Meredith represented. The provocateur pokes and prods and sometimes intimidates his or her guests and fellow commentators. The goal is to create sparks and full-fledged fireworks that will draw attention to important issues and attract viewers who love the spontaneity and confrontations. And, almost without exception, provocateurs are also intent on attracting attention to themselves in order to make their stars burn brighter.

The challenge for producers is to select the proper roles and the best people to fill them based upon the parameters of their specific telecasts or series. There are pitfalls in either choosing too few or too many talent for any particular program. If the producer puts a play-by-play commentator and two analysts in the booth, but does not use a sideline reporter, he or she could be vulnerable when news breaks down on the field or courtside.

In January, 1995, I was in Melbourne, Australia as ESPN's coordinating producer for tennis. Our three primary tennis commentators at the time were Cliff Drysdale, Fred Stolle, and Mary Carillo. For major events, and at that time the Australian Open was the only grand slam on ESPN, all three regularly sat in the same commentary booth. Their interaction, particularly with Mary Carillo prodding her two colleagues, was insightful and entertaining.

The budget for tennis was not large enough to bring a sideline reporter with us. That deficiency in the production plan became glaringly obvious when Pete Sampras met Jim Courier in one of the men's quarterfinal matches that we were televising. Courier won the first two sets, and Sampras came back to win the next two. In the fifth set Pete Sampras unexplainably began to cry. He was serving through his tears. At one point Courier came to the net and apparently asked Pete if he was okay.

We were unable to adequately tell the story of what was going on and why Sampras was crying because all three of our talent were in the TV booth near the top of the arena. I quickly directed Mary Carillo to get off headset and go down to the courtside area to get the details. When she returned a few minutes later she told the audience that Pete was crying for his coach, Tim Gullickson, who had been diagnosed with brain cancer. A fan had yelled out, "Do it for your coach," and that triggered Sampras' painful emotions. Amazingly he played on and beat Courier 6-3 in the fifth set. Tim Gullickson died in May of 1996 at the age of forty-four.

After this episode revealed how vulnerable a telecast can be without eyes and ears courtside, we never did another major tennis championship without a sideline reporter.

At the other end of the spectrum, a studio show with one host and four, five, or more studio analysts can lead to confusion as to who talks next and about what. And it can suffer from under-utilizing the one analyst who has the best angle on the game or topic, because everyone else has to get their share of air-time too. One or two really good analysts will usually make a studio show better than having four or five analysts, some of whom may be good reporters and communicators, and the others who may just be famous.

THE PIONEERS

An entire book could be devoted to telling the stories of the pioneers of sports commentary. In the pages of this text we have already mentioned Bill Stern, Red Barber, Jim McKay, Brent Musburger, Howard Cosell, Keith Jackson, and others, all of whom are deserving of their own biographies. And so is Irv Cross.

For the first thirty-two years of television sports, from 1939 until 1971, every face the public saw doing commentary was white. No members of any minority group had ever been hired to do sports on TV. That changed in 1971 when CBS hired Irv Cross as an analyst on regional NFL game telecasts.

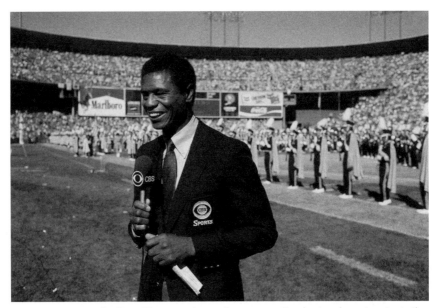

Figure 8.2 Irv Cross, the first African-American to become a national network sportscaster in the United States
Source: reprinted with permission of Getty Images

Irv Cross played defensive back for the Philadelphia Eagles from 1961 to 1966, when he was traded to the Los Angeles Rams. He made the Pro Bowl twice as an Eagle, and in 1969 he returned to Philadelphia as a player-coach. He retired as a player in 1970, and continued as an assistant coach for the Eagles. Cross joined CBS the next year and spent twenty-three years with the network. He is best remembered for his role as the original studio analyst for *The NFL Today*, which was launched in 1975.

In 2009, Irv Cross was honored by the Pro Football Hall of Fame as the recipient of the Pete Rozelle Radio-Television Award. In remarks prepared for the occasion, Irv Cross said, "I always enjoyed thinking about football, thinking about strategies, coming up with ways to break offenses and design defensive concepts," so the move from player and coach to television analyst was a natural one. But Cross said that, as his playing career was coming to an end, he had envisioned himself one day becoming a general manager, not going into television.

Ever since Irv Cross became the first minority sportscaster on national television, and thanks to his groundbreaking work, thousands upon thousands of young people who weren't born white have seen the commentator's job as something to which they could aspire, and which would be open to them based upon their knowledge, education, and communications skills.

Young women have also been able to do the same thanks to Jane Chastain and Donna de Varona. Jane Chastain started doing a weekly sports report on WAGA-TV in Atlanta in 1963, just two years after she graduated high school. She was called "Coach Friday," and she made her predictions for Saturday college football games. When Chastain moved to WTVJ-TV, the CBS affiliate in Miami in 1971, she became a respected sports reporter and got her first network sports assignments. CBS hired her in 1974, making her its first woman sports commentator. Chastain only stayed at CBS one year, unhappy with her assignments, which she complained were mostly interviews with cheerleaders and athletes' wives.

Figure 8.3 Jane Chastain
Source: courtesy Jane Chastain/Facebook

Figure 8.4 Donna de Varona
Source: courtesy International Swimming Hall of Fame

Donna de Varona was only thirteen years old when she swam for the USA in the 1960 Olympics in Rome. She won two gold medals at the 1964 Olympic Games in Tokyo and was named the outstanding female athlete in the world that year by the Associated Press. When de Varona retired from competitive swimming in 1965, and still only seventeen, ABC put a microphone in her hand to do reports on *Wide World of Sports*, making her the first female sports commentator on any American television network.

Donna de Varona covered every Olympics for ABC through 1988, also doing reports for the *ABC Evening News* and *Nightline*. She was the co-founder of the Women's Sports Foundation, along with tennis legend Billie Jean King, and served as the foundation's first president from 1976 until 1984.

BECOMING A SPORTS COMMENTATOR

Getting a job broadcasting sports on television is the dream of young sports enthusiasts, boys and girls, all across the country. For a few talented individuals, the dream will come true. But it is a very small number who have everything that it takes, and are lucky enough to find themselves at the right place at the right time, to get that on-air job. These criteria set the baseline for success as a television sports commentator.

- Interest in and knowledge of a broad spectrum of sports.

- An expert knowledge of one or more sports that comes from being a life-long fan and studying the players past and present, the teams, history, rules, venues, and contemporary issues.

- Self-confidence. When the lights and the camera come on, the successful on-air talent has the confidence to know that they don't have to imitate anyone else. They are self-assured, knowing that the information they have is solid and authoritative, and that giving the best they have from within will be good enough, better than any imitation could ever be.

- Personality. Television viewers want to like the people who deliver their sports. They want credibility, but they also want to feel that the commentator loves the sport just as much as they do, and that it would be fun to meet and just "talk sports."

- Sincerity. Television viewers can spot a phony in five seconds or less. The successful television sports talent has sincerity in his or her voice, face, and, most importantly, in the eyes. Virtually everyone watches the eyes of whoever is talking, in person or on television, so, if the commentator is sincere and believes what he or she is saying, it will be there in the eyes.

- Humility. This is a requirement for every sports talent with the possible exception of a "provocateur." Admiring the work and skill of others, not yourself, is what sports reporting is all about. For example, when Bob Costas makes a self-deprecating comment about his short stature, he makes himself human and vulnerable, and therefore all the more likeable.

- A quick wit. Live television is full of unexpected turns and events. Having a quick response that's appropriate for the situation, and which adds context or relaxes tension, is a talent that is hard to teach.

- Patience. The very best commentators let live scenes play out, take the time to get the story right, and never sound rushed or out of breath. Patience reinforces their command regardless of how fast things are happening.

The people who will succeed as sportscasters are the ones who work the hardest. It's true in school and in every profession. It's true in sports television. It takes dedication and an unswerving love for the sport and the profession to put in the hours reading and studying for each assignment. Research packets sometimes contain hundreds of pages of statistics, past results, backgrounds, analysis, and stories from newspaper and online services. Travel from home to game to game to studio and back is not in the least glamorous or easy. There are early morning meetings for games later that night, and late night meetings for shows the next day. There are assignments like basketball tournaments and tennis grand slams that have the talent working multiple games and matches in the same day, with barely any time in between to go to the bathroom. It is hard work. And only those committed to working hard will become the next generation's stars.

There is one final key. Even a prospect with 100 percent of the skills and attributes listed above who is missing this key is doomed to hit a door that will not open. The people who make their living communicating sports on television need excellent interactive personal communications skills. They will be working long hours with their fellow talent, producers, directors, researchers, technicians, and assistants. They will face challenges together, travel together, and get stuck in airports together.

Sports commentators will always have to interact with players, coaches, team executives, and their own network executives. They will be interviewed and quizzed almost as often as they themselves do interviews.

Through it all, the key is to show every individual genuine respect. Ask for help; never demand it. Thank those who provide their services; never take them for granted as if you were entitled. And always hold onto the love of sports that made you want to get into the profession back when you were a kid talking sports with your buddies.

SUMMARY

The television sports commentator serves the audience by turning the reality of a live event into dramatic reality. As stated by ABC Sports veteran Keith Jackson, the job is to amplify, clarify, punctuate, and enjoy. The commentator amplifies by adding information about the teams and players, and putting the game in context. He or she clarifies by answering the questions that any journalist would pose: what is happening, how and why, and who is responsible. Punctuation adds emphasis and drama to live telecasts with an excited exclamation or a pause that allows the sound of the event and its players to tell the story. And, with their passion for the game, the very best commentators share the enjoyment of being there in person with those who watch on a screen.

When sports television began, the only talent job was play-by-play. "Color" commentators were added to major events beginning in the late 1950s and early 1960s to tell viewers about the pageantry and everything that surrounded the game. The arrival of instant replay in late 1963 gave birth to the modern sports television analyst, very often a former player or coach who could use the replay to dissect and explain plays.

In the decades since, several new talent roles have evolved, adding layers of texture and interest to sports programs. Many have been created by necessity because of the increased number of shows from studios and game sites that require more people to report on and analyze more aspects of a sport or event. The attributes needed to succeed in any commentary role start with a passion for sport and a willingness to work hard for long hours on nights and weekends. And it takes self-confidence, personality, sincerity, humility, a quick wit, patience, and excellent inter-personal skills. Those few people who have it all become the television stars whose names are recognized by fans nationwide.

The industry owes a debt of gratitude to the pioneers who broke through the racial and gender barriers that had existed in sports television for its first few decades. Donna de Varona, on ABC Sports, and Jane Chastain, on local television and then CBS, were the first women to become sportscasters in the United States, and Irv Cross became the first African-American to report sports on a national network when he retired from professional football and started working for CBS in 1971.

DISCUSSION TOPICS/ASSIGNMENTS

1 Who do you think the best play-by-play announcer is currently on television? Using the list of job functions from this chapter, explain what you think this announcer does better than any other.

2 Do the same assessment for the best analyst on television using the description of that job's key elements from this chapter.

3 Research the career of one of the sportscasters listed below. How did they get their start in broadcasting? On which events did they work over what period of time? What was their lasting contribution to the profession?

Red Barber.
Jim McKay.
Curt Gowdy.
Brent Musburger.
Howard Cosell.
Donna de Varona.

3   Watch any televised sporting event and make notes on how the commentators affected you. What did they add to your understanding of what was happening? How well did they explain the *how* and *why*, or did they just tell you *what* the players did? Were they enhancing what you saw, or were they doing "radio on television," describing every action?

9 INTERNATIONAL SPORTS BROADCASTING

All sports for all people.

(Pierre de Coubertin, founder of the modern Olympics)

Table 9.1 Chapter 9: The Rundown

- Comparison of domestic and international sports programming.
- International rights agreements.
- The role of host broadcasters.
- Host broadcasters make a variety of signal feeds available.
- What are discreet and unilateral feeds?
- The host broadcaster model changes.
- International broadcast centers.
- Producing sports television overseas.

America's appetite for sports from around the world was whetted by the coverage of the Olympics from foreign venues like Rome in 1960, and Tokyo and Innsbruck, Austria, in 1964, and by *ABC's Wide World of Sports*, which aired every weekend beginning in 1961. It was fed by the launch of communications satellites over the Atlantic and Pacific and the laying of trans-oceanic fiber cables along the ocean floors. The sports programs coming back to the United States from foreign countries however just didn't look like American sports. Many of the sports themselves were different, sometimes bordering on exotic, definitely "foreign." And the picture and sound were never quite as clear or synchronized as they were in shows that originated in the US, because the European networks used a different technical broadcast standard called PAL that had to be converted to the American NTSC standard, which had fewer lines of resolution.

What international sports programming did for American television viewers was to open our eyes and broaden our horizons. We found that several sports considered "minor" here at home like tennis, soccer, and horse racing were the major sports in many countries overseas. Some sports with virtually no domestic television coverage like cricket, rugby, and Formula One racing had millions of devoted fans on continents other than North America, with stars who were celebrity icons, and expensive TV rights contracts. And the major sports with the largest fan bases and most valuable TV deals in the United States, gridiron football and baseball, were of limited interest in only a few scattered countries around the globe, and they were played in even fewer. Pierre de Coubertin, who we quoted above, apparently was wrong: all sports are definitely not for all people.

Regardless of the sport or where it is played, the basics of the sports television product are pretty much the same: words and pictures telling dramatic and entertaining stories live as they happen. The terms we use may be different: our commentator or announcer is called a "presenter" in many countries. When the presenter is seen on camera, he or she is "in vision." Our TV truck is their "OB van," for "outside broadcast," and what American television professionals call a "site survey" is a "recce," short for "reconnaissance," in English-speaking countries outside the US. Translations and variations abound in the non-English-speaking world. But, regardless of terminology, the goal of sports production personnel worldwide is the same: deliver compelling live television to millions of eager viewers.

With different cultures come different approaches to televised sport, which makes it all the more interesting when American TV networks go overseas to originate programming for their audiences back home in the US, and when foreign broadcasters come to the US to send coverage of events here back to their home countries. Every nation and every network does business in its own fashion. When they have to work together to televise international events to multiple nations, there are three universal common denominators: 1) international rights agreements, 2) host broadcasters, and 3) international broadcast centers.

INTERNATIONAL RIGHTS AGREEMENTS

In Chapter 6 we discussed how television rights agreements work: a television network or station pays an amount of money specified by contract to an event organizer or league for the exclusive rights to televise a set number of games or shows over a specified period of time. For domestic events, the network or station that pays for the broadcast rights is then responsible for producing the coverage, providing all of the necessary personnel and technical equipment, and transmitting all programs to its affiliated stations and systems.

International rights agreements work differently. A network or consortium of networks pays the organizer for the exclusive rights to televise an event in a specific territory, which could be just one country or a number of countries that may or may not be contiguous. In return the networks get 1) access to the international feed of that event to relay back to their territory, 2) a fixed number of credentials for their personnel who will be on site, and 3) the exclusive rights in their home territories to sell advertising in and to promote the event on their networks. Obtaining the international rights to an event such as World Cup Soccer, the Olympic Games, or Wimbledon does not automatically allow a network to set up its own cameras or bring in its own personnel or technical equipment. That would be impossible to control if only because of the space limitations at the sports venues. Imagine if all 199 nations or territories that held rights to televise the 2010 World Cup in South Africa had sent their own cameras, microphones, and crews to each soccer stadium. There would have been little room left for spectators or players.

Instead the organizer, which in the case of the World Cup is the Fédération Internationale de Football Association (FIFA), makes available a host feed of the event to its rights holders. The feed is available at the organizer's International Broadcast Center (IBC), and it contains basic coverage of all action from the event. Every national network that has paid for broadcast rights can then customize the programming for its specific audience by adding a voice-over and graphics in its preferred language. It is responsible for securing transmission of that feed back to its home country.

If a network wants greater access and its own studio, technical facilities, and production personnel on site, then it has to pay more for these expanded rights. NBC paid $1.181 billion dollars for the exclusive rights to televise the 2012 London Olympics in the United States and its territories. For that kind of money, NBC was allowed to set up a number of studio and commentary positions and its own cameras and microphones at several Olympic venues, and the network's voice carries weight when issues arise that affect the network's programming schedule or production needs. NBC added multiple control rooms, edit facilities and offices staffed by thousands of network personnel, all of whom needed credentials issued by the International Olympic Committee (IOC). Traditionally the rights payment from the American broadcaster represents half of all the money the IOC collects in television licensing fees. The payments from every other country in the world combine to make up the other half.

It is very common for several nations' broadcasters in regions such as Europe and Africa to band together into a consortium. The aggregate size of the consortium gives them more bargaining power and influence than if individual small nations tried to negotiate one-on-one with an international organizer such as FIFA or the IOC. For example, in 2009 a group known as SportFive, which is based in Hamburg, Germany, paid $312.5 million dollars for the broadcast rights to the 2014 Winter Olympic Games in Sochi, Russia, and the 2016 Summer Games in Rio de Janeiro, Brazil, for forty European nations and territories. SportFive then in turn will collect payments from its partner television networks in each of those forty nations to cover the cost of the rights fee, any production equipment, enhancements to the feed, or staffing required, plus its transmission of the broadcast feeds.

The basic international rights agreement gives broadcasters license to televise the event just once: live or on tape-delay, an option they may choose if the site is several time zones away from their home region. Almost invariably, broadcasters do not get rights to re-air any games or shows, and their use of highlights from the event is also limited to a set period of time after which all rights to all video revert back to the organizer. ESPN may have aired the World Cup in the United States, but FIFA owns all the video.

The rights-holding network in turn gets to decide if or how any other video medium will be allowed to use recorded highlights from the event. These restrictions or prohibitions are distributed to all news and sports media in the form of "embargo notices" in advance of an event. Normally news coverage by non-rights holding networks or stations is strictly forbidden until after the rights holder's show goes off the air. And there are limitations imposed on how many seconds of video can be used in bona fide news programs in any twenty-four-hour period. It is not uncommon for rights holders to also put expiration dates on their video. NBC for example does not allow any highlights to be used by non-rights holders after forty-eight hours have elapsed from the time the event occurred live. Highlight usage of any kind on internet video platforms is rarely allowed by rights-holding networks. They want to encourage fans to look for video on their proprietary websites, not on those owned by any competitor or third party.

HOST BROADCASTERS

The amount of work involved in organizing an international sporting event is enormous. The IOC must work with multiple sport federations from each nation that will be sending athletes to the Games. It works with the host city on the design and construction of arenas, stadiums, athlete housing, and amenities. And it does the marketing and licensing of the Olympics and its merchandise. FIFA coordinates the three years of international competition that will yield the sixty-four teams that play in a World Cup. Then it works with the soccer federations of those sixty-four nations in much the same way the IOC connects with the governing bodies of each individual sport. And there are stadiums to build or renovate and marketing to be done. Organizing events and competitions is their specialty. Broadcasting is not.

In order to handle all television production matters and relationships with broadcast rights holders, international organizers contract with third-party production entities, or set up subsidiaries to serve as the host broadcaster. The role of the host broadcaster is to produce the television and radio coverage of an event that is made available to every network that has paid for broadcast rights. To do so it must:

- Design, build, install, and operate the IBC. And then dismantle it when the event has concluded.

- Design, build, install, operate, and then remove television facilities and equipment at the competition venues and select non-competition venues such as medal stands or news conference and interview rooms.

- Coordinate and provide various facilities and services to each rights-holding broadcaster. These can range from routers that allow a network to select various venue or camera feeds, to office furniture and catering. The host broadcaster has a rate card that specifies the pricing for everything down to the very last chair or meal.

- Represent the needs of the rights-holding networks to the organizer. For example, a Chilean network may want a match featuring its number one player to be scheduled for a time that coincides with prime evening viewing hours back in Chile. The host broadcaster can't guarantee that the schedule will be adjusted, but it is responsible for taking that request to the organizer's scheduling committee.

- Produce various features and video teases and opens that any network can use as part of its programming from the event.

- Assist the organizer with the design and construction of infrastructure needed at the venues to accommodate broadcasting needs. These could include camera towers for the coverage of expansive outdoor events such as a major golf tournament, enlarged press boxes, or additional commentary positions.

- Provide all the data and scoring feeds that show race timing or game clocks, or, in the case of tennis, the game, set, and match score plus serve percentages, unforced errors, and every other statistic that is tracked in the sport, from every television court or arena. These data feeds are part of the graphics that are incorporated into the basic world feed, and they are also available for the rights-holding networks on site to interface into their own network graphics machines.

This host broadcaster template dates back to the 1972 Olympic Games in Munich where an international signal for global distribution was produced for the first time, separate and distinct from the domestic broadcast in the nation that was hosting the Olympics. The German broadcasters ARD and ZDF created a separate team to produce the international feeds. Prior to that the primary network in the host nation, NHK for the 1964 Summer Games in Tokyo for example, was responsible for providing a feed of its domestic coverage to any network that had paid the IOC for television broadcast rights. For smaller, less complex international competitions such as a three-day Davis Cup tennis event, the home nation's primary network is still responsible to act as host broadcaster and make a feed of its coverage available to any foreign network that has purchased rights from the organizer, which in the case of Davis Cup tennis is the International Tennis Federation.

CUT CABLES AND PAYING BRIBES IN MOSCOW

In my two decades of producing international sports television, one of the most challenging events was the Davis Cup Final, the US team led by Pete Sampras vs. the Russian national team, in Moscow in December of 1995. We had three days of coverage to produce and feed live back to ESPN. The Russian television network ORT was serving as host broadcaster.

The event was staged inside the cavernous arena that was built for the 1980 Moscow Olympics. One clay tennis court was constructed in one corner of the huge building, which had rarely been used in the fifteen years since the Olympics and was in serious need of cleaning.

We brought our tennis commentators, Cliff Drysdale, Mary Carillo, and Fred Stolle, along with our producer, director, operations manager, associate producer, and a translator from the US. Woods TV from Paris transported all the technical equipment that we had hired and set up our control room in one of the backstage rooms at the Olympic arena.

The day before play was to begin, our ESPN crew was anxious to test the camera feeds from ORT, but the Russians kept putting us off. We offered to make the connections ourselves, but we were advised through our translator that "that could be dangerous."

Late that Thursday afternoon our exasperated technical director, an American named Bernie Kraska who was living in Germany, had had enough. He made the connections, tested the cameras, and we all went back to our hotel.

Friday morning we arrived back at the arena to find that our cables had been physically cut. We were due to start feeding live tennis back to the US just a few hours later. When I went to our ORT contact to find out what was going on, the response was, "We told you it could be dangerous for you to connect your cables." The Russian director had an assistant at his side who clearly explained that he needed "one grand" in cash before the connections could be restored. I had gone to Russia knowing I might have to grease some palms, but I didn't have $1000 in cash in my pocket.

My solution was to go to the executive director of the International Tennis Federation at the time, Christopher Stokes, who was on-site. I had worked closely with Christopher many times before and our good relationship made all the difference that day. He agreed to take the cash out of his fund for local expenses. We paid off the Russians, the cables got re-connected, and that afternoon we went on the air with live tennis from Moscow.

Perhaps it's fitting that the American team beat the Russians to win the Davis Cup that weekend.

HOST BROADCASTERS MAKE A VARIETY OF SIGNAL FEEDS AVAILABLE

A host broadcaster that is separate from the home nation's network will provide a variety of feeds allowing any other network that has purchased the television rights a number of options. The rights-holding network can simply air the finished program that is produced by the host broadcaster with its graphics and commentary, or it can customize the program for its home audience. These feeds are available in four configurations:

- *Dirty feed* includes all video, ambient sound audio from the venue, announcer commentary, and all world graphics including scoring data with no network logos.

- *Clean feed* includes video, venue audio, graphics, and scoring but with no commentary.

- *Clean/clean feed* is only the video and venue audio. No graphics (except scoring and clocks as desired) and no commentary.

- *Discrete feed* is a direct signal from a selected camera, such as the camera in the interview room, or from a specific venue at the event like the figure-skating arena at the World Championships or Winter Olympics.

If a network chooses a clean feed, it can add its own commentator's voice-over in its native language. The world graphics and scoring data are designed to be understandable in most languages that use the Roman alphabet. The commentators can be at the site of the competition, or in a studio in the IBC, or back in their home studios adding their voices to the final product by calling the action as they watch the video feed on a monitor. Calling the show "off the tube" is the most cost-efficient method of customizing a feed, saving the network travel costs and any fees associated with setting up production equipment at site or in the IBC.

Discrete Feeds

At an event such as the Olympics or Wimbledon, there is simultaneous action at several venues or on various tennis courts. The rights holder can select which competition to broadcast back to its home country based upon who is playing where. If the champion shot-putter from Croatia is competing on the athletics field, the Croatian television network can choose the feed from that venue, even though the rest of the world may be focused on a swimming race that is underway simultaneously at the aquatics center. Or if the number-one ranked tennis player from Japan is on Court 13 at Wimbledon, NHK as the rights holder for Japan can punch up "Court 13" in their router and show it to all their viewers regardless of who is playing the match over on Centre Court. These discrete feeds from arenas or courts are directed and produced by professionals hired by the host broadcaster.

It is very common for broadcasters to take a discrete feed from one specific camera, such as a fixed aerial beauty shot of the grounds that can be used when the network chooses to go to commercial, or as the background shot for graphics that promote what's coming up next. An ambitious rights holder will request several discrete camera feeds that it can use to cut into and augment the host feed, further customizing the coverage that it sends back to its home audience. The only danger in cutting to one of these discrete camera feeds during a live telecast is that the only director the camera operator hears is the host broadcast director. You have probably seen a camera suddenly pan to another shot or re-focus live on air. The host broadcast director has told that camera operator to change his or her shot, but, since the director for the network you're watching can't hear that change being made, it looks like a mistake in the show you see. All camera operators at international events know their coverage assignments so they tend to be very reliable for a rights-holding network to cut to and from. But, with several different network programs integrating that shot into their feeds, directed by people speaking a variety of languages, the operators can only take direction from one voice: the director of the host broadcast feed. So they would never know if your network is showing that camera live when they pan or change focus.

The host broadcaster charges extra for every additional discrete feed that a rights holder adds onto the basic coverage feed. It can also set up studios, provide production and office space in the IBC, assign and equip announce booths, provide interview rooms, relay your network's signal to the nearest uplink or fiber terminal, supply computers, furniture, and even the catering. When you add up every item selected from the host broadcaster's rate card, a large production over several days or weeks can be very expensive.

THE HOST BROADCASTER MODEL CHANGES

In 1984 at the Summer Olympics in Los Angeles a new option was added to the mix for international broadcasters. For an additional fee a rights holder could add one or more of its own unilateral cameras at an arena or other venue in order to further personalize the coverage for its viewing audience. This allowed networks for the first time to focus their coverage even more specifically on athletes from their home nations. To mix these unilateral signals into the programs being fed back to viewers at home requires that the network set up a small production integration facility in the IBC on site.

Until the 1992 Olympic Games in Barcelona, the host broadcaster had always been the network in the host country that had secured the exclusive television rights. For example, ARD and ZDF worked together in Germany in 1972, and ABC was the host broadcaster for the 1984 Los Angeles Olympics. The IOC changed its rules in 1992 to allow a broadcast organization that was *not* from the host country to serve as the host broadcaster. In that year Radio Television Olimpica (RTO '92) was set up by the Olympic organizing committee for the Barcelona games to serve as host instead of any Spanish television network. For subsequent Summer and Winter Olympic Games, bids were solicited from independent production groups to fill the host broadcaster role. That ended with the Beijing Olympics of 2008 and the Vancouver winter games of 2010. For these and all future Olympics a private company funded by and supervised by the IOC became the permanent Olympic host broadcaster. The company called OBS, for Olympic Broadcasting Services, gives the IOC more control over the content and tone of its television product, and it establishes production continuity from one Olympics to the next regardless of what country is hosting the Games.

The same model of setting up host broadcasters that are independent from domestic networks has been adopted by FIFA for the soccer World Cup, as well as by several other international event organizers.

LIVE FROM THE SPORTS CENTER IN HARARE, ZIMBABWE

You could probably count on the fingers of one hand the number of live events that have originated in Zimbabwe for American television. And you'd have a few fingers to spare. The Davis Cup draw for the year 2000 had the American team playing its first round matches against Zimbabwe in that nation's capital, Harare. ESPN had the US TV rights, so it was my job to put together the production.

As mentioned in this chapter, the host broadcaster for any international sports event is traditionally the television network in the nation where the event is played. That would have made ZBC, the Zimbabwe Broadcasting Company, the host broadcaster for the matches against the US, and ESPN would have been taking camera feeds from their host truck.

But the ZBC had only televised tennis once or twice in twenty years, and our ESPN team was turning out a hundred days of coverage every year. So early on I decided that ESPN should offer to serve as host broadcaster providing our feeds to ZBC. Making this kind of suggestion could have been seen as an insult by the people at ZBC, so I had to be very diplomatic in raising the topic. My strategy was to offer the ZBC three days of superior tennis coverage, directed and produced by the most experienced professionals from the United States. We could make their shows look better by sharing our expertise and personnel.

After a series of conference calls that put my international diplomacy and "sweet-talking" skills to the test, ZBC agreed to take the secondary role and let ESPN serve as host broadcaster.

There were only two mobile television production trucks in all of Zimbabwe. They had been built by Thomson Electronics in France and were a gift from the French government. During their years of use in Zimbabwe, one truck was producing television and the other was being used for parts to keep the first truck operational.

We needed two trucks for the tennis coverage: one in which our ESPN crew would produce three days of shows, and the second for ZBC to add their own graphics and commentary audio to the feed we provided. When I arrived at the Harare Sports Center arena early in the week before the start of play, I only saw one truck. When I asked where the other truck was, I was informed that there was only one functioning battery. So a couple of ZBC staffers had driven the first truck to the Sports Center, removed its battery, and put it into the trunk of their car to go get the second TV truck.

Perhaps the second most important decision I made next to making ESPN the host broadcaster was hiring Woods TV from Paris to provide technical assistance and personnel. They were able to get the blueprints of the two ZBC trucks from Thomson Electronics, and they brought along an engineer who used every ounce of his resourcefulness to get both trucks up and running in time for our telecasts.

Zimbabwe's economy was in rough straits then and has deteriorated seriously in the years since. There was very little foreign currency in the country, and gasoline suppliers would not accept Zimbabwe dollars to pay for their shipments. Many gasoline tanker trucks were being turned away at the border.

That made getting gasoline to run the electrical generator that powered both TV trucks problematic. Tom Woods of Woods TV had run the technical operations for some televised auto racing events in South Africa, and he had a few relatives and acquaintances in Zimbabwe. Through these connections we got some "black market" gasoline for which we paid a premium. Our ESPN production office was in a small room off the arena floor. And that's where we stored the gasoline. One big red container was under my desk, and we wound up using that gasoline when our generator ran dry.

Overcoming the obstacles we faced and working alongside the ZBC people we hired to operate cameras or serve as stage managers and production assistants, and the Woods TV professionals from France, made this little three-day event, "live from the Sport Center in Harare," one of the most gratifying of my career.

THE INTERNATIONAL BROADCAST CENTER

When hundreds of television networks have all paid for broadcast rights to an event and they or their representatives all come together in the same place at the same time speaking different languages and serving different audiences in widely separated time zones, the result could be chaos. To control if not eliminate the chaos, the organizers of major international events work with their host broadcasters to build an IBC or designate an international broadcast compound.

The IBC is the locus of all the production facilities, services, phone and internet connections, and signal feeds for an international sports event. Every offering made by the host broadcaster is available in one place. How each rights holder network or consortium of networks decides to use the facilities and services varies widely.

When ESPN took over the US cable rights for Wimbledon in 2003, we knew we would need a lot of space for control rooms, edit suites, offices, and a studio. So we contracted with the All England Club (AELTC) and its host broadcaster, the BBC, to use virtually an entire wing of the broadcast center, upstairs and down. The network paid a set fee per square meter for all that space. Then we hired production equipment from vendors to outfit the rooms we had rented at an additional expense. We selected which discrete court and camera feeds we wanted routed to our control rooms from the BBC distribution center, which is nicknamed "Oscar." Then we populated our wing of the IBC with well over a hundred people to work two weeks or more on the ESPN shows, some of which combined to last up to ten hours per day.

By contrast some networks from Europe and Asia only had one person working for them on site at Wimbledon. Their purpose was to make sure the right feed from the courts where their players of interest were competing was routed to the correct transmission path, which would deliver that audio and video back to their network's home base. That's where their tennis commentators could watch the feed come in and add their voices to the coverage. Fans in their countries got to see the live tennis matches, and so did fans in the United States. The difference was in the

Figure 9.1 The quiet outside the IBC at Wimbledon belies the activity inside and in the technical compound behind. Notice the camera positions and technicians on the roof
Source: Dennis Deninger

Figure 9.2 Just one corner of the BBC television compound adjoining the IBC at Wimbledon
Source: Dennis Deninger

ambition level of the respective networks and how much each was willing to spend to customize the programs.

At many international venues there is no permanent building for an IBC. At these events a parking lot is fenced off as the broadcast compound. The individual rights holders can hire all the technical facilities needed from the host broadcaster, or, in many cases, from independent vendors. The video and audio feeds, electrical power, phone lines, broadband internet service, portable offices, and restrooms are all moved in, and surcharges are applied for each network that puts them to use. These broadcast compounds are by their nature less organized than a permanent IBC, but they have the same function: for organizers to serve all the rights-holding broadcasters who are providing coverage of and publicity for their events around the globe.

PRODUCING SPORTS TELEVISION OVERSEAS

It takes a special set of skills to successfully produce sports programming from foreign countries for broadcast in the United States. Adaptability is paramount. Broadcasters in different countries do things differently than we do in the United States. That doesn't make them wrong; it just means they are different. Learning how to work within new systems that come with a variety of challenges and limitations will make all the difference. No amount of complaining or tantrums will get a foreign network to change its way of doing business. Instead diplomacy, understanding, and resourcefulness are necessary.

Communication with host broadcasters, organizers from a variety of countries, and foreign network personnel is vitally important. It needs to be respectful, cordial, and, above all else, clear. Making an assumption that a message got through or was relayed to the right person can be a big mistake. Comprehensive planning, specific requests with all proper documentation, and vigilant follow-up should be part of any enterprise, but they become that much more vital when you are thousands of miles away from your home base with no safety net of fellow employees ready to assist if and when things go awry.

Communicating with that home base is just as important. The people to whom you will be sending your programming need to know every detail of its content, timing, and transmission. They need to know which matches or events will be in each show so that promotion can be produced for broadcast, online, and print media to build your audience. And, when you are several time zones away, your network needs to know what time it is at your overseas venue. Morning for them may be the middle of the night for you.

In many ways international broadcasting is like learning a new sport. You have to learn a new set of rules, there are different players, and you have to use different equipment and put new resources to work for your advantage. And, just like sport, it can be exciting and extremely rewarding, providing you with a new set of friends and a new perspective for your lifetime. But, to succeed, you have to know how to play and make the most of what you have.

Figure 9.3 Sets like this one for ESPN at the 2010 World Cup are constructed inside the international broadcast centers at major sports events. From left: host Chris Fowler and analysts Alexi Lalas, Steve McManaman, and Roberto Martinez
Source: courtesy ESPN

SUMMARY

The American public's appetite for sporting events from around the world was whetted by tape-delayed coverage from the 1960 Summer Olympic Games in Rome, the debut of *ABC's Wide World of Sports* in 1961, and the coverage of both the Summer and Winter Olympics in 1964. That appetite has continued to grow, along with the expectation that every major event will be made available live on television from anywhere on the planet.

The television rights agreements for international sports differ from domestic events because of the multitude of broadcasters who want to air the games and matches in their home countries. The organizers of major international events such as the Olympics, World Cup Soccer, or Wimbledon each set up a host broadcaster to provide a world feed to the networks that have paid for television rights. The world feeds can be supplied with or without commentary, and with or without any graphics. Host broadcasters also offer rights-holding networks discrete feeds from specific venues and from individual cameras that they can use to customize the programs they send back home. Buying the rights to an international event does not allow networks to set up their own "unilateral" cameras unless special arrangements are made and additional fees are paid.

The IBC is where every rights-holding network from around the world gets access to feeds from the host broadcaster. The feeds come into the IBC from every arena, stadium, or court and are made available on a router so that each network can choose which of several concurrent competitions to televise. These decisions are most often based on the nationality of the competitors and their appeal in each network's home country. The IBC is also where networks can set up their own studios, edit suites, and control rooms to augment their live coverage, if they choose to lease the space and hire all the equipment and personnel needed.

Working with broadcasters and event organizers from other nations who have priorities, processes, and practices different from American networks can be challenging. It requires a broad set of skills that include diplomacy and resourcefulness, and careful, concise communication with everyone at the international site and back at home base.

DISCUSSION TOPICS/ASSIGNMENTS

1   Go online and find a foreign network's coverage of any sport that is also played in the United States such as soccer, tennis, or auto racing. Make notes about what is different about the program and compare it with how the sport is produced for television by American networks.

2   Interview anyone who grew up outside the United States and ask about what sports they watched on their home nation's television networks. What do they remember fondly? What do they like better or worse about American sports coverage?

3   In January, go to the Australian Open website and, using the schedule of matches for two consecutive days, put together a plan for how you would build a four-hour block of television from 7–11 p.m. Eastern Time. Which players would you want to feature, how do the local times of their matches synchronize or conflict with the 7–11 ET air window, and from how many different courts would you need to get feeds?

4   Do a short research paper on the history of host broadcasters for the Olympics, FIFA, and the Tour de France. How many different nations air each event? Which nations are represented by broadcast consortiums? Who will the host broadcaster be for the next Olympic Games, World Cup of soccer for men or women, and for the next Tour de France?

10 WHO'S WATCHING TV SPORTS, AND WHY?

That action is best which procures the greatest happiness for the greatest numbers.

(Francis Hutcheson, 1694–1746)

Table 10.1 Chapter 10: The Rundown

- TV viewing on the rise in the US.
- Sports help drive television consumption.
- The factors that affect what Americans watch, and how much.
- Non-traditional television viewing.
- The "best available screen."
- Sports audience demographics.
- Why measure the audience?
- Broadcast vs. cable networks.
- More options splinter the audience.
- Audience trends in the 21st century.
- "Time-shifters" and "cord cutters."

In America's pursuit of happiness, television viewing is the leisure "activity" of choice by a wide margin over anything else we choose to do when not working. Watching TV is something virtually all Americans have in common. In 2010, there were televisions in 98.9% of American homes. That's 115 million homes, with a total of 290 million residents and an average of three televisions per home. And those TV sets get a lot of use. The average American spends just over five hours per day watching television.

It is remarkable that, despite the ever-expanding options we have that could be pulling us away from the TV, such as video games, social media sites, online fantasy sports, or simply surfing the internet, the amount of television watching that Americans do has not been eroded. It has increased. The Nielsen Company, whose reports are the source for most of the statistics in this chapter, found that from the first quarter of 2009 to the first quarter of 2010, the average monthly viewing actually increased by more than two hours per month. When you add time-shifted viewing of television shows recorded on digital video recorders (DVRs) or TiVo to traditional viewing, the average American spent an average of 167 hours per month watching TV in 2010.

Table 10.2 Average daily time spent viewing television per person

Country	Hours/Minutes
Serbia	5:39
Macedonia	5:18
United States	5:04
Greece	5:03
Croatia	4:49
Hungary	4:47
Italy	4:18
Turkey	4:17
Poland	4:14
Puerto Rico	4:06

Source: copyrighted information of Nielsen, licensed for use herein

But that number still doesn't put the United States in first place in the "couch potato" race. People in Serbia and Macedonia spend more time watching TV every day than Americans. Why that's the case could be the subject of another book.

Sport is one of the driving factors in the consumption of television here as well as around the world. In the United States in 2010, there were over 40,500 hours of live sporting events televised on either broadcast or cable television. That does not include sports programs such as ESPN's *SportsCenter*. When you combine the hours that ESPN programs on its six domestic cable networks—ESPN, ESPN2, ESPNU, ESPNews, ESPN Classic, and ESPNdeportes—their total content comes to 52,560 hours per year. Consider that twenty-four hours per day times multiplied by 365 days in a year gives us all just 8760 hours in a year. There's a lot more sports on television than any one of us could consume, even if we chose never to sleep.

A number of important factors determine how much television each of us consumes, how much sports viewing we do, and which sports we watch. Start with age. Americans over the age of sixty-five watch more television than any other age group: almost forty-nine hours per week. That's seven hours a day sitting in front of the TV. The amount of viewing declines for each younger age demographic, hitting its lowest point among teenagers aged twelve to seventeen. They watch the least amount of television on average: twenty-four hours and twenty-eight minutes per week. Children from age two to eleven watch slightly more TV than teens: twenty-five hours and forty-eight minutes per week.

The variance in viewing for different age groups obviously relates directly to the amount of activities and leisure options available or feasible for individuals, depending upon their vitality, mobility, and connections to family and peer groups. If you are active and your recreational options take you away from the home, the amount of traditional television viewing you do will be diminished. That is where "TV Everywhere" technology kicks in. Content providers are making it possible for more people each year to access the television programming to which they subscribe on mobile devices and computers. All you need is a user log-on, and you can watch the same shows you'd turn on at home anywhere there is a cellular signal or broadband internet access.

This non-traditional viewing has been adopted quickest by adults aged 25–34, who watch more video via the internet than any other demographic segment, and teenagers are watching the most video on their mobile phones. These viewing totals are measured in minutes not hours, but they are growing steadily. The Nielsen Company has confirmed that the more video content a person consumes via streaming on the internet or on mobile devices, the less time he or she is spending in front of a traditional TV. But the balance favors the TV viewing at home by a factor of one hundred to one for most people. One hundred minutes of viewing at home for every one minute of remote viewing.

The "best available screen" theory posits that viewing on mobile or remote devices will never surpass traditional viewing in the home. Question: if you have a 50-inch high definition set in your family room and a smart phone in your pocket, which screen will you use to watch the game? Answer: the best available screen, which is not the one that fits in your pocket.

The number of televisions in the home and the level of technology to which you have access are two more important factors that determine how much television you will watch. Homes with multiple TVs and subscriptions to digital television programming on hundreds of HD channels will have those sets turned on for more hours than homes with standard-definition sets and fewer viewing options. And Nielsen research has found that people with HD TVs watch more sports compared with people in their same demographic group who do not have high-definition sets. HD penetration in the United States surged past 50 percent of the population in 2010, a statistic that would appear to bode well for sports programmers if the HD sports-viewing trend holds.

The factors that demographers use in measuring television viewing totals and the size of the audiences for specific types of programming are:

- Age.

- Gender.

- Education level.

- Income level.

- Employment status.

- Marital status and family size.

- The season or time of the year.

The majority of sports viewing is done by males, but it varies widely by sport and event. The audience for the Super Bowl has been roughly 54 percent male and 46 percent female in recent years. But the audience for regular season NFL games and sports such as Major League Baseball, the NBA, college football, college basketball, and auto racing tends to be more than 70 percent male. The shows about sports like ESPN's NFL Live and Pardon the Interruption have the highest concentration of men in the audience with the gender split being 80–20 or more.

Women's sports on television do attract more female viewers, but the majority of the audience is still male. More women watch the Olympics on TV than men by a ratio of 56 to 44 percent. Outside the Olympics, the only sport measured that consistently has more female viewers than male is figure skating.

Olympic Viewers by Gender

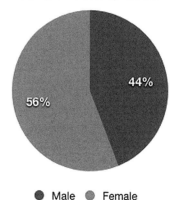

44%

56%

● Male ● Female

Super Bowl Viewers by Gender

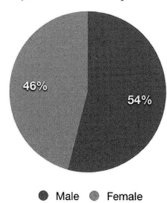

46%

54%

● Male ● Female

Olympic numbers through Feb. 21 - does not include opening ceremonies.   Source: The Nielsen Company

Figure 10.1 Olympic and Super Bowl viewers by gender
Source: copyrighted information of Nielsen, licensed for use herein

Sports viewers tend to be slightly better educated than average TV viewers. Sampling data show that 29 percent of adults who watch sports on television have at least one college degree. Only 21 percent of the total viewing public has that level of education. The disparity in income is even more dramatic: fully one-third of the sports viewing audience can be found in households with over $100,000 in annual income. Only 15 percent of all television viewers make that much money. And the more money men make, the more sports they watch compared with other forms of programming. Bigger income plus bigger HD screens equals more sports viewing.

Marriage is also popular among sports TV viewers. Six out of ten adults who watch TV sports are married as opposed to just 50 percent of the non-fan population. That's important to advertisers who market different products to different audiences. (There is more about advertising in Chapter 11.)

Regardless of your age, gender, or any other demographic distinctions, more people watch more television when the weather is cold and wintry. TV viewing levels are highest in the winter and lowest in the summer, except in the case of major events. People will tune in for the Olympic Summer Games even if it's beautiful weather outside. If the Super Bowl were in August instead of February, it would undoubtedly still be the most-watched show of the year, but it's likely that the total audience would be slightly smaller because of the competition for people's time from outdoor recreation. As "TV Everywhere" takes root, however, those outdoor activities could include watching the Super Bowl.

WHY MEASURE THE AUDIENCE?

The numbers that the Nielsen Company and other audience research organizations gather are used to make decisions that affect the livelihood of thousands of people working on shows and at networks, millions of viewers, and the expenditure of billions of dollars. The interpretation of ratings data for networks and sponsors is a valuable specialty that can determine how efficiently those dollars are being spent, and predict future audience trends. Here are some of the reasons why the ratings are so important:

Audience Growth

When networks know which of their programs or series are drawing large audiences, and which ones are lagging behind, they can expand the strong franchises and drop the under-performers. By eliminating low-rated programming from the schedule a network can increase its overall daily and weekly ratings, and make room for new shows that may attract more viewers. When networks are fortunate enough to develop ratings winners, they can increase the number and/or length of those shows, or create similar programs that will appeal to the same mass audience.

For example, when ESPN started producing preview and analysis shows leading up to the Super Bowl, the network never envisioned doing close to one hundred hours of programming before the "big game." But the ratings success of their Super Bowl "shoulder" programming led to the creation of more new shows and longer hours for the existing ones.

Pardon the Interruption became such a hit in the late weekday afternoons that its ratings surpassed those for the *SportsCenter* show at 6 p.m. Eastern Time. So ESPN created a *Pardon the Interruption* segment within that *SportsCenter* as a way to entice more viewers from "PTI" to stay tuned.

Program Development

Identifying who is watching at what hours makes it possible for networks to design programs and acquire series and events that will be attractive to those demographic segments. If a network has a strong 18–34-year-old audience, it is more likely to go after new mixed martial arts programming than PGA Tour golf tournaments.

Ratings data on how the viewership builds and slips during specific day parts can lead to the development of new lead-in shows, or shows that can capture a large percentage of the audience that was watching the program preceding it on the network's schedule. The goal of every network regardless of its content genre is to keep you watching for longer periods of time. The longer you watch, the longer you are part of the total audience being measured. Therefore networks can increase their ratings *without* adding more viewers, if they can find ways to entice their current viewers to simply watch for longer periods of time. One of the best ways to achieve that goal is by surrounding successful shows with programs that will appeal to the same large audience.

Compete and Win

Networks that subscribe to the Nielsen ratings service get information not only on who is watching their programs, but also who's watching the competition. (There are some networks that choose not to subscribe to Nielsen ratings. In many cases their audiences are so small that ratings data could actually hurt their positions in the marketplace.)

The tracking is available minute by minute, not just for every half-hour or quarter-hour. With minute by minute data, programmers and audience research professionals can accurately identify which segments within a show drew the most viewers and which segments failed to hold viewers. Segments that repeatedly cause audience erosion will quickly be dropped in favor of new ones. It is predictable that viewers will tune away when the live action in an event comes to a halt, but it is remarkable how many loyal fans will stay tuned to a NASCAR race telecast even if it's in a rain delay. Ratings data can identify what type of reports and interviews cause viewers to keep watching during a pause in racing action, and for how long.

The network competing against that NASCAR series will study the demographic characteristics of the audience and then decide whether its best option is to counter-program with a series that appeals to non-racing fans, or to steal viewers away with shows that race fans will find attractive. The audiences for NASCAR and NFL programming are very similar, so scheduling an NFL game or highlights and analysis show opposite a competing NASCAR telecast could cause a significant number of viewers to change channels.

Maximize Advertising Revenue

The key to success and survival for any television network that sells advertising is to sell the largest number of commercials and sponsorships at the highest possible prices. Ratings data are used to convince advertisers that buying commercial time, or entitling a sponsored feature within a popular program's content, will be effective ways for that company to increase the sales of its product or service. Advertisers use several factors when deciding which shows they will sponsor, the most important of which is the size and composition of the audience they can reach with their commercial messages.

The advertiser's goal is to spend efficiently for the greatest effectiveness. Advertisers and the media measure efficiency using CPM, cost per "mille," which is Latin for "thousand," like the "M" in Roman numerals. Dividing the total dollars spent advertising in a program by how many thousand viewers are reached by that program yields the CPM. Cost per thousand is the standard by which cost and efficiency are measured for advertising in all media: television, radio, the internet, newspapers, magazines, outdoor/billboards, even signage in arenas and stadiums.

Even more important to advertisers than the total number of viewers they reach for every $1000 they spend is how many potential customers they reach for that money that are in their target audience. If Cadillac or Lexus is targeting men who earn more than $100,000 per year, it's a waste of money if their commercials are being seen by lots of women under thirty or teenagers with limited buying power. The makers of Viagra, Pfizer Pharmaceuticals, have become one of the largest advertisers in Major League Baseball games because they know that the audience is predominantly older men who are Pfizer's target market.

The networks use the details of how many viewers in each demographic category are watching their shows to devise the pitches they make to each advertising client. The series such as MLB and PGA Tour golf that have older male viewers will be offered to advertisers such as Pfizer and Lilly Icos, which makes Cialis, because the CPM for reaching potential customers is much more favorable than it would be for shows that have a younger or more female audience.

Track Seasonal Trends

Ratings information can be especially useful in designing future programming schedules when it is tracked over a period of several weeks and months, not simply day to day or week to week. Sports leagues and organizers and their television network partners identify when interest starts to build for their product, and when it wanes. When decisions are made to start the season a week earlier or later, or to expand the post-season playoffs, or to move an event to a different date, the ratings can be a determining factor. For example, for its first several years ESPN's *Espy Awards* show was scheduled in February a week after the Super Bowl. Viewing levels in the winter and sports interest were both high. But the *Espy*'s went up against the *Westminster Kennel Club Dog Show* on USA Network, and, despite attracting a large audience, the *Dog Show* perennially won the night among cable viewers. So the *Espy*'s moved to the week of the Major League Baseball All-Star Game. It did well there until Black Entertainment Television programmed its annual BET *Awards* in the same time slot.

Assess the Effects of Change

Television networks constantly change show formats, features, and talent in hopes of increasing audience and profits. The feedback they get via the ratings provides an unbiased report card on whether they succeeded or failed. If the number of sponsored features within any sports telecast reached the saturation point where their accumulated weight annoyed viewers so much that they started tuning out or watching for shorter periods of time, that network would be forced to cut back on sponsor sales in favor of audience retention.

Any programming change that a network sees as positive, such as a new series, host, or segment, is more than likely going to be launched with a major promotional campaign. Decisions have to be made at the network regarding how many promos will run in what day-parts, on which non-TV platforms, and how far in advance of the premiere to reach potential viewers. When that new show finally hits the air, its ratings will tell the network how effective its promotional campaign was, and it will provide valuable information as to how to improve promotion for the next network initiative.

Determining Net Worth

A network with a record of consistently high ratings year after year will have a higher net worth than a network that always finishes third or fourth in the ratings, regardless of their respective assets. There are several other factors that go into calculating the value of media ownership such as the percentage of return on investment. But making a lot of money on low-rated, low-budget shows is not the formula for a network's success. If NBC had been the number-one network in overall ratings for several years in a row, instead of third or sometimes fourth behind CBS, ABC, and FOX, it is unlikely that it would have been acquired by Comcast in 2011.

BROADCAST VS. CABLE

Sports came to American television and flourished in an era when broadcast networks and stations ruled. There was no competition from cable systems and networks or from video on the internet. The birth of ESPN in 1979 was not seen as a serious threat to the executives at CBS, NBC, and ABC because they had the exclusive rights to televise all the major sports and events, and they had a large majority of the viewing audience. Less than 15 percent of television viewing was on independent stations and another 3 or 4 percent went to public television. Cable was only in 20 percent of American homes when ESPN was launched, so the ratings for any one of its shows would have been insignificant compared with say *ABC's Monday Night Football*.

However, as cable's penetration increased along with the number of entertainment options it offered viewers, the percentage of people who watched the broadcast networks started a gradual, inexorable decline. In 1987, when ESPN's reach hit 50 percent of the nation's TV homes, prime time viewers on the three broadcast networks (CBS, NBC, and ABC) outnumbered viewers watching all the basic cable networks combined by a factor of seven to one.

Fifteen years later, in 2002, the playing field had been leveled. In that year the combined prime time ratings for all basic cable networks pulled even with the total ratings for the four broadcast networks, which since 1991 had also included FOX. When viewership was measured for the total day, not just the prime time hours of 8–11 p.m. on Monday through Saturday and 7–11 p.m. on Sundays, basic cable had already taken the lead.

The ratings for cable programming collectively have continued to grow at roughly 5 percent per year since 2002, and broadcast viewership has continued to erode by that same 5 percent per annum. By the year 2010, cable networks had six out of ten American homes tuned to their shows, with just four in ten watching the broadcast networks and public television combined. Since the number of broadcast networks has remained small, they divide their total audience into fewer pieces, which yields a stronger rating for many of their shows compared with cable programs. By comparison, there are a hundred or more cable network choices available to homes from cable systems, direct-broadcast satellite (DBS) services such as DirecTV and Dish Network, or digital delivery systems like Verizon Fios and AT&T U-verse. So the larger total cable audience gets divided into a lot more smaller pieces.

The highest-rated sports programming on cable however is drawing viewership totals that rival the highest-rated broadcast shows. The top-ten rated cable network shows in the years 2010 and 2011 were all *Monday Night Football* games on ESPN. Nielsen ratings figures show that these games averaged from 15 to 18 million viewers per minute. That placed each game ahead of all the shows on television on Monday nights, and in the top-five rated shows during their respective weeks, broadcast or cable. The highest-rated series of any kind on television in 2010 was NBC's *Sunday Night Football*, which only serves to underscore the dominance of sports on television as a means of attracting mass audiences. (In 2011 the only broadcast series with more weekly viewers than NBC's *Sunday Night Football* was *American Idol* on FOX.)

AUDIENCE TRENDS IN THE 21ST CENTURY

Time-Shifted Viewing

Americans have continued to increase their consumption of television programming, but technological innovations have provided new methods by which it can be consumed. Before the introduction of TiVo at the Consumer Electronics Show in January of 1999, and the generation of DVRs that followed, "time-shifted viewing" was limited to a fraction of the population who taped shows for playback on VHS recorders. By 2011, there were DVRs in more than 50 percent of American homes, with projections that the rapid double-digit rate of growth in the spread of this technology would continue unabated.

In its *State of the Media: Consumer Usage Report* for 2011, The Nielsen Company reported that 111 million Americans were storing television shows on their DVRs for viewing whenever they choose. Time-shifted viewing had grown to an average of more than ten hours per month for most adults, so Nielsen has devised new ways to measure the audience for these programs, combining the numbers who watch the show when it first airs with those who watch at a later date or time. Time-shifting has affected live sporting events less than any other genre of programming because of their perishable nature. The suspense is in watching the action as it happens. Only a very few diehard fans will watch a game or match on the DVR once it has been completed and the result is known.

The Decline in Cable Subscriptions

Veterans of cable distribution may one day look back fondly to the year 2001, and reminisce about the good old days when 66.9 million homes subscribed to cable television service. The figures from the National Cable and Telecommunications Association (NCTA) show that competition from other digital video delivery services has gradually cut into the number of American homes that are connected to the local cable company. By 2010, the total had dropped below 60 million for the first time since 1994.

During the same period of time, digital delivery of television via services such as Verizon Fios and AT&T U-Verse has steadily increased, along with the number of homes receiving high-speed broadband internet service. Add to this the competition from DBS services such as DirecTV and Dish Network, and it's easy to see why cable systems may wax nostalgic about the way the world used to be in 2001.

The impact of cable subscription erosion, however, has not been felt by the "cable" networks that never delivered their signals over the air, such as ESPN, USA, CNN, etc. To them it matters little who delivers their content or by what electronic means, as long as that content is distributed to the largest number of homes possible. The networks benefit from the monthly fees collected by their distribution partners and from selling advertising to companies that want to reach their viewers. ESPN could not have been possible without the cable television industry when it launched in 1979, but, if suddenly every cable system disappeared and everyone chose to subscribe to a DBS or digital television service, ESPN and its fellow content providers would survive and continue to flourish.

Cord cutting

More than half the US population is now watching at least some video online with regularity. The ratings service comScore, a leader in measuring the digital world, reported in 2011 that 180 million unique users were watching an average of 18.5 hours of streaming video each month. Nielsen's survey puts those numbers considerably lower: 143 million users and less than four hours per month. But even if comScore's higher numbers are correct, that's still only a fraction of the 167 hours that the average American spends watching traditional television each month. In many households that have high-speed broadband connections, which have dramatically improved the quality and resolution of internet video, it is estimated that 10 to 20 percent of all television viewing is now being done online.

The growth of broadband distribution and the huge increase of television programming that is available online have led a number of people to cancel their cable, satellite, or digital telecommunications subscriptions and retain only their broadband connections. They have chosen to do 100 percent of all their viewing online. The number of "cord cutters" as they are called has been in the range of 100,000 to 200,000 per quarter nationwide. For the first quarter of 2011, cord cutters represented just 0.18 percent of television homes. It is a trend, though, that the television industry as a whole will continue to watch closely because of its potential impact on subscription revenues.

ESPN reports that among medium and heavy sports viewers, the people who represent 87 percent of their audience, there is "zero cord cutting." The leagues, conferences, and organizers who make millions of dollars by selling the television rights to their games and events have made it extremely difficult for consumers to bypass their rights holders and access any live video free online. If their television network partners were to suffer losses in audience ratings and subscription fees because of cord cutting, the value of those rights packages would decline accordingly.

The live sports programming that can be viewed free online, such as the CBS "March Madness on Demand" package and ESPN3's offering of games, is part of a strategy to increase total audience ratings by expanding the number of screens on which the programs can be seen. Online viewers add to the number of people who see the network's commercials and promotion, but they don't have to pay a subscription fee. CBS and the NCAA love the fact that their "March Madness" college basketball tournament games are playing to millions more fans, but it's safe to say that cable systems, DBS, and digital television distributors are wary observers. If more organizers in the future were to develop similar online packages for their live events, the temptation to "cut the cord" may become more enticing for fans who'd like to stop paying a monthly bill for television service, but don't want to miss out on their favorite sports action.

SUMMARY

Watching sports on television has never been more popular, but who is watching which sports on the expanding variety of video platforms via multiple distribution services is constantly in flux. Average viewership of the Major League Baseball World Series fell steadily from an average of 44 million people in 1978, to just 16.6 million in 2011. Those 27 million lost viewers didn't stop being sports fans or disappear. They simply changed their allegiances to watch other sports. Or they became highlights viewers only, choosing not to devote three to four hours to watching a baseball game. After all 1978, the year of the highest-rated World Series, was just one year before *SportsCenter* gave birth to the "highlights culture."

The number of viewing and entertainment options available to all fans has risen dramatically, and it shows no signs of abating. That makes the measurement of audience totals and demographics all the more important for the owners of the sports content, the leagues, teams, and organizers—as well as the television networks, their advertisers, and the distribution services that deliver live sports into your home. When each of these segments of the sports television industry knows who's watching what and why, they can apply their resources efficiently to reach their target audiences, and give sports viewers more of the programming they want on the screens they use the most.

DISCUSSION TOPICS/ASSIGNMENTS

1   Keep a ratings diary for one full week, recording all of your television viewing by quarter hour. How many hours did you watch in a week? What percentage

of that total was sports? How much was on traditional live television? Online? Time-shifted?

2   Research the latest "TV Everywhere" offerings being made by television networks and content distributors. How are these marketed to sports viewers? How many people in the United States are making use of these options like "Watch ESPN," and what are their predominant demographics?

3   Do a report on how the Nielsen Company measures television viewing in the United States. How do they account for multiple viewers in front of the same set? What information do they provide about out-of-home viewing: all those sports fans who watch games at bars or other locations away from home?

4   What impact does the matchup of teams have on the television ratings for the following? Chart your findings over the past five years.

The Super Bowl.
The World Series.
The NBA Finals.
The Stanley Cup Finals.

11 Advertising and Sponsorship

Advertising is the life of trade.

(*Calvin Coolidge*, President of the United States 1923–29)

Table 11.1 Chapter 11: The Rundown

- The first connections between sports and advertising.
- Advertising delivery systems.
- Why advertise in sports programming?
- Borrowing the "emotional capital" of sports.
- Sports television is virtually DVR-proof.
- Advertising within sports content instead of commercial breaks.
- The Super Bowl: the Holy Grail of advertising.
- Effective advertising and its measurement.
- The integrated advertising packages cross platforms.
- The potential pitfalls of sports advertising.

Advertising has been part of sports since long before anyone owned a television. In 1869, the Peck and Snyder Company of New York City was one of the first manufacturers of baseballs. They started printing "trade cards" to give away that had the picture of a baseball team on one side and an advertisement for their product on the other. Trade cards became a popular form of advertising in the 1870s and 1880s, and pasting them into scrapbooks developed into a hobby for thousands of collectors.

The mass distribution of baseball cards as national advertising began in the 1880s when Goodwin and Company, makers of Old Judge tobacco products, started putting pictures of baseball players on the pieces of cardboard that they used as "stiffeners" in their packs of cigarettes. The cards served a practical packaging purpose, and they helped boost the sales of Old Judge among the increasing number of men who were starting to follow the young sport of organized baseball.

The delivery systems available now to advertisers who want to connect with sports fans in the 21st century include every communications innovation that has been developed in the years since Old Judge baseball cards.

- Television ads on broadcast and cable networks and stations.

- Sponsorship of features within television programs and series entitlement.

- Naming rights of stadiums, arenas, and events.

- Signage in sports venues and virtual signage that is electronically inserted into television coverage.

- Radio ads and sponsorship.

- Online advertising via display ads, video, search, and social networking.

- Mobile devices such as smart phones and tablets.

- Newspaper and magazine ads.

- Advertisements in event programs and on tickets.

- Direct-mail advertising and coupons.

Regardless of the method used, the goal of the advertiser is to borrow the *emotional capital* of the sport or event and its stars. By connecting its brand with the action, achievements, and excitement of sport, the advertiser's goal is to link its product to the passion felt by fans, and over the course of time become identified with the positive attributes of that sport or event, or the excellence and winning personality of the star they have chosen to sponsor. It's what Leo Burnett, the founder of one of America's leading advertising agencies meant when he said, "Good advertising does not just circulate information. It penetrates the public mind with desires and belief."

WHY ADVERTISE IN SPORTS PROGRAMMING?

On any given day, nine out of ten Americans watch at least some television. That's a larger percentage of daily users than any other communication or entertainment medium. And, as we demonstrated in Chapter 10, the majority of people consume TV by the hour, following their favorite shows and sampling new ones. Sports on television provides advertisers with a loyal core audience that is more predictable than that of any other programming category. Anyone who has grown up as a fan of a particular team, or attended a university and followed its sports, will tend to watch television when that team is playing. These lifelong loyalties are far stronger than any allegiance to a situation comedy, dramatic series, or "reality" show. Advertisers can count on sports fans, which makes targeting them by demographics much more reliable than predicting who will tune in and in what numbers for the premiere of any new entertainment series.

The live, unpredictable, and perishable nature of sports television also guarantees that well over 90 percent of viewers who watch the games will do so live as they happen. Avoiding time-shifted viewing via digital video recorders (DVRs) means that there is a greater likelihood that the commercial messages will be seen and not sped through by hitting the "Fast Forward" button. That's not to say that sports viewers don't do their share of channel-surfing during commercial breaks to check out what else is on. To deal with that challenge, advertisers are putting greater emphasis on incorporating their sponsorship and branding into the content of the sports telecast through the use of entitlement, sponsorship, billboards, signage, product placement, overlay and hybrid ads.

ADVERTISING WITHIN SPORTS CONTENT

A commercial message delivered as part of sports content can have a greater impact on potential customers than a thirty-second commercial that shares time in a three-minute break with at least five other spots. New methods to integrate commercial branding into content are constantly being developed and refined. Advertisers pay a premium for the increased exposure, but they see it as added value that improves their connection to and recognition by the people in their target market. Here are a few that are currently in use:

Entitlement

This is adding a brand name to the title of an event, as with the "Discover Orange Bowl" or the "AT&T Pebble Beach National Pro-Am." The company pays an entitlement fee to the event organizer, and there is usually a stipulation that a certain number of commercials also must be purchased from the broadcast network partner that televises the event.

Instead of naming an event, an advertiser may decide that it is more advantageous to entitle the shows or series that cover the events on television. Networks put together entitlement packages for the "Chevy Pre-Game Show" or the "Toyota Halftime Report" that include naming the show for the sponsor, commercials within the show, and "brought to you by" billboards at the beginning, middle, and/or end of the program.

Naming Rights

This is a form of entitlement that applies to the naming of venues. The new Meadowlands Stadium became "Met Life Stadium" in 2011 after Met Life Insurance paid the New York Giants and Jets an estimated $400 million for a twenty-five-year contract. None of that money goes directly to any television network, but all teams and leagues require broadcasters to refer to stadiums and arenas by their sponsored names or risk losing privileges such as highlights usage or credentialed access to the venues.

Sponsorship

A "presenting sponsorship" links a brand to the name of the event or to the telecast. The Tournament of Roses organization has never consented to having a sponsor put its name on the "left side" of the Rose Bowl title, but it does share its title with a presenting sponsor on the "right side." So from 2011 through 2014 the annual game is officially entitled "The Rose Bowl presented by Vizio." Vizio's chief sales officer, Randy Waynick, told *AdWeek* that:

> Sports fans, particularly football fans, are a critically important audience for our brand as it continues to grow and expand. Serving as presenting sponsor of the "granddaddy of all Bowl Games" provides a rare opportunity to reach a captive audience on New Year's Day. It also provides tremendous marketing potential leading up to the game during the critical holiday buying season.

Sponsored features within telecasts identify advertisers with specific pieces of content. When you think of "cold," Coors wants you to think of their beer, so for years they sponsored the "Coors Cold Hard Facts" in ESPN's *SportsCenter* shows. Everything from the "Starting Lineups," to the "Play of the Game" is for sale. Some telecasts like NASCAR auto races have well over a dozen features available for purchase by sponsors. If all of these are sold the network's profit goes up, but it does present a problem for the show producer. To accommodate all the sponsored features within a program takes time that would otherwise be spent telling the story of the unfolding event or of an emerging star. Too much sponsored content can crowd out some of the story-telling and the proper documentation of the games that sports fans tune in to see. One of the great challenges for sports television professionals is maintaining a balance between sponsored and editorial content as more sponsors seek inclusion within programs.

Billboards

When buying commercials in a sports telecast advertisers can pay an additional premium for one or more billboards within content to tell viewers that the show is "brought to you by . . ." (Or customized depending upon the sponsor's line of business to read: "delivered by," "built by," "served by," or any other applicable variation.) Accompanied by the brand logo or a short video/animated message and the play-by-play host's voice-over, the billboard serves to make a better connection with viewers than a simple commercial between innings or during a stoppage of play. A sponsor usually does not need to pay for a full entitlement package to get a billboard.

Signage

Signs inside a stadium or arena are strategically placed to be visible on camera. The better the chance that a sign will be seen on television, the higher the price the venue management can charge for that sign. Signage is also common on studio sets and in television monitors behind or alongside the talent. When coupled with television commercials in the telecasts or on the in-house video boards, these signs serve to reinforce brand awareness and presence.

"Virtual signage" is electronically inserted by the broadcaster behind home plate in a baseball game, on a soccer or football field to appear as if it is painted on the turf, or in any number of positions, but these are not visible to the fans in the venue. The advertiser pays the network for this logo placement. However, agreements must be reached beforehand with the event organizer, the venue management, and the league or team to allow the insertion of these "virtual" signs. Virtual signage can be particularly problematic for a venue if the intention of the television network is to cover up or replace the actual signs in the stadium that have been sold to local or regional team sponsors.

Another form of signage is on athlete apparel. NASCAR and European soccer teams are the undisputed masters of this advertising, which is gradually making inroads in other sports. Several NFL teams have sold sponsorship deals that place corporate branding on their players' practice jerseys. The league has frequently been approached with, and then declined, lucrative offers to place advertising messages on their teams' game day uniforms. At some point in the future the size of the offers may become just too lucrative for the NFL to maintain its policy regarding signage on uniforms.

Product Placement

This can be as subtle as a logo on a coffee cup or a bottle of soda or water on the TV set desk or news conference table. Or it can be as overt as a giant inflatable soda can or a brand new car or truck situated behind the end zone or along the sideline where it will get maximum exposure to the stadium and television audiences.

Overlay Ads

Using graphics and logos super-imposed over action, these ads can turn coverage of the game into commercial content. When a batter is stepping up to the plate in the World Series and a graphic appears at the bottom of the screen with a Taco Bell logo and the play-by-play announcer says, "If he hits a home run, everyone in America gets a free taco this Wednesday," that's a commercial. When the manager walks to the mound to change pitchers, add a graphic and a phone company logo with an accompanying live voice-over, "This call to the bullpen is sponsored by . . .," and you have an overlay ad. The possibilities are endless.

Hybrid Ads

Here is perhaps where the line between sports content and commercial message gets blurriest. Elements of the event coverage are blended with commercials to create the impression that they are one and the same. A commercial that uses the game being covered as its backdrop and the network commentator as its voice is designed to look and sound like editorial content. An example of a hybrid commercial would be a spot in *SportsCenter* that is set in a living room with its actors watching ESPN and consuming the beer or snack food being advertised, while the *SportsCenter* theme music is heard playing on their television. More brands are working closely with television networks to develop advertising that will directly engage the target audience, and the result is sure to be more hybrids.

Table 11.2 Top advertisers by sport, 2009

NFL	Anheuser-Busch InBev
Major League Baseball	Pfizer Pharmaceuticals
NBA	T-Mobile
NHL	Verizon
College Football	Nissan
College Basketball	AT&T Mobility
NASCAR	Sprint Nextel
Men's golf	Lilly Icos LLC
Tennis	Geico
Soccer	Volkswagen

Note: you can tell a lot about what demographics are watching which sports by doing no other research than tracking which advertisers are most prominent in the telecasts of each sport. If the company spending the most money in your sport is the maker of prescription medicines for erectile dysfunction like Pfizer and Lilly Icos, it's a clear indication that you have an aging male audience.

Source: copyrighted Information of Nielsen, licensed for use herein.

Each of these advertising vehicles moves the brand from the "real estate" outside the game or event, the commercial breaks that take viewers away from the action, into the action itself. It's as if the commercial messages that were available only in the parking lot outside the venue or during time-outs, could now all be delivered "inside the lines" and during play. Brands that share the spotlight within the content of live television coverage recognize the value of being so closely associated with the sports, teams, and athletes. Their research tells them that these close connections work best at borrowing "emotional capital," and will therefore attract fans in their target market. For that they are willing to pay a premium.

THE SUPER BOWL: THE HOLY GRAIL OF ADVERTISING

The most prominent event of the year in advertising is the Super Bowl. If you want your brand to be identified with the biggest game of the year, the Super Bowl is where you'll spend your advertising dollars. It is the most-watched television program every year, a virtual holiday that celebrates so many of the things that Americans hold dear: football, television, socializing with family and friends, and consumption. For millions of viewers, the primary reason to watch the game is to see the commercials. That puts tremendous pressure on the companies buying thirty-second spots at $3 million or more per unit in the Super Bowl, and on their creative and marketing partners whose job it is to produce messages that will be memorable AND sell product.

In the decade from 2001 through 2010, the Super Bowl accounted for $1.62 billion dollars in television network advertising, according to a comprehensive study done by Kantar Media, one of the leading advertising and marketing research firms in the world. That $1.62 billion bought 850 commercial announcements that occupied 425 minutes of Super Bowl telecasts: more than seven full hours. More money is spent each year on advertising in the Super Bowl game itself than is spent on all the commercials in every World Series game combined, or on all three games of the NCAA's Final Four men's basketball championship weekend.

The Super Bowl represents the largest mass audience that an advertiser can reach at any one time on American television. An average of over 111 million viewers was tuned in during every minute of Super Bowl XLV in February of 2011 as the Green Bay Packers defeated the Pittsburgh Steelers. More than half the population of the United States watched at least part of the FOX telecast: 162.9 million total viewers according to research published by the Nielsen Company. And each year those viewers are seeing more commercials from more advertisers, and more promotion of programming by the network that airs the game. There's a word for that many messages in one television show: clutter.

The Kantar Media study found that in 2001, when the Baltimore Ravens beat the New York Giants in Super Bowl XXXV on CBS, there were eighty-two commercials that took up forty minutes and fifteen seconds of the telecast. The average price per thirty-second commercial then was $2.2 million. In the year 2011, Super Bowl XLV still had just sixty minutes of playing time, but the commercial time had grown to forty-eight minutes, during which 115 different advertising messages were delivered. And the price per spot had grown to $3 million.

Fifteen to 20 percent of the advertising time in any Super Bowl telecast is used by the televising network to promote its upcoming programs. If the network sold that time to advertisers, it's estimated that an additional $50 million would be piled on top of the more than $200 million that is spent on commercials in the Super

Table 11.3 Advertising on the Super Bowl

Super Bowl XLII, February 2008	97.5 million viewers per minute $2.7 million per thirty-second spot on FOX $27.69 CPM—cost per 1000 viewers
Super Bowl XLIII, February 2009	98.7 million viewers per minute $3.0 million per thirty-second spot on NBC $30.40 CPM
Super Bowl XLIV, February 2010	106.5 million viewers per minute $2.94 million per thirty-second spot on CBS $27.61 CPM
Super Bowl XLV, February 2011	111.0 million viewers per minute $3.0 million per thirty-second spot on FOX $27.02 CPM

Source: Kantar Media

Bowl each year. It would be very tempting to take the extra profit and sacrifice the program promotion, but the broadcast networks see the value of reaching that huge audience just as clearly as do the companies buying commercials.

The price of $3 million for one thirty-second commercial may seem outrageous, but, when you divide that figure by the 110 million viewers who see it, the cost to reach 1000 viewers is only $27.02. The cost per thousand people reached, or CPM (the "M" is the Roman numeral for one thousand), is the standard by which advertising is priced in all media. If a company wants to make a national impact on a broad, heterogeneous audience, the Super Bowl is the place to be. The Kantar study found that as many as one-third of all the companies that buy time in the Super Bowl are devoting at least 10 percent of their entire annual advertising budgets to that one telecast.

The question then becomes one of effectiveness. How does one company stand out from the thirty-nine or forty other advertisers in the game? For brands like Bud Light the solution to the "clutter" problem is two-fold: buy multiple ads in the game and strive for cutting-edge creative messages that will be memorable. Not every company, however, has an advertising budget the size of Anheuser-Busch InBev. And the other obstacle that the Super Bowl presents to effective advertising is the very size of the audience that makes it so attractive. An audience that huge includes all demographic groups: men and women, young and old, high and low income, advanced or limited education. The percentage of women in the TV viewing audience for the Super Bowl is usually 40–45%. A company targeting its sales at men, or at a specific age or income demographic, may make more effective use of its advertising budget by not buying commercials in the Super Bowl, but rather by finding a sports property that has a larger percentage of its target market in an albeit smaller total viewing audience. Even NFL regular season games and playoff games leading up to the Super Bowl have a much larger percentage of male viewers than does the Super Bowl.

EFFECTIVE ADVERTISING

In advertising the goal is to reach the largest number of potential customers per dollar spent with a persuasive message that will prompt them to buy a product or

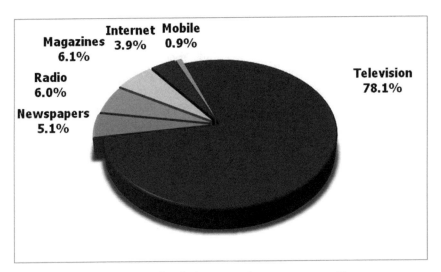

Figure 11.1 Television advertising has the best perception among persons 18+
Source: TVB Media Comparisons Study 2010. Knowledge Networks Inc. Custom Survey

service. Television is by far the most persuasive advertising medium, which explains why close to six out of every ten dollars spent on advertising in the United States goes to television.

Using sports as an advertising vehicle, however, is about more than just total audience reached. It's about brand identity for advertisers and products: tying their names and most favorable attributes to athletes and events that will be admired and remembered for great performances and the powerful emotions they evoke. When fans make the connection, the advertiser accrues *brand equity*, a value that goes beyond actual sales figures because it reaches customers at an emotional level. That is important because the decisions people make about what to buy are far more often emotional decisions, not rational decisions.

Success in sports advertising requires a *functional congruence* between the brand and the sport, event, or athlete it chooses to sponsor. The objective is to transfer the attitude and characteristics of the popular sport or admired athlete to the brand. A maker of precision watches will connect its advertising with a sport such as golf or tennis where precision is of utmost importance. The prestige and exclusivity of these sports are also congruent with the characteristics of well-made, expensive timepieces. Manufacturers of trucks or tires will connect with sports where endurance and durability are the most valuable traits. Advertisers whose products are not functionally congruent with the sports or athletes they sponsor run the risk of achieving lower levels of effectiveness in their media campaigns.

The cost of advertising in prime time network television averages from $20–$30 per thousand viewers reached. Compare that at the high end to the approximately $250 it costs to reach 1000 people via direct-mail advertising, or at the low end of the price spectrum, to the approximately $10 CPM for radio. Price is important, but advertisers need to know a lot more than simply *how many* people they reach for every dollar spent.

One of the key factors is the percentage of the total audience who are in the advertiser's target market. This is what makes advertising in sports attractive to a select number of brands. The sports demographic is predictable in its 1) percentage of men, 2) age range by sport, and 3) loyalty to team, which assures a consistent level of viewership. This goes back to the concept of "narrow-casting." An advertiser who can guarantee that the commercial content it buys in a sports program is reaching a higher concentration of its target market than ads in broad-interest entertainment shows will be willing to pay a premium for that kind of advertising efficiency. That's why the CPM to advertise in prime time sports is in the range of $35 or more, five to ten dollars above the cost to advertise in any other type of prime time programming.

The seasonal nature of sports is another advantage for advertisers, because reaching the target audience *when* they are ready to buy is far more effective than reaching those very same people when they aren't in the market for an advertiser's product or service. Airlines and travel services offering tropical vacation getaways will buy time in hockey or basketball games, as will the makers of snow tires and snow blowers, because that's when the sales of these products peak. Summertime sports like baseball, tennis, and golf may have many of the same viewers, but the networks televising these sports won't get any ad buys for products that don't coincide with the season.

Another important factor in measuring the effectiveness of advertising is the *share of voice*. Of all the commercial messages about the products or services in their category, each advertiser needs to know what percentage it commands. This carries even more weight in sports because of the limited set of product categories that primarily target men. The brewer of Sam Adams beer, for example, may have targeted a specific sport that is watched by a large number of its potential consumers, but, if competing beers already represent half or more of the advertising in those games, Sam Adams' share of voice would be minimal. Their advertising strategy would probably shift to another sport or event that appeals to the same target audience, but in which their brand would have a greater share of voice.

Measuring the share of voice goes beyond the actual advertising in the programs to the impact that advertising has on social media traffic. Research companies are able to do what is called "listening," the process of tracking every mention of brand names on Facebook, Twitter, or any other social network. Brands can gauge the effectiveness of their advertising campaigns by comparing the share of mentions they receive to how often people are mentioning their competitors. It is also possible to determine what percentage of social media or blog posts regarding a product contain positive or negative comments since not every mention of a product or service will be a "rave review."

To achieve maximum effectiveness in advertising, professionals in the field prescribe *integrated packages* that deliver brand messages across multiple platforms. Several research studies show that people have significantly greater recall of the brands and messages they see in television commercials if those messages are reinforced by product placement, entitlement, or signage within TV programs, and by online video, radio, or print media advertising. Branding the same sports product or series across all communications platforms increases reach and binds the advertiser even more closely to that sport.

THE POTENTIAL PITFALLS OF SPORTS ADVERTISING

Identification with a sport, team, or athlete can represent a tremendous market advantage for an advertiser when public perceptions are positive. But the unpredictable nature of sport and the imperfections of its stars can quickly erode that market advantage if those perceptions change from positive to negative. The same emotional capital that an advertiser gains from its close association with a sport or athlete can become a deficit when bad news overshadows the good, or when championships and victories one year turn into losses the next. Advertising in other forms of entertainment that are scripted, recorded, and edited before distribution is far less susceptible to the effects of negative publicity.

A sport's standing in the court of public opinion can be adversely impacted by reports of performance-enhancing drug use, fatal or debilitating injuries, cheating, illegal gambling or point-shaving, financial irregularities, or labor strife and work stoppages such as the player strike that forced the cancellation of the final weeks of the 1994 baseball season along with the World Series that year, and the NHL lockout that wiped out the 2004–05 season. These are associations that advertisers obviously do not want to share.

The use of an athlete as a brand's standard bearer can be even more tenuous. The last thing that any company wants is to have the athlete who is on their box of cereal or is selling their sneakers get arrested or become implicated in scandal. Suddenly all the positive characteristics and accrued brand equity can evaporate into an endorsement nightmare.

A number of specialized research organizations serve the advertising and marketing industry by evaluating a sports celebrity's ability to influence brand affinity and consumer purchase intent. These include Market Evaluations Inc., which compiles its "Q" scores, the Davie Brown Index, and the Nielsen Company, which has introduced "N" scores, all of which measure a sports figure's positives, negatives, and level of recognition.

Tiger Woods topped the list of America's favorite athletes after Michael Jordan retired, and he also was the runaway leader in brand endorsements. That all changed following his Thanksgiving 2009 auto accident and the ensuing revelations of marital infidelity. Negative impressions soared, positives dwindled, and several brands that had valued their connection with Tiger Woods severed those ties. These unpredictable reversals underscore the wisdom of advertisers like Wheaties or Nike that use multiple sports endorsers, reducing their liability should the behavior of one athlete suddenly replace adulation with animosity.

SUMMARY

Advertising in sports programming gives brands the opportunity to identify their products and services with the qualities that fans hold in high esteem: superior performance, determination, loyalty, teamwork, perseverance in the face of obstacles, and stamina. Advertisers borrow emotional capital from the sports, teams, and athletes that they sponsor by sharing the joy and excitement of dramatic victories and remarkable, inspiring achievements. It works best when there is a functional congruence between the distinguishing characteristics of the sports product and those of the product being advertised.

Sports audiences tend to be more predictable than those for other television entertainment programming, and overwhelmingly they watch games and events live as they happen, making the programs virtually "DVR-proof." Sports fans are loyal to their favorite teams and athletes, providing sports advertisers with a reliable core of viewers in their targeted demographic groups, who can be reached via a diverse and ever-expanding set of delivery platforms.

Increasingly advertisers see the value in connecting their messages directly with the live content of televised sport, as opposed to simply sharing space in commercial breaks during pauses in game action. This has led to a blurring of the lines between the editorial and commercial content.

The Super Bowl is annually the most-watched television program in the United States, making its 110 million plus viewers the year's most heterogeneous sports audience. The "big game" is a showcase for creative commercials that must be distinctive and memorable to stand out among the forty or more different advertisers and warrant the pricetag of $3 million or more per thirty-second spot.

The cost of advertising is measured in CPM, which stands for "cost per thousand" viewers reached. The most effective advertising targets a specific audience that is most likely to buy the product or service being offered for sale. The greater the concentration of these targeted viewers in the television audience, the more efficient the advertising buy will be. An integrated package of ads that reaches potential customers multiple times on multiple platforms is likely to have the most impact on brand and message recall when purchasing decisions are being made.

The unpredictable nature of sport and the inability to control the behavior of its stars can present a risk to brands that identify themselves too closely with one athlete endorser or one particular sport or team.

DISCUSSION TOPICS/ASSIGNMENTS

1 Watch one hour of live television sports and count the number of commercial messages that you see or hear. How many different advertisers? How many of the messages were presented in the show content itself and not during commercial breaks?

2 Compare the commercial content of various sports on television. Which advertising categories are common to more than one sport? What does the advertising tell you about which demographic groups are being targeted in each sport?

3 Take a product that you buy regularly and design an integrated advertising campaign for that product based upon what you know about who uses the product and the values that they share with you. What percentage of your advertising budget would you apply to televised sports, online video or other digital applications, radio, or print media?

4 Research the history of ratings and advertising on Super Bowl telecasts. Identify important milestones in the level of viewership and in the creative presentation of commercial messages. Discuss the impact that the Apple "Big Brother" commercial of 1984 has had on Super Bowl advertising since.

5 Discuss how sports celebrity endorsers affect the impressions you have of specific brands. Has the endorsement of any sports star influenced a purchasing decision you have made? If so, how?

12 POWER AND ECONOMICS

Show me the money.

("Rod Tidwell" in the film *Jerry Maguire,* written by Cameron Crowe)

Table 12.1 Chapter 12: the rundown

- The power of content ownership: organizers, leagues, conferences, and teams.
- Television rights contracts.
- The power of television
- Controlling video usage.
- The TV impact on college conference realignment.
- The synergy of media conglomerates.
- The disintermediation of sports television.
- Media ownership of sports franchises.
- The power of television distribution services.
- Retransmission consent and "must-carry."
- The power of the performers.
- Free agency changes the sports power equation.
- The power of sports agents.
- Mark McCormack and the IMG model.

Power in sports television, as in most businesses, is derived from control. A varied array of organizations and individuals control the content, the rules, the assets and capital, the media production and distribution. These groups interact and share power with the stars who attract vast audiences, their agents, the governmental bodies that sanction and regulate their activities, and the fans who exercise their power with their wallets and their eyeballs. No power over content, rules, distribution, assets, or capital has any value unless it includes the capacity to attract and maintain public support.

THE POWER OF CONTENT

Organizers, leagues, conferences, and teams own the events and series that comprise the content of American sports. Those who control the events that generate the largest audiences and revenues have the most power. The NFL and its member teams own the content that is every game played: pre-season, regular season, playoffs, championships, and the Super Bowl. They set the rules of play, including how many individuals will wear the uniform of each team, and they establish the schedules: who will play whom, and when. Every professional league in the United States functions in the same manner and has the same level of control.

The NCAA is an organizer that owns and controls thirty-three national championships in men's and women's sports including the wildly popular "March Madness" men's national basketball tournament. The tournament is so successful that television rights for fourteen years of coverage sold for $10.8 billion in 2010, and tickets to the Final Four games are in such demand that fans have to enter lotteries in hopes of buying a seat.

The International Olympic Committee (IOC) and the Fédération Internationale de Football Association (FIFA) are the two most powerful global organizers of sport. The IOC owns the Olympics, which includes every minute of every contest at the Winter and Summer Games, the name "Olympics," and its five rings logo. FIFA owns the World Cup of Soccer for women and men, as well as every qualifying event played to select the field of teams that gathers to compete for the cup every four years.

The list of sports organizers includes groups that control just one annual event like The Masters golf tournament, which is the property of the Augusta National Golf Club, and series of events such as Southeastern Conference (SEC) and Atlantic Coast Conference (ACC) football games, which are owned by those conferences and their member colleges.

Each sports organizer decides when and where their contests will be held, dramatically affecting local and national economies. Decisions made by the IOC or FIFA as to which countries will host the upcoming Olympic Games or World Cup have billion-dollar impacts on those nations, and adversely on the countries whose bids were unsuccessful.

Organizers get to choose their partners for marketing, sponsorship, stadium and site construction, transportation, supplies and services, and television. No governmental body and no set of laws can dictate who they must choose to work with: neither the highest bidder for TV rights nor the lowest bidder for any service is guaranteed selection. The power to choose is at the sole discretion of the organizer.

Close attention is paid to the annual calendar of sports in order to capture the largest television audiences available and avoid competing with other major events. It makes sense for the Augusta National Golf Club to schedule The Masters for the weekend after the NCAA Final Four each year, but it doesn't have to abide by that schedule. The club has the power to choose any weekend it wants regardless of whatever time conflicts that may cause for some other sporting event. The power of The Masters would more than likely force any conflicting events to find alternative dates.

The organizers, leagues, and teams that own content also control how their games and events will be televised and covered by the news media. This includes when the games or matches will be played. Television networks are able to set start times only if the organizers sell them the rights to do so. Any league can retain its freedom to play games at any time of day or night it chooses, if it is also willing to accept fewer dollars from the television network to whom it sells the television rights. The network would offer less money if it projected that televising the games on the organizer's schedule would not generate a large prime time audience or the corresponding increased advertising revenue. The economic reality is that no league commissioner is going to risk going back to his or her team owners after negotiating a television contract and tell them, "I could have gotten you another x million dollars to share, but I thought retaining the right to set our start times was more important." The next stop for a commissioner delivering that message would be his or her office to start packing.

Broadcast contracts with the owners of content specify how many games or events will be featured on television over a set period of time for an agreed upon figure. As discussed in Chapter 6 on "Programming Sports on Television," these rights contracts cover every excruciating detail including:

- Access to camera positions, sidelines, and locker rooms.

- The list of advertisers approved by the organizer and the amount of advertising time that can be sold per hour of an event.

- Which sponsorship, logos, and graphics may or may not be added to live content.

- The extent of the promotion that the television network must provide leading up to the event.

- How the two parties will work together on the internet in the development of social media sites, interactive games, and the streaming of any live coverage or highlights video.

- The number of minutes of highlights per game or event that can be used by the television partner while play is underway or following its conclusion. How long those highlights can be used before all rights revert back to the organizer, and what access is provided, if any, to historical archive footage from past games or events.

- The procedures for negotiating contract extensions or renewals.

- Even the number of tickets that will be made available free or for purchase in order that the television network may entertain clients, executives, or guests.

By approving or denying requests for media credentials, the organizer decides who will be allowed to enter its venues for the purpose of reporting on, recording, or photographing: competition, interviews with players, coaches, or other participants, or any other activity or person on the grounds controlled by that organizer. If you are an analyst or columnist who the organizer believes has been overly or unfairly critical, you can be denied a credential and banned from access to press areas. Your first-amendment rights are not abridged because you can still buy a ticket and write about the event, but an organizer doesn't have to let you in free and grant you access to the press box, locker rooms, or news conferences.

The greater the public interest and demand for a sports product, the greater is the power that comes with the ownership and control of that content. Any reduction in audience or demand will correspondingly reduce the power of that organizer.

THE POWER OF TELEVISION

The media has the power to increase the reach, demand, and popularity of sports, which makes for a symbiotic relationship between content owners and the media.

Sports as programming benefits television networks because it attracts a loyal core audience of fans. The networks make money by selling commercial time in sports programming to advertisers who have targeted those fans as their potential customers, and by charging monthly fees to the cable systems or other distributors who want sports fans to buy their programming packages. The sports events that each network carries also help them to define their media brands. One of the signature events of CBS Sports is The Masters golf tournament, which it has televised every year since 1956. NBC has branded itself as the Olympic Network by virtue of its being the TV home for every Summer and Winter Olympic Games since the year 2000. The successful launch of the FOX network relied in no small measure on tying its brand to the NFL Sunday package that it obtained in 1994 by outbidding CBS.

On the other side of this symbiosis, the teams, leagues, and organizers benefit because television introduces their sports and stars to more people, thereby expanding their drawing power and increasing value. The rights payments made by television networks to content owners represent the lifeblood of sport, pumping billions of dollars into their operations each year. Signing a television rights deal also guarantees sports organizers, leagues, and teams broad distribution of their marketing and promotional messages, which helps build the fan base and sell tickets.

There is no better example than ESPN's contract with the NFL, which was renewed in 2011 for eight years at $1.9 billion per year. NFL owners share television revenues equally, so over the course of the contract the thirty-two teams should receive in the neighborhood of $500 million each from ESPN alone. In exchange for paying all this money ESPN receives the rights to televise seventeen *Monday Night Football* games and a few pre-season games each year through the 2021 season. The network pays more than double what FOX, CBS, or NBC pays, but does not receive the rights to televise a single Super Bowl. What it does get, however, is the NFL as television content 365 days a year with highlight rights across all media platforms including its ESPN.com websites. That constant coverage

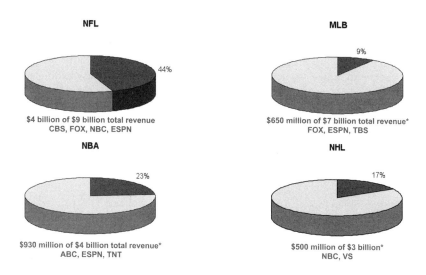

NFL

44%

$4 billion of $9 billion total revenue
CBS, FOX, NBC, ESPN

MLB

9%

$650 million of $7 billion total revenue*
FOX, ESPN, TBS

NBA

23%

$930 million of $4 billion total revenue*
ABC, ESPN, TNT

NHL

17%

$500 million of $3 billion*
NBC, VS

*Excludes regional coverage, e.g. YES Network [$3 billion]

Figure 12.1 Percentage of league revenue from network TV, 2012
Source: copyrighted Information of Nielsen, licensed for use herein

and analysis of the NFL, its teams, and players is valuable publicity and promotion that the league could never buy, and its impact on sustaining and building the NFL's fan base cannot be underestimated.

When more than one television network bids for the rights to an event or season of games, the advantage goes to the content owner. Competition almost always increases the amount of money offered in rights bids. It's a simple example of the law of supply and demand. However, if networks choose not to bid on rights packages for any number of reasons—from changing their target audience to pursuing other forms of programming that could prove less expensive to buy or produce and therefore generate higher profits—the sport could lose all the benefits of the symbiotic relationship with television including a major portion of their annual revenues.

Controlling Video Usage

Television networks are very protective of the rights they buy at such a premium. The value of a rights package can be seriously compromised if "pictures, descriptions or accounts of the games" are easily accessible on competing stations or websites. For each telecast of an event included in a television rights contract, the rights-holding network issues a set of "news access guidelines" that it distributes to every broadcaster and internet video website in the territory covered by the agreement. The network that buys the rights to a season of games or events like the Olympics has the power to dictate how and when any video from its telecasts can be used by anyone who is not a rights holder. Most rights holders will embargo the use of any highlight video by non-rights holders until the live telecast is over. That is not necessarily right when the games ends, but rather it's when the rights-holding network signs off following its post-game interviews and analysis. The show isn't over until the copyright notice is displayed at the bottom of the screen.

Rights-holding networks also have the power to dictate how many seconds of video may be used in what types of programs (usually *bona fide* newscasts only), and over what period of time. For example, NBC allows non-rights holders to use no more than two minutes of Olympic highlights in their newscasts and only within twenty-four hours after the original telecast. After that twenty-four-hour window closes, only NBC can use any of those video excerpts. Rights-holding networks and organizers want the broadest possible coverage of their events as a means to generate the largest possible audience for their live games and events, but they don't want to lose viewers who might choose to just watch comprehensive highlights packages shown by a non-rights holder instead of the actual live event.

College Conference Realignment

The combined forces of 1) higher television rights fees and 2) expanded audiences for marketing and promotion have together fueled the re-shuffling of college conferences in the early 21st century. If a university with a major athletic program can continue fielding the same number of teams, employ the same number of coaches, keep its expenditures virtually unchanged, and at the same time increase its revenue by millions more dollars each year by joining a conference with a better media rights deal, why shouldn't it consider realignment?

That was the question the University of Nebraska answered in June of 2010 when it announced that it would leave the Big 12 Conference to join the Big Ten

Figure 12.2 Big Ten Network logo
Source: courtesy Big Ten Network, LLC

beginning in 2011. IRS filings for the 2009–10 school year show that Nebraska received $9.3 million as its share of Big 12 television rights revenue. For the same year each of the eleven members of the Big Ten Conference got $19.4 million, equal shares of a $214 million pot. The primary reason for the huge disparity in television revenues for the two conferences is the Big Ten Network (BTN), which was launched in 2007 as a joint venture by the Big Ten and FOX Cable Networks. BTN delivers programming twenty-four hours a day, 365 days a year, to more than 40 million homes. Its content is virtually every Big Ten sporting event that isn't televised by ESPN/ABC or CBS. The network sells advertising and returns over $70 million per year to the conference to share among its member schools.

That's in addition to the $100 million that ESPN pays the Big Ten each year for the rights to televise up to forty-one live college football games on either ESPN or ABC through the 2015–16 season, and another $20 million a year that CBS pays for a minimum of twenty-four live college basketball games. The CBS contract extends through the 2016–17 season. Adding the revenue stream from BTN has made membership in the Big Ten Conference very attractive, it has spurred the efforts of the Pac-12 and other conferences to establish new television programming arrangements to maximize their respective bottom lines, and it has universities actively seeking the best opportunities for higher returns on college athletics.

Synergy

The power of media conglomerates is directly related to the number of networks and platforms each controls. Their aggregated power is greater than the sum of their individual parts because of synergy: the cooperation among all co-owned platforms to achieve corporate priorities and cross-promote their products. ESPN is obviously the center of the sports synergy universe with ESPN, ESPN2, ESPNU, ESPNews, ESPN Deportes, ESPN Radio, ESPN.com, ESPN3, *ESPN The Magazine*, ESPN Mobile, and ABC Sports all promoting each other's content in order to reach potential customers wherever and however sports is viewed, listened to, read about, or discussed.

But consider the synergistic forces that Comcast NBC Universal can marshal to deliver the largest possible audience to the opening game of its *Sunday Night Football* series: the *Today Show* live from the site of the game along with correspondents from CNBC, MSNBC, E!, the Weather Channel, *Access Hollywood*, Telemundo, any of their eleven Comcast regional sports networks or the 233 affiliated NBC local television stations. The Comcast NBC Universal conglomerate also owns the NBC Sports channel (formerly Versus), the Golf Channel, USA Network, Bravo, SyFy, Oxygen, and the Universal movie studio and its resorts. The lists of multi-platform media assets for News Corp./FOX, Time Warner, and Viacom/CBS are just as impressive.

Whenever one of these conglomerates identifies a priority such as increasing the ratings for a series or special event, it has the power to reach millions of people across all demographics through a variety of delivery systems to insure that each potential viewer gets the message on multiple occasions and in several different forms. That power of synergy is precisely what leagues and organizers want from their media partners so it can be applied to enhance the value of their content.

POWER FROM THE DISINTERMEDIATION OF SPORTS TELEVISION

Perhaps the ultimate power and synergy in sport is for the content owner, the league or team, to also own the media that covers its sport or events. In economics, "disintermediation" refers to the elimination of an intermediary in a transaction. By removing the middleman, leagues, teams, and organizers add the power of the media to the power of content that they already possess. The league, team, or organizer that controls its own television network has effectively removed the media as a "middleman" who would otherwise be independently deciding the relative importance of stories and content. The ability to deliver messages directly to an audience without an intermediary to analyze, question, or criticize your actions is a public relations dream come true. Opposing opinions need not be solicited.

Each of the major professional leagues has established its own network, starting with NBA TV in 1999, the NFL Network in 2003, NHL Network in 2007, and the MLB Network in 2009. It is also very common for regional sports networks to be owned by the teams they cover. And college conferences that appeal to large audiences across several states are joining the ranks of those organizations that also own their own networks, led by the huge success enjoyed by the BTN.

When the same organization is signing the paychecks for the general manager, coaches, and players on a team as well as the commentators and producers who tell their stories on television, the tendency can be for the network to become the public relations arm of the team. If that general manager, for instance, makes a stupid trade that hurts the franchise, how much will he or she be criticized by commentators who are fellow employees of the same owner? Will you see a graphic comparison showing how much better the traded player is doing for his new team than the player your team got in exchange on a regional sports network telecast that is controlled by your team?

The ultimate success of the team will result in higher profits for all, so any criticism or stories that could jeopardize that success or tarnish the image of the organization are less likely to be part of the program on a network that is owned by the team. This is not to say that there isn't an economic partnership between each league and the independently owned television networks that have purchased their broadcast rights, which can have an impact on what is said in a telecast. The rights agreements that bind the network and league together are worth hundreds of millions of dollars per year. And they rely upon each other for mutual success. But there is a greater chance that viewers will see and hear more unbiased reporting and objective criticism on networks that are not owned or controlled by the leagues they cover.

A few simple examples may help make the point. The best camera shot of a baseball pitch is from centerfield, framing the pitcher and the batter with the catcher and the umpire. The longer the lens on that camera, the closer it can zoom in on these four so the viewer can see their actions, their faces, and their reactions. However, if the team's priority is to sell season tickets for next season, and billboards have been installed behind home plate with the number to call or website to click on for ticket purchases, you can be sure that a director working for the team-owned television network will instruct the camera operator to widen the shot so that the promotional message can be seen on every pitch. It's a subtle change that most fans might not notice, but the priority is no longer delivering the best, most powerful camera shots to the home viewer. It is helping the team make a profit.

Another less subtle example: Penn State and Ohio State are both part of the Big Ten Conference, which in partnership with FOX Sports Networks owns BTN. When news broke regarding the allegations of sexual abuse and its ensuing cover-up at Penn State, or the trading by Ohio State football players of their awards and memorabilia for tattoos, it was not broken by the Big Ten Network.

To be fair, the Big Ten Network does not represent itself as a news-gathering entity, but the point is that no television network owned by a league is ever going to go digging for stories that might have a negative impact on that league or any of its teams or members. The more media outlets that are controlled by the sports they cover, the less chance there will be for this kind of investigative reporting to see the light of day.

No one is more sensitive to this than Mark Quenzel, who heads programming and production at the NFL Network. "People have to believe they will get accuracy from us," he said. "Any time someone can point to an example of the NFL Network soft-peddling a story, it's going to hurt our credibility." Quenzel says that the key for his network is to report stories and "add opinions based on fact." Covering labor disputes represents a very clear dilemma for any network owned by the league. The league's position and point of view have to get preference, even if only subliminally, when everyone's paycheck comes from the league. Fair and balanced reporting is more likely to come from independent media.

The in-house networks for each of the major sports leagues in the United States realize that their fans are sophisticated enough to see right through any attempt to gloss over controversial stories. To differing degrees, these networks and the regional sports networks that are owned by teams, such as the YES Network in New York, which is owned by the Yankees, or NESN in Boston, which is owned jointly by the Red Sox (80 percent) and the Bruins hockey team (20 percent), recognize the value of controversy. Stories that get the public talking about your league, team, or players serve to attract attention and viewers. So it is not in their interest to suppress controversy, but ownership of the media does provide content owners with the power to set the agenda as to what will be discussed on the air, and how and when related information and background will be released.

THE POWER OF TELEVISION DISTRIBUTION SERVICES

Less than 10 percent of American homes get their TV signals the old-fashioned way, over the air from their local television stations. Nine out of ten receive television via subscription from cable systems, direct-broadcast satellite (DBS) services such as DirecTV and Dish Network, multi-channel video programming distributors like AT&T U-verse, Verizon Fios, and broadband internet providers. That dominance over the distribution of broadcast content endows this sector of the industry with tremendous power, and profits to match.

Cable systems, DBS, and the digital communications providers are free to choose which networks they will include in the lineups they offer. There is no statute or regulation that requires them to distribute sports networks, or any

TED TURNER AND MEDIA OWNERSHIP OF SPORTS FRANCHISES

Media ownership of sports franchises is a phenomenon that goes well back into the 20th century. CBS was broadcasting the baseball *Game of the Week* on Saturdays when the network bought the New York Yankees following the 1964 season. CBS owned the team for a year before the *Game of the Week* moved to NBC. During that year as a team owner, CBS had the opportunity to influence the sport it was televising, sharing in decisions with the other owners and in Major League Baseball revenues. CBS sold the Yankees to George Steinbrenner's ownership consortium after the 1972 season.

Ted Turner took media ownership of franchises to an unprecedented level because he saw the games as television content. Turner took over the family's small Atlanta radio and billboard advertising business when he was 24 years old, following his father's suicide. In 1970 he bought Channel 17 in Atlanta, an independent TV station known primarily for its seemingly endless reruns of *The Andy Griffith Show*. Six years later Channel 17 became America's first "super station," when Turner started beaming its signal to cable systems around the country via RCA's Satcom I geo-synchronous communications satellite, which had been launched in 1975.

To program the station Turner added old movies to the TV sitcom reruns, and he bought the Atlanta Braves baseball team in 1976. A year later he purchased the Atlanta Hawks of the NBA, and added those games to his super station lineup. More live sports content for which Turner did not have to pay rights meant he didn't have to buy as many old movies and syndicated TV series. In 1979, Ted Turner changed the call letters of Channel 17 from WTCG (for Turner Communications Group) to WTBS, the flagship of the Turner Broadcasting System. He dropped the "W" in 1987 and the TBS cable network was born, in no small measure on the strength of owning the sports content that it televised.

A number of media groups, newspaper and broadcast, have bought sports franchises and events to give them more control over the product they cover or televise. For many it's a business formula that works. For others, making the sports business as successful as their communications businesses has proven difficult or impossible. But, given the consistent rise in the purchase prices for sports franchises over the past several decades, selling the team to a new owner can be a very profitable business decision for a media group.

Figure 12.3 Ted Turner
Source: reprinted with permission of Getty Images

Table 12.2 Top-ten multi-channel video programming distributors, June 2011

1	Comcast Corporation	22,525,000 homes
2	DirecTV	19,433,000
3	Dish Network Corporation	14,056,000
4	Time Warner Cable, Inc.	12,235,000
5	Cox Communications, Inc.	4,838,000
6	Charter Communications, Inc.	4,413,000
7	Verizon Communications, Inc.	3,848,000
8	AT&T, Inc.	3,407,000
9	Cablevision Systems Corp.	3,284,000
10	Bright House Networks LLC	2,139, 000

Source: courtesy NCTA. Contains data estimates from SNL Kagan

particular category of programming. Market forces and subscriber demand make it unrealistic that distributors would not include sports channels. But, if they thought they could save money by eliminating the monthly fees charged by those networks and not lose too many customers, some would definitely be willing to experiment with an altered channel lineup.

Consider the power that Comcast has by virtue of its 22.5 million home subscriber base, the largest of any distribution service. If Comcast decided that it was no longer willing to pay ESPN the $4.50 to $5.00 per home per month that the "Worldwide Leader" charges for its programming, ESPN's reach would shrink overnight from 100 million homes to less than 78 million. Reaching a smaller audience, ESPN would have to reduce its advertising rates. With less money coming in from advertising and subscriber fees, the network would be forced to re-evaluate which sports it could afford to buy rights for, and which ones it might have to drop. That's the kind of power distribution services have, in varying degrees according to the number of homes they reach, over any of the networks they carry.

It's obvious that Comcast has never enjoyed writing a check for over $100 million a month to ESPN (22.5 million homes multiplied by the $4.50+ charge per home). Over the course of a year Comcast pays ESPN more than $1.2 billion. In an attempt to take over ownership of the network, and in so doing put an end to the check writing, Comcast made a bid in 2004 to buy ESPN's parent, the Walt Disney Company, for $49.1 billion. Disney was able to rebuff the Comcast takeover bid, but that didn't dissuade Comcast from its conviction that the company's future success lay in acquiring more control over the networks it distributes.

Competition from DBS and the multi-channel digital distributors that include broadband internet video sources has hurt the cable television business. The National Cable and Telecommunications Association (NCTA) reported that in the year 2001 there were 66.9 million homes subscribing to cable TV in the United States. There has been steady erosion since that high water mark, with the total falling to 58.9 million homes in 2011. Comcast could have chosen to resign the company to the reality of declining cable distribution, but instead it built a stable of owned networks including Versus and the Golf Channel. And in 2009 it reached agreement with General Electric to buy controlling interest in NBC Universal for $30 billion. When that deal won federal regulatory approval in 2011, it made Comcast a giant in both media programming *and* distribution. The company still pays ESPN huge sums of money, but, as it strengthens the content of the NBC Sports channel and the Golf Channel, Comcast will be in an improved bargaining position when it comes time to renew its subscriber contracts with ESPN.

Distribution services definitely hold the upper hand when it comes to their negotiations with sports networks that are smaller and therefore less powerful than ESPN. They can choose to put these networks on a premium sports tier for which subscribers would pay an additional fee each month, thereby limiting distribution, or they can choose not to carry the networks at all. The NFL Network dearly wants to add Time Warner Cable's 12.2 million homes to its audience total, but negotiations that began before the network even debuted in 2003 had still not been resolved nine years later.

Recognizing the power of the distributors, the MLB Network took a different tack when it launched in 2009. Major League Baseball retained two-thirds ownership of the network, but they partnered with Comcast, DirecTV, Time Warner Cable, and Cox Communications, who together own the remaining one-third. This guaranteed that the MLB Network would be seen in more homes on its first day, January 1, 2009, than the NFL Network, which had already been on the air for five years.

Must-Carry and Retransmission Consent

When cable television first began its transition from community antenna television (CATV), a means by which rural areas could receive broadcast signals, to a distributor of programming to cities and towns alike, the Federal Communications Commission (FCC) imposed what it called "must-carry" rules. Beginning in 1972, cable systems were required to include every TV station within a sixty-mile radius (later revised to fifty miles) as part of their basic subscription offering. Local stations feared that, if they could not be seen in homes where cable had been installed, they would lose market share. By invoking "must-carry" status, the stations were guaranteed carriage on cable, but they could not demand compensation from the cable distributor.

After a series of regulatory revisions and findings in the 1980s by the US Circuit Court of Appeals that "must-carry" violated the free-speech provisions of the First Amendment, the FCC in 1994 gave broadcast stations the option of charging cable operators in exchange for granting permission for their signal to be retransmitted. The cable companies were required to obtain "retransmission consent" before carrying any broadcast signal. This ruling gave strong local stations, most with network affiliations and large audiences, the power to charge cable systems for the programming they provided and negotiate terms including channel number preference. (See Chapter 13, "Politics and Government in Sports Television," for more detail.)

As cable networks tallied huge annual profits from their dual-revenue streams of advertising and subscriber fees, the broadcast networks—ABC, CBS, NBC, and FOX—began to look at retransmission consent fees as their potential second revenue stream. With over 90 percent of homes receiving television via subscription, the distinctions between "broadcast" networks and "cable" networks have all but vanished. For most people, each network is simply another number on the box. That being the case, the broadcast networks made the argument that if CBS, ABC, NBC, or FOX had content like the Super Bowl, the Olympics, and NCAA "March Madness," plus plenty of highly rated entertainment shows that could deliver more viewers per minute than ESPN, TBS, or any cable network, they should be able to set a fair market value on their programming and collect it by increasing the retransmission consent fees charged by their affiliated stations.

The additional revenue now flowing to ABC, CBS, NBC, and FOX, which they share with their local affiliate stations, has improved the business model for broadcasters in the US, and helped them achieve more of a competitive balance with the networks that were born on cable and never transmitted their signals over the air. It has also served to put a check on the power of the distribution services, limited to the extent however that they can pass along the increased prices they pay for programming to their subscribers. The true winners in this equation are the conglomerates that own networks and distribution services. The retransmission consent fees that Comcast cable systems pay to NBC TV stations is money Comcast pays itself. The same is true for Time Warner when its cable systems pay monthly subscriber fees to the networks owned by Time Warner, which include TBS, TNT, CNN, and the Cartoon Network. Power is multiplied by the number of industry sectors in which any one company can establish a significant presence.

THE POWER OF THE PERFORMERS

Television has the power to create stars by showing the greatest successes of individuals and teams live to millions of fans, followed by close-ups of jubilant celebrations and smiling faces. Stars who become regional or national celebrities in turn have the power to draw paying customers to live events and to television coverage of those events. Star status can bring endorsement contracts worth more than their salaries to athletes like Michael Jordan and Shaun White, with whom the public makes an emotional connection. The value of endorsements and their power within their respective sports is multiplied geometrically by having their stories told and legends built on television.

Each year a number of publications release their lists of "most powerful athletes," and each year performers in individual sports such as golf and tennis tend to have far greater representation than these sports and their lower television ratings would seem to deserve. The two primary factors in their favor are that they don't share the spotlight with any teammates when they win championships, and as individuals they can decide where and when they will compete. That gives them tremendous power over the organizers of events whose success at the gate is heavily dependent upon having stars in their golf or tennis tournaments. The impact on television ratings and therefore on the value of the television rights to these events is even more important, which gives individual performers power with the media as well.

In 2008, before his fall from grace, Tiger Woods was at the top of every "most powerful athlete" list. Here's an example that explains why: that summer Woods won the US Open golf tournament in a playoff. The live coverage on NBC got a 10 rating and a 20 percent share of all the televisions that were in use that Sunday afternoon in June. Woods won the playoff the following day but injured his knee, so he did not compete in the next major golf tournament that year, the PGA Championship in August. Without Woods in the field, the PGA got a 3.0 rating for its Sunday telecast on CBS, a precipitous drop in viewership from the US Open.

Events that rely on star power are subject to much wider fluctuations in attendance, TV ratings, the value of rights, advertising, and sponsorship deals than do the leagues and team sports that have built up fan loyalty over generations. The power that stars in the individual sports have to affect the bottom line for organizers and the media can translate into steep appearance fees, bonuses, and special treatment in addition to the income they receive for wearing branded apparel and endorsing products.

The only appearance fee that athletes in team sports get is their salary, which does rise and fall with their star status and the caliber of their performances. The greatest power that team athletes have is collectively through their respective unions and player associations. Withholding their services until they receive a contract offer they deem acceptable shuts down leagues and teams, which don't make much money if games aren't played and televised. As in most businesses, however, the upper hand in contract negotiations is usually held by the side that has the deepest pockets. In sports, that is invariably the owners.

Athlete compensation became much more a function of the marketplace with the advent of free agency, which allows stars to realize their true value by selling their services to the highest bidder. The power of performers was insignificant compared with owners and organizers before free agency.

Free Agency Changes the Sports Power Equation

Every professional baseball contract from the 1880s into the 1970s had a "reserve clause" that allowed the team to automatically renew a player's contract every year of his career at a salary set by the team. This left players virtually powerless, bound to their teams for life. Major League Baseball also enjoyed an antitrust exemption, which stemmed from the US Supreme Court's *Federal Baseball Club of Baltimore vs. National League of Professional Baseball Clubs* decision in 1922. The Federal League was being organized as a rival to the National and American Leagues, but it was unable to sign any players away from their NL or AL teams because none could escape the reserve clauses in their contracts. The Federal League claimed that the two established leagues were in violation of antitrust laws, but the Supreme Court disagreed. Justice Oliver Wendell Holmes stated that baseball was not subject to antitrust regulation and that "the charges against the defendants were not an interference with commerce among the states."

This 1922 ruling was upheld in 1972 when Curt Flood, an outfielder for the St Louis Cardinals, sued baseball in order to void his trade to the Philadelphia Phillies. Flood argued that he should have the option to sign with any other club that may seek his services when his contract with the Cardinals expired. The Supreme Court ruled against Flood, calling baseball "an exception and an anomaly," making it clear that the only way the antitrust exemption could ever be overturned would be by act of Congress.

Curt Flood did not win free agency for baseball players, but three years later a combination of factors nullified the reserve clause and ushered in a new era of power for the performers in American team sports. The players had organized a strike against baseball owners in 1972 when they failed to reach agreement on a new collective bargaining agreement. When an agreement was reached in 1973, a salary arbitration clause was included that would allow a player to seek the assistance of an arbitrator if he could not agree with his team on an appropriate level of compensation. The reserve clause remained in effect.

A pitcher for the Los Angeles Dodgers, Andy Messersmith, did not accept the team's contract offer, so he played out his contract in 1975 and looked for other teams to bid for his services. Not one team made him an offer, so Messersmith filed a grievance and invoked the arbitration clause. The arbitrator found in Messersmith's favor, saying that teams could only renew an existing contract for one year after it expired, not for every year of a player's career. By playing out that one option year, a player would then be legally free to offer his services to any team. It's what Curt Flood had envisioned and fought in vain to achieve.

Free agency gave each player more control over his career and diminished the power of owners, forcing them to pay fair market value or face losing their stars. In 1975 when Andy Messersmith filed his complaint, the average major league baseball player was earning $51,501. Ten years later that average had grown to $371,157, evidence that before free agency owners were not paying players what they were truly worth.

Every work stoppage in professional sports since has been a struggle to tip the balance of power between those who own the product—the team owners and their leagues—and the performers, without whom there would be no product for fans to watch in person or on television. Each side wants more control over its percentage of revenues, the work rules, schedules, and a host of lesser but not inconsequential issues. Resolution is usually achieved when it becomes apparent that when games aren't played, like the World Series lost to a player strike in 1994 or the entire 2004–05 National Hockey League season, the media rights dollars that fuel professional sport disappear.

THE POWER OF SPORTS AGENTS

The subject of sports agents probably deserves its own chapter or an entire book. Their presence has added leverage and expertise to the power of the athletes they represent, forcing leagues and organizers to negotiate terms that would otherwise be unilaterally enforced. In the era of free agency, agents can affect the fortunes of professional franchises on and off the field by facilitating the movement of one or more stars from one team to another.

The most powerful agents are those who represent a group of stars in one sport. An agent who has thirty or more clients in the NBA, for instance, becomes a force in professional basketball far greater than an agent who has only one or two clients. He or she can set standards for what will or will not be included in contracts, and relative pay scales for comparable performers. Powerful agents have contributed behind the scenes to the settlement of labor disagreements by building consensus among their player groups. Their vested interest in solving disputes is obvious: when players aren't being paid, agents don't get their commissions. An agent such as David Falk, who represented Michael Jordan during his playing career, can attract new advertisers to a sport through his clients and expand the influence of the sport by marketing its stars outside the game.

The father of modern sports representation is undoubtedly Mark McCormack, who founded the International Management Group (IMG) in 1960. As a college golfer at William and Mary in the early 1950s, McCormack met Arnold Palmer, who played for Wake Forest. He went on to Yale Law School and was working at a Cleveland law firm in 1960 when he proposed the idea of representing Palmer, who had become the most charismatic golfer on the PGA Tour. McCormack's pitch was that he could make more money for Arnold Palmer through endorsements and appearances in a year than the golfer could earn winning golf tournaments. The two men sealed the deal with a handshake. A year later, having seen his success with Palmer, golf's two other top players of the era, Jack Nicklaus and Gary Player, also signed with IMG. It was just the beginning of what would become the world's largest athlete representation firm.

Figure 12.4 Mark McCormack, 1930–2003, the founder of
International Management Group

Mark McCormack's greatest contribution however was his vision of how to integrate every level of the sports business to maximize profits and power. It's what I call "the IMG model," and it has been copied many times over, but never duplicated at McCormack's level of success.

- He started with representing individual athletes, and then he created or bought events for them to star in.

- IMG would sell sponsorships to these events to advertisers, as well as do all the marketing, brand management, and licensing. The company extended these services to organizers and leagues around the world like the All-England Lawn Tennis Club, the English Premier League, the PGA, LPGA, the US Golf Association, the US Tennis Association, and, through its IMG College division, to the NCAA and more than 200 universities. IMG's reach has grown to the point that year after year its sports catalogue has over 250 pages of client and partner listings.

- IMG's subsidiary, Trans World International (TWI), became the world's largest independent producer of sports television by packaging the coverage of owned and non-owned events and shows alike. (TWI was re-named "IMG Media" after IMG was purchased by Ted Forstmann's private equity firm following McCormack's death in 2003.)

- In many cases the television commentators for the shows produced by IMG Media, as well as the shows produced by others for organizers who are IMG partners, are IMG clients themselves.

- And to keep fresh young talent flowing into the IMG pipeline, the company established the IMG Academies to train promising athletes, many of whom doubtless one day will become professional clients. IMG trains over 12,000 athletes from eighty nations.

IMG has a role in every sector of the sports business, which means there is a commission or fee at every level for IMG, and its structure gives the company power to affect change and create synergies for clients and partners that would not be possible if it weren't simultaneously a content owner, media producer and distributor, agent, marketing, branding, and licensing representative, and sports academy.

SUMMARY

Power in sports television is derived from control. The leagues, teams, and organizers that own content which is in demand control how and on which networks their contests will be televised, as well as the rules and schedules of play. Content owners have a symbiotic relationship with their broadcast media partners. The owners get exposure and promotion that expands their fan bases, plus huge television rights fees that fuel their businesses. The television networks and stations get programming that is proven to draw large, loyal audiences and attract advertisers who will pay dearly to reach viewers who are in their target markets.

The leagues and teams that have established their own television networks have increased the power over their content through "disintermediation," which removes the media as the "middleman" between the league or team and its fans. The messages and stories that the content owner delivers on its owned network are less likely to contain any criticism than those delivered by independently owned broadcasters.

The companies that control the distribution of television programming have the power to choose which networks they will offer to viewers and set subscription rates for their channel lineups and any specialty tiers of service. This affects the size of the audience any network can reach, which in turn dictates how much a network can charge for its advertising.

The players and performers have power that comes from their ability to put fans in seats and in front of televisions. The power of athletes in individual sports is disproportionate to the relative strengths of the sports themselves because they can decide where to play and when. Star power at an event will increase attendance, revenue, and TV ratings. The events that stars choose to skip will very often suffer steep declines in each category. The players in team sports gained far more power with the advent of free agency, elevating them from the status of virtually indentured servants that prevailed until the 1970s.

The creation of player unions gave them the power to shut down leagues and the flow of revenue that comes from live games, until they reach bargaining agreements they believe are fair. Player agents aggregate power by representing several players in the same league, or by building organizations such as IMG, which vertically integrate representation, marketing, sales, brand management, licensing, television, and player development.

The ultimate power in sports, however, rests with the public. Win the support and allegiance of fans, and power is yours. Sports products with strong attendance and the television ratings to match can charge more for their broadcast rights, sell more advertising and sponsorships, build new arenas and stadiums, and develop new opportunities in new markets. Take fans for granted or make changes they don't like and attendance and viewership will slip away, and with it power and earning potential.

DISCUSSION TOPICS/ASSIGNMENTS

1 Select one sports league or organizer and study its history on television. When did its events first appear on American television? Who have its media partners been? How have its television audience and attendance figures changed over the years? And what role has television played in its popularity?

2 Decide which of the following has the most power in the sports business and explain why.

   a The leagues and organizers.
   b Players, unions, and agents.
   c The television networks.
   d Distribution services.

3 Compare the coverage of one event or story on a league-owned television network with the coverage of that same event or story on a network that is not controlled by the league. Were any story lines omitted or emphasized by one and not the other? Were you able to separate reporting from promotion? Which network did the better job?

4 Take one of these media conglomerates and assemble its entire list of holdings. Then discuss its opportunities for synergy and how the priorities of one division could possibly affect the product of another.

   a News Corporation/FOX.
   b The Walt Disney Company.
   c Comcast/NBC Universal.
   d Time Warner.

5 Research the ownership of sports franchises and events by television networks and media groups. Which have been the most successful? How has network ownership affected the team and the league in which it plays?

6 Find a current "Most Influential" or "Most Powerful in Sports" list and discuss why certain figures are near the top and why others are not. Do you agree with the rankings? How would you rearrange or change them, and why? Who do you think is the most powerful individual in sports? How did that person achieve that level of power?

13 Politics and Government in Sports Television

A sporting system is the by-product of society and its political system, and it is just boyhood dreaming to suppose you can ever take politics out of sport.

(Peter Hain, Member of British Parliament)

Table 13.1 Chapter 13: The Rundown

- Sports and political symbolism.
- Sports as a forum for politics.
- The event as a political statement.
- Berlin 1936 and Olympic boycotts.
- The event as a political stage.
- Mexico City 1968 and Munich 1972.
- Sports stars as political icons.
- Economics makes sports political.
- Public vs. private funding for stadiums.
- NCAA College Football and the Supreme Court.
- The Federal Communications Commission.
- Media ownership limitations.
- Public access to television programming.
- Must-carry and retransmission consent.
- The congressional connection.

If there were a sports utopia, the vast majority of fans would want it to be a place of festival and spectacle where all games were contests of skill and will, matching the best athletes and teams in competitions that would, with each renewal, reach new heights and create ever more amazing highlights for us all to cheer and enjoy. In sports utopia politics and government would play no role whatsoever. But as each of us knows all too well, there is no such place.

SPORTS AND POLITICAL SYMBOLISM

Games and matches are more than simply competitions; they are events that play a role in the construction and representation of local, regional, and national identities. The quest for victory and the unwillingness to settle for anything less is paramount in sports, and in politics. Winning tells all challengers that your city, region, or nation is better than theirs. It sets the highest standards, works the hardest to reach its goals, will endure all struggles and overcome all obstacles to prevail. For much of the world, and for millions of Americans, gridiron football represents the United States. Success is built on superior strength, teamwork, and the ability to impose one's will by any means necessary on the opposition. The symbolism of baseball as the original "national pastime" is tied up in the values upon which the country was founded, where boys and girls played on open fields and pastures, and, regardless of an individual's humble beginnings, working hard and striving to excel, would reap the rewards of success.

The power of symbolism is not lost on politicians. Nor is the ability to simultaneously reach a vast audience of potential voters. President William Howard Taft started a tradition that has connected politics and sports since 1912: throwing out the ceremonial "first ball" of the baseball season. From their seat in the stands, Taft and successive presidents presented a smiling, positive image as men of the people who enjoyed taking in a game just as much as the average guy. The symbolism changed when presidents stepped out of the stands and onto the field to make the "first pitch" from the mound. Now the president is "one of the players," a man of action standing shoulder to shoulder with elite athletes on ground

Figure 13.1 President William Howard Taft started a tradition when he threw out the first ball to open the 1912 baseball season
Source: reprinted with permission of Getty Images

Figure 13.2 President Barack Obama playing basketball presents the image of a fit and active leader, connecting him to younger generations
Source: reprinted with permission of Getty Images

where only they, and a select few who receive special permission, are allowed to tread. Sitting in the stands was fine for newspaper photos; pitching from the mound makes better television.

SPORTS AS A FORUM FOR POLITICS

The first pitch is symbolic and largely devoid of any political message beyond that of a leader openly sharing his or her love for the sports that the nation holds close to its heart. However, any gathering with thousands of spectators in the audience and millions watching on television can be used as a political forum by individuals or groups who will exploit the captive audience to make their stands known. There are three broad categories to examine.

The Event as a Political Statement

Throughout the 20th century and into the 21st there are numerous examples of sports events that by virtue of their very existence, timing, and competitors have become political statements. The very fact that the Olympic Games were held in

Berlin in 1936 made a political statement even before sprinter Jesse Owens, an African-American, won the first of his four gold medals. In 1931, two years before Adolf Hitler rose to power, the International Olympic Committee (IOC) had selected Berlin over Barcelona to host the games. When it became evident that Hitler's Third Reich was an oppressive dictatorship that trampled the rights and endangered the lives of anyone who was not a member of the white "Aryan" race, there was an international outcry and demands that the games be moved out of Germany.

The president of the American Olympic Committee in 1933 was Avery Brundage. His initial reaction to news that Jewish athletes in Germany were being persecuted and would not be allowed to compete was to say that, "The very foundation of the modern Olympic revival will be undermined if individual countries are allowed to restrict participation by reason of class, creed, or race." However, after the Germans invited Brundage to see for himself in a carefully orchestrated visit to the country in 1934, he became a staunch advocate in favor of sending the American team to compete in Berlin. His message to anyone who believed that sending a team would be an endorsement of Hitler's hateful policies was, "The Olympic Games belong to the athletes and not to the politicians."

The boycott movement fell apart in December of 1935, after the Amateur Athletic Union (AAU) voted in favor of American participation. Hitler and his Nazi Party got their international stage upon which to demonstrate the "natural supremacy" they claimed. The German team did win the largest number of medals in Berlin: thirty-three gold, twenty-six silver, and thirty bronze for a total of eighty-nine, but it was Jesse Owens' world records and four gold medals that made the most powerful political statement: Hitler's racial convictions were wrong.

The staging of the Olympics in Moscow in 1980 was seen as a political statement by those who opposed the Soviet invasion of Afghanistan in 1979. A total of sixty-seven nations refused to send their teams to Moscow, joining a boycott led by US President Jimmy Carter. The number of nations that did participate was eighty, the smallest field for a summer Olympiad since the 1956 games in Melbourne, Australia. NBC had purchased the rights to televise the 1980 Summer Games in 1974, long before the Afghanistan invasion or subsequent boycott. The $72.3 million in rights that NBC paid, along with all other expenditures made by the network in preparation for the telecasts from Moscow, was lost. No American team meant there would be no American television coverage.

Every international sporting event held before 1994 that excluded the Republic of South Africa can be interpreted as a political statement in opposition to that nation's apartheid policy that separated the races into a hierarchy with whites at the top. That was the year in which South Africa held its first democratic elections open to all races. Following the election of Nelson Mandela as president, teams from South Africa again were welcomed at international competitions.

The Event as a Political Stage

The larger the audience for a sporting event, the more the reward outweighs the risk to use it as a stage upon which to make a political statement. The world was watching on October 16, 1968, when American sprinters Tommie Smith and John Carlos used the Olympic medal stand in Mexico City to make a controversial statement about racial repression in the United States. In the months leading up to the Olympics, America was in turmoil. Dr Martin Luther King, Jr. and Robert F.

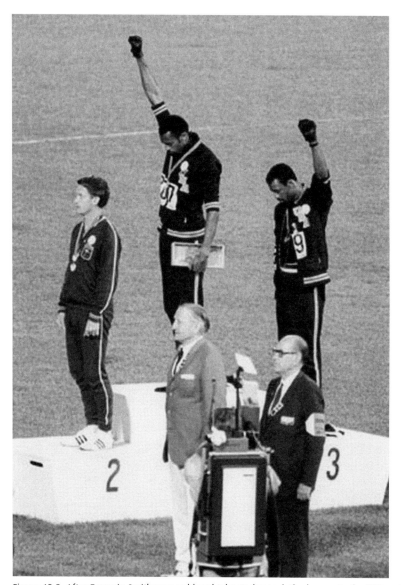

Figure 13.3 After Tommie Smith won gold and John Carlos took the bronze in the 200-meter dash at the 1968 Summer Olympics in Mexico City, they raised gloved fists to make a political statement about racial conditions at home in the United States. Australian Peter Norman won the silver. All three men wore badges showing their support for the Olympic Project for Human Rights
Source: reprinted with permission of Getty Images

Kennedy had both been assassinated. Riots in American cities had led to recriminations and heightened racial tension. A sociologist at San Jose State University in California, Dr Harry Edwards, established the Olympic Project for Human Rights and attempted to organize a boycott of the games by African-American athletes.

The boycott did not occur, but Smith and Carlos felt compelled to make a silent statement in Mexico City to show their solidarity with blacks who they saw as being oppressed back home. Tommie Smith won the 200-meter dash in a then world record 19.83 seconds at the 1968 Summer Games, and John Carlos finished third. Both men had trained at San Jose State.

When they walked into the stadium to receive their medals they shed their shoes to portray the poverty that African-Americans had endured. Smith wore a black scarf and Carlos a beaded necklace that they later explained represented their black pride and memorialized "those individuals that were lynched, or killed, and that no one said a prayer for, that were hung and tarred. It was for those thrown off the side of the boats in the Middle Passage."

When the "Star Spangled Banner" began to play, Americans watching on ABC and a global audience saw Smith and Carlos, with their medals around their necks and Olympic Project for Human Rights badges on their chests, each raise a black-gloved fist. "We are black and we are proud of being black," said Carlos after the demonstration. "Black America will understand what we did tonight." The IOC did not understand, reacting sternly and immediately to what it saw as an inappropriate insertion of domestic political issues into the Games. The IOC chairman was Avery Brundage, who thirty-two years earlier had supported American participation in the Berlin Olympics. "If these boys are serious," he said, "they're making a very bad mistake. If they're not serious and are using the Olympic Games for publicity purposes, we don't like it."

Smith and Carlos were immediately evicted from the Olympic village, sent home, and banned from all future international competition. They each suffered economically and personally for decades for what heavyweight boxing champion Muhammad Ali later called "the most courageous act of the 20th century."

A tragic attempt to use the Olympics as a stage for political coercion was at the 1972 Summer Games in Munich. Germany had not hosted an Olympics since the

Figure 13.4 Jim McKay reported for ABC Sports from the 1972 Summer Olympic Games in Munich and anchored coverage of the terrorist attack that resulted in the deaths of eleven members of the Israeli Olympic delegation
Source: reprinted with permission of Getty Images

Berlin games in 1936, and its goal was to show how the nation had changed since the end of the Third Reich and World War II. Palestinian terrorists from the "Black September" movement dashed those hopes when they invaded the Olympic village, killed two members of the Israeli team and took nine others hostage. The terrorists demanded the release of 234 Palestinians and other prisoners in Israeli jails as well as freedom for the two German founders of the violent Baader–Meinhof group, Andreas Baader and Ulrike Meinhof.

Americans watched in horrified disbelief as Jim McKay anchored ABC's coverage. When the eighteen-hour standoff ended in a hail of gunfire that left all the hostages dead aboard a helicopter at the Fürstenfeldbruck NATO airbase, they heard him say in utter sadness, "They're gone. They're all gone."

The Munich massacre forever changed international athletic events and their television coverage, pushing the security of participants and spectators to the forefront. The selection of host nations is now viewed through the lens of geo-politics for potential targeting by factions who see an opportunity to put their ideologies and demands on a stage to be seen by a worldwide television audience. And the screening, credentialing, and access for media to venues and athletes were tightened to prevent infiltration by elements that might seek cover for their extremist motives by masquerading as members of the press.

Sports Stars as Political Icons

The athletes we see on television are themselves icons for a broad range of political constituencies. They represent who we are: people who grew up in our city, state, or nation, members of our ethnic, social, or affinity groups as varied as fellow alumni from the college we attended, children who grew up in poor families, who had blue-collar dads, people who have come through divorce or recovered from serious injury, or who volunteer in their hometowns. We celebrate the athletes' superior skill, their determination, stamina, strength, resourcefulness, and fair play, the qualities we value most in ourselves *and* in our elected representatives.

Dozens of athletes have parlayed cheers into votes by convincing constituents that the leadership and positive attributes they demonstrated in their sports careers could be successfully applied to government when coupled with their education and civic interests and/or experience. Some notable examples:

- Bill Bradley—New York Knicks forward, then US Senator from New Jersey for eighteen years.

- Steve Largent—Record-setting NFL receiver, served eight years as Congressman from Oklahoma.

- J.C. Watts—University of Oklahoma quarterback, who also served eight years in Congress representing Oklahoma.

- Jim Bunning—Hall of Fame Major League pitcher who threw no-hitters in both leagues, elected to Congress and then to two terms in the US Senate representing Kentucky.

- Jack Kemp—Buffalo Bills quarterback, and then congressman from Buffalo, secretary of Housing and Urban Development for President Ronald Reagan, and Republican nominee for vice-president in 1992.

- Dave Bing—Basketball Hall of Famer who was an All-American at Syracuse and then a perennial NBA all-star with the Detroit Pistons; he was elected mayor of Detroit in 2009.

- Kevin Johnson—NBA All-Star guard who was elected in 2008 as the first African-American mayor of Sacramento, California, eight years after he had retired from play.

ECONOMICS MAKES SPORTS POLITICAL

Nothing stirs as much political interest and ire as how elected representatives spend the tax dollars that government collects. Symbolism may get some candidates elected. How they spend the public's money can get them voted out of office. When tax dollars are spent to stage sports events or to build and maintain venues, government and sports organizations become partners. As a result, the actions, decisions, and statements made by each partner take on considerable political weight. These partnerships can be volatile due to the fact that government is subject to the shifting mood of the public come Election Day each year. Officials who support sports partnerships or new stadium building projects can quickly be replaced by combative antagonists who will raise questions about how every public dollar is being spent. Media coverage of such debates merges news with sports, and suddenly the game is not the "only thing."

Recent history is replete with examples. The hundreds of millions of dollars in tax-free financing that was provided for the new Yankee Stadium became a campaign issue in the New York City mayoral election of 2009. The debate over what percentage the public should pay, if any, for the construction of a new football stadium for the Minnesota Vikings was an issue in the 2010 election for governor of Minnesota. The Securities and Exchange Commission (SEC) subpoenaed documents to investigate if any federal securities laws were violated in connection with the public financing of Miami's new retractable-roof baseball stadium built for the Marlins. The overwhelming proportion of publicly financed sports venues, compared with the very few that have been built exclusively with private funds, has turned tax subsidies for sports into a political issue almost everywhere there are professional franchises.

Table 13.2 Public financing of stadiums and arenas

NFL	Eleven stadiums built with 100% taxpayer financing:
	Atlanta, Buffalo, Green Bay, Kansas City, New Orleans, Oakland, San Diego, San Francisco, St Louis, Tampa Bay, Tennessee
	Three stadiums built with 0% taxpayer financing:
	Carolina, New England, New York (Meadowlands)
MLB	Seven stadiums built with 100% taxpayer financing:
	Anaheim, Atlanta, Chicago White Sox, Kansas City, Oakland, Tampa Bay, Washington
	Four stadiums built with 0% public financing:
	Boston, Chicago Cubs, Florida, Los Angeles Dodgers

Source: National Sports Law Institute Sports Facility Reports

Figure 13.5 Fenway Park in Boston, which opened on April 20, 1912, is one of only four current Major League Baseball stadiums that were built with no public financing

The economics of sports and the extent of its availability to the public on commercial television have also led to government intervention, leaving organizers and leagues with less than the total control they enjoyed in the days before TV. Any action that limits or restricts commerce in the United States is bound to be challenged in court. The billions of dollars that are spent on television rights and advertising each year most certainly qualify sports as "commerce," and as a result the courts have had an impact on what is seen and how it is delivered.

Perhaps no court ruling has had a greater effect on the availability of sports content on American television than the decision handed down by the US Supreme Court in 1984 in a case brought by the Universities of Oklahoma and Georgia, representing the College Football Association (CFA), against the National Collegiate Athletic Association, the NCAA. Beginning in 1951, and continuing through a succession of contracts with NBC, CBS, and ABC, the NCAA had tightly controlled how many college football games would be televised per weekend and per season. The original fear shared by the NCAA and its member universities was that games on TV would diminish the number of fans attending in person. So the first contract limited NBC to a total of twelve Saturday afternoon telecasts during the college football season, and no school could be featured more than once.

The restrictions were loosened over the years as the popularity of college football on television raised the sport's profile and attendance. But, in 1981, the NCAA contract with ABC still limited the appearances of any team to no more than six over the course of two seasons. The newly formed CFA, which represented the Division I schools with major football programs, signed a separate deal with NBC that year which would dramatically increase television exposure, and with it the rights fees, for these universities. In response, the NCAA announced in September of 1981 that it would take disciplinary action against any CFA member that complied with the NBC contract.

That's when Oklahoma, Georgia, and their fellow CFA universities filed a complaint in Federal District Court charging that the NCAA had been violating the Sherman Antitrust Act by placing anti-competitive limitations on how many games could be sold to television networks, and the price that could be charged for that content.

The case went all the way to the US Supreme Court, which ruled in 1984 in favor of the CFA, opening the floodgates to allow the hundreds of games that are now televised each year and for which the universities are compensated at the highest rates the market will bear. In his majority decision Justice John Paul Stevens wrote, "the finding that many more games would be televised in a free market than under the NCAA plan is a compelling demonstration that the plan's controls do not serve any legitimate precompetitive purpose." The judicial branch of government gave more fans more games and made college football a bigger sport with far more revenue than the NCAA on its own may have ever achieved.

THE FEDERAL COMMUNICATIONS COMMISSION

Before there was sports television there was a Federal Communications Commission (FCC). The agency was established by the Communications Act of 1934 to regulate interstate and international communications in the fifty states, the District of Columbia, and US possessions. At the time, those communications included just radio and telegraph, but with advancements in technology the scope of the FCC's regulation has been broadened to encompass television, satellite, cable, wireless, and broadband.

The airwaves used to transmit broadcast and data signals are a public resource that, just like the air we breathe, cannot be owned by any individual or organization, corporate or otherwise. The spectrum of airwaves has no borders that would allow for local, regional, or state regulation, so it fell to the federal government to make the decisions as to how the airwaves would be used, by whom, and for what purposes. The fact that today there are media that communicate exclusively via fiber optic or coaxial cable, or other devices that do not go "over the air," has not given them license to operate in an unregulated environment.

The areas of FCC oversight that relate most directly to sports television are:

• Media ownership.

• Public access to television programming.

• "Must-carry" and retransmission consent.

Media Ownership

The number of frequencies available for broadcasting is not unlimited, so the FCC early on instituted a licensing application procedure by which it approves the allocation of space on the broadcast spectrum to only those companies or individuals who meet or exceed a set of federal standards. The granting of broadcast licenses is never in perpetuity, but rather they are reviewed every five years, or more frequently if judged necessary by the FCC, to ensure that all standards are being met.

As the regulator of communications for a democratic nation, the FCC has from its beginning included as an important part of its mission a guarantee to the public that no one corporation, no matter how powerful, will ever be able to control all the messages that any American receives via television, satellite, cable, wireless, broadband, or any future medium not yet invented. The FCC's stated goal is to protect the public interest by fostering competition, localism, and diversity. It enforces a set of media ownership rules and restrictions that it reviews and adjusts every four years to ensure that there will be a multitude of "independent voices" accessible to all Americans.

The current rules prohibit any merger among the top-four broadcast networks in the United States: ABC, CBS, NBC, and FOX. There are no limits on the number of television stations that any one company can own; however, collectively no media owner is allowed to control stations that would reach a market universe larger than 39 percent of the total US population. If one entity owns a television station in New York City, Chicago, and Los Angeles, its total market universe is approximately 10 percent of all the TV homes in the United States. It would be allowed to own or buy more stations, but only until its universe as a group hit 39 percent. (The 39 percent figure was a compromise in 2003 when the FCC had approved a change in the ownership limit from 35 percent to 45 percent of the population. Congress voted to keep the limit at 35 percent. A compromise brokered after a threatened veto by then President George W. Bush set 39 percent as the mark.)

The FCC also governs how many television and radio stations any company can control in one designated market area (DMA). Multiple ownership is allowed for up to two TV stations and six radio stations in large DMAs, as long as the FCC can verify that there are at least twenty individually owned "independent voices" in that metropolitan area.

The impact on sports television of these regulations is that there will always be competition for broadcast rights, local teams and events will have equal opportunities for coverage even if they are not owned by or in partnership with a dominant media company, and, when controversies arise, a multitude of reports and opinions can share the airwaves.

Public Access to Television Programming

The FCC "is committed to fostering a strong and independent broadcast media that provides Americans with multiple and diverse sources of news, public affairs and entertainment programming," said FCC Chairman Julius Genachowski in May of 2010 when the latest four-year review of broadcast ownership rules began. Access to television sports is a major part of that "entertainment programming." That's why it is highly unlikely that the Super Bowl will ever move to a cable channel exclusively: anyone who didn't subscribe to a service that distributed that channel would be denied access to the game. That would not be tolerated by either the FCC or the senators and representatives whose constituents live in the small percentage of homes (less than 10 percent) that still get their TV signals over the air.

A succession of public access disputes over sports programming have been brought to the FCC over the past several years, notably a discrimination complaint lodged in 2006 by the NFL Network against Comcast. The NFL claimed that Comcast had unfairly placed its network on a pricey digital sports tier, which had only 2 million subscribers, while sports networks owned by Comcast including Versus and the Golf Channel were made available to more viewers on one of its more popular tier offerings. In October of 2008 the FCC ruled in favor of the NFL, and in May of 2009 Comcast moved NFL Network to the same tier as its owned networks, making it accessible to approximately 10 million homes.

Just a few months later Comcast and its networks were back in the FCC's public access sights when the company announced plans in December of 2009 to acquire controlling interest of NBC Universal from General Electric. The FCC and the Justice Department did grant approval for the takeover in January 2011, but not before clearly stipulating that the combined Comcast NBC Universal had to allow rival cable and broadband distributors reasonable access to each of the programming networks that it owned. That would prevent the conglomerate, if it ever chose to do so, from making any of its networks exclusive to Comcast customers only.

The FCC also put in place conditions requiring Comcast to negotiate fairly with rival programmers, the networks that it does not own, to give them an equal opportunity to deliver their content to Comcast subscribers. The combination of NBC Sports with Versus and the Golf Channel gives Comcast a formidable sports presence and puts the company in a stronger bargaining position when its contracts with ESPN come up for renewal.

The FCC had previously adopted rules that forbade cable companies that own programming channels from refusing to allow competing multi-channel video programming distributors, such as AT&T and Verizon, to offer those channels. Comcast and Cablevision had challenged those rules, but the US Court of Appeals for the District of Columbia Circuit decided the case in the FCC's favor in March of 2010. The result is more public access to more content including sports. Comcast, and all other multi-channel distributors that own regional sports networks, must make their content, including hundreds of live games, available at market prices to services like U-Verse and Fios with which they compete for subscription customers.

Must-Carry and Retransmission Consent

The FCC first adopted "must-carry" rules in 1972 responding to the fears of local television station owners that they would lose audience and advertising dollars if people could get entertainment, news, and sports from a cable running directly into their homes as an alternative to their over-the-air signals. (See Chapter 12 for more on the economic implications of "must-carry" and retransmission regulations.)

Federal courts found the must-carry rules to be a restriction of the First Amendment right of free speech following challenges in the 1980s by several cable operators and by Turner Broadcasting. Congress stepped in and passed the Communications Act of 1992, which still required cable companies to carry local commercial and public stations, but allowed them to drop redundant signals if, for example, there were two college stations within the fifty-mile radius that both carried the same PBS programming. Two years later the FCC gave stations a choice of maintaining their must-carry status with the local cable systems, or be carried under a new regulation that required the cable operator to obtain "retransmission consent." The retransmission consent rules gave strong local network affiliates and independent stations increased power to negotiate their terms of carriage, including channel preference, with the cable company.

Paying for content from broadcasters that had always been free did not sit well with multi-system operators like Cablevision, who in October of 2010 chose to drop FOX from its channel lineup rather than pay the monthly per home fee that the network had demanded. The public relations battle lines in this and in similar disputes are almost always about the sports that viewers would miss if no agreement were reached. In fact 3 million Cablevision homes did miss a New York Giants game and the first two games of the 2010 World Series on FOX because of the dispute. A settlement was agreed to and FOX returned to the Cablevision lineup just before the first pitch of World Series game three.

Issues that affect millions of people inexorably spawn proposed legislative remedies from representatives who are either truly concerned about the services provided to the citizenry, or anxious to win votes from disgruntled constituents, or both. Less than a week after the Cablevision homes in New York, New Jersey, Connecticut, and part of Philadelphia lost FOX in the fall of 2010, Senator John Kerry of Massachusetts sent draft legislation to the FCC chairman that would protect consumers during retransmission consent disputes. If millions more viewers are affected by similar service interruptions in the future, and especially if live sports programming is blacked out, it will surprise no one if this bill or one like it starts to gain momentum on Capitol Hill.

THE CONGRESSIONAL CONNECTION

The level of congressional interest and intervention in sports television issues has grown in direct proportion to the industry's growth in audience and income, as would be the case with any expanding sector of the economy. A major milestone was the Sports Broadcasting Act of 1961, which we discussed in Chapter 4. It allowed leagues of individually owned teams in multiple states to act as single entities in negotiating broadcast rights with television networks, without fear of being found in violation of any federal antitrust statutes.

As cable television reached into the majority of American homes in the late 1980s and early 1990s, and live sports coverage began to migrate to ESPN, TBS, and other networks that were not available free over the air, legislation was proposed by a number of representatives on Capitol Hill to limit the "pay-per-view siphoning from free TV." The FCC had adopted rules in 1975 to restrict the programming that cable or subscription TV services could offer as a means of protecting broadcast stations, but these "anti-siphoning" regulations were struck down as invalid, arbitrary, and capricious in 1978 by the US Circuit Court of Appeals in the case of HBO vs. FCC.

That ruling did not however halt the efforts by some representatives to win congressional approval of laws that would impose restrictions on cable sports programming. None succeeded. The cable industry was able to demonstrate that,

Figure 13.6 The House Committee on Oversight and Government Reform heard testimony in 2005 from Major League Baseball players, left to right: Mark McGwire, Rafael Palmeiro, and Curt Schilling

Source: reprinted with permission of Getty Images

despite the fact that hundreds of hours of sports were being shown exclusively on cable stations, the volume of sports programming on broadcast networks had increased, not declined.

More people paying more attention to sports, and consuming more of it on television, has had the effect of bringing a far wider range of issues before Congress for discussion if not resolution. At the epicenter of the sports debate in Washington, DC, has been the House Committee on Oversight and Government Reform. In 2005, the committee held hearings on the use of steroids in baseball that included testimony from, among others, former Baltimore Orioles slugger Rafael Palmeiro, who waved his finger in his strident denial, and Mark McGwire, who hit seventy home runs for the St Louis Cardinals in 1998, but famously told the congressmen that he was not there "to talk about the past."

The Committee on Oversight picked up the mantle again in 2008 following the December 2007 release of the Mitchell Report that the commissioner of baseball had commissioned to investigate the illegal use of performance-enhancing substances. The star witnesses were Roger Clemens, who won 354 games in his twenty-four seasons as a Major League pitcher, and his former trainer, Brian McNamee, who claimed that he had administered banned substances to Clemens with the pitcher's knowledge and approval.

Neither of these sets of hearings resulted in the passage of federal legislation to impose governmental jurisdiction over the testing of athletes for any substances, but it is noteworthy that the proceedings were carried live on television and generated national publicity. It is unlikely that television would have paid attention if the House Committee on Oversight and Government Reform had strictly limited itself to its list of legislative responsibilities as set forth in House Rule X, clause 1:

- Federal civil service, including intergovernmental personnel; and the status of officers and employees of the United States, including their compensation, classification, and retirement.

- Municipal affairs of the District of Columbia in general (other than appropriations).

  - Federal paperwork reduction.
  - Government management and accounting measures generally.
  - Holidays and celebrations.
  - Overall economy, efficiency, and management of government operations and activities, including federal procurement.
  - National archives.
  - Population and demography generally, including the Census.
  - Postal service generally, including transportation of the mails.
  - Public information and records.
  - Relationship of the federal government to the states and municipalities.
  - Reorganizations in the executive branch of the government.

The Committee uses as justification for its investigations and involvement that part of its overall charge that calls for it to review and study on a continuing basis "any conditions or circumstances that may indicate the necessity or desirability of enacting new or additional legislation addressing subjects within its jurisdiction (whether or not a bill or resolution has been introduced with respect thereto)."

High-profile sports that attract millions of television viewers, which are played by athletes who compete at the risk of personal injury to themselves and others, who become national celebrities with multi-million dollar contracts and are emulated by young people across the country, in an industry with an annual economic impact in the billions will always come under the scrutiny of government and elected representatives. There could be no other reasonable expectation. Nor is it likely that politicians will miss many opportunities to increase public awareness of issues they deem important to the public welfare, which at the same time increase awareness of themselves.

SUMMARY

The ideal long clung to by the IOC and lifelong sports fans that politics should play no role whatsoever in sport is antiquated and unrealistic. It may have been possible in the era before television when sports were neither a stage nor an economic powerhouse, but not now. The innocence is gone forever, but the symbolism of sport remains in its celebration of athletes as icons representing their nations, regions, racial, ethnic, and affinity groups, and people who share the same personal history.

Sporting events that draw the attention of millions are often used as forums for politics, in the very fact that they are staged in a certain city or country, or that they include or exclude certain competitors. With the guarantee of national or international television coverage, sports is also seen as a political stage from which controversial positions can be espoused, and, in the case of extremists, burned into the public consciousness through acts of terrorism like the Munich Olympics invasion of 1972.

The vast amounts of money involved in sports, television, and the construction of venues naturally invites government oversight and involvement. The leagues and teams that use public funding for a new stadium or arena, or to stage a major event, automatically find themselves as partners with the governmental bodies that oversee the distribution of tax revenue. These partnerships can abruptly change depending upon whether supportive government representatives get re-elected or replaced by opponents of the project at hand.

The FCC exercises authority over the ownership of all electronic media, public access to programming, and the retransmission of television signals by any video distributor. Each of these areas has an impact on how Americans receive their sports on TV, and on the business of sports television.

Congress steps in when issues arise that require a change in the law, or when representatives believe that an investigation or public hearing is necessary to increase national awareness or focus the spotlight on conditions that exist within sports that they want to see changed. Any spillover from the glare of television coverage that might brighten a politician's chances for re-election is a welcomed side-effect.

DISCUSSION TOPICS/ASSIGNMENTS

1   Research one or more of these Olympic Games and discuss how the events were used as either a political statement or as a stage for political reasons: the 1936 Berlin Games, the 1968 Mexico City Games, or the 1972 Munich Games. How has what happened at these events changed sporting events and their coverage on television?

2   Do a study of the stadiums or arenas where your favorite teams play to determine how they were financed. How has the use of public funding, or the lack of it, affected how the team does business in the community?

3   Study the 1984 US Supreme Court ruling that changed how college football is distributed on television in the United States. Compare the number of games and individual team exposure before the ruling to after.

4   How have different committees such as the House Committee on Oversight and Government Reform or the House Judiciary Committee investigated sports issues? What legislation or changes have resulted?

5   Examine the disputes between cable systems and broadcasters that have resulted in the suspension of service to customers. An example is the Cablevision dispute with FOX in 2010. How has sports been used as a negotiating tool in each dispute?

14 THE SOCIAL AND CULTURAL IMPACT OF TELEVISED SPORT

The media is a primary site for the construction and constitution of identities, collective and individual, rather than merely a secondary reflection of already formed identities.

(Ben Carrington, Ph.D., University of Texas Dept. of Sociology)

Table 14.1 Chapter 14: The Rundown

- The impact of sports on personal identity.
  - What we wear.
  - What we consume.
  - What we do.
  - What we say.
- The passion for sports drives behavior.
- The portrayal of women in TV sports.
- "The Battle of the Sexes."
- Women sportscasters.
- The impact of television sports on racial attitudes.
- Minorities assume leadership positions.
- The black quarterback.
- Muhammad Ali.
- The race and gender report card.
- Althea Gibson and the impact of TV coverage.

In the same way that sports is part of the identity of nations it is also integral to how millions of Americans define themselves. Consider the people you know, or simply look in the mirror, to see the evidence of how the mass distribution of sports in the United States and around the world has affected what people wear, the food and drink we consume, the words and phrases we use in daily speech, how we spend our leisure time, and our attitudes about race and gender.

THE IMPACT OF SPORTS ON PERSONAL IDENTITY

What We Wear

It is difficult for most people alive today to remember a time when sports apparel and footwear were worn only by athletes and did not constitute such a large percentage of an average person's wardrobe or closet. Look back at photographs or film of sporting events from the 1940s, 50s, or 60s and take a close look at the crowds. In the summer they wore shirts and blouses, many men with ties and felt hats, and in the winter you see overcoats and jackets. But you don't see the proliferation of team jerseys and caps proudly proclaiming one's team loyalty that fill the stands at games in the 21st century. The transition from fans who dressed like average people to fans who dressed like their favorite athletes, or in the colors of their favorite teams, is concurrent with the expansion of sports on television in the years since 1970.

Michael Jordan's role in the growth of Nike presents an excellent example of how sports on television and the marketing of sports celebrities has changed how Americans identify themselves through their choice of clothing. In fiscal 1984, the year that Nike signed an endorsement deal with Jordan as he was leaving the University of North Carolina, the company had total revenues of $919,806,000. Jordan led the NBA in scoring in his first season with the Chicago Bulls and again in the 1986–87 season. Nike sales went over the $1 billion mark for the first time in 1986, and another crucial milestone came in 1987. That's when ESPN's cable penetration exceeded 50 percent of American homes, putting Michael Jordan's amazing highlights in front of a growing national audience every night on *SportsCenter*. Jordan won the first of his five NBA Most Valuable Player (MVP) awards at the conclusion of the 1987–88 season just as Nike introduced its "Just Do It" advertising campaign. The company's sales hit $1.7 billion in fiscal 1989, an increase of more than 70 percent in the five years following their signing of Michael Jordan.

By 2003, the year in which he played his last NBA game, then as a member of the Washington Wizards, Nike's annual revenue had reached $10.7 billion, which translates to millions of Americans wearing Nike sneakers and athletic gear, "just doing it" dressed like their favorite professional athlete. If the NBA's exposure on television had remained limited to one or two games per weekend on the broadcast networks, and video from every Bulls game was not being featured on a nightly basis, it is safe to conclude that Jordan's impact on consumer behavior and on Nike's sales would have been geometrically smaller.

What We Consume

The impact that Michael Jordan had on behavior went beyond what Americans put on their feet and on their backs, to what they put in their stomachs. Gatorade signed Michael Jordan as its brand spokesman in 1991 and launched its "Be Like Mike" advertising campaign. He led the Bulls to their first NBA Championship that season, winning awards as the NBA regular season and finals MVP, and Gatorade sales increased faster than the rest of the soft-drink industry. The product got plenty of television air time with its bright orange coolers and green cups visible on the sidelines at basketball and football games. Gatorade was what the viewing public saw the best athletes use to keep themselves hydrated, so it became a more popular choice among active young people and adults who had the same kind of thirst that could be satisfied with a beverage offering the same beneficial effects.

The pattern repeats itself over and over with products from energy bars to golf clubs and baseball caps. Each of us makes a social statement about ourselves through the products we use and wear, and for millions the decision to buy those products is made as a way to emulate the star athletes we see on television.

What We Do

Gatorade became part of how Americans in communities large and small celebrate championships at all levels of sport as the result of what they saw after New York Giants games in the 1985 and 1986 seasons. During the week of practice leading up to a nationally televised New York Giants vs. Washington Redskins game on October 20, 1985, New York Giants coach Bill Parcells had been riding his nose tackle Jim Burt, telling him that his opponent on the Redskins line, Jeff Bostic, was going to "eat him up" on Sunday. Burt was infuriated and when the Giants won 17–3, he took his revenge with a cooler full of Gatorade. "I was the only one who had the guts to do it without knowing what his reaction was going to be," Burt told Darren Rovell for his book about the Gatorade brand, First in Thirst.

Jim Burt and teammate Harry Carson continued the Gatorade showers the following season, turning them into a ritual after every Giants victory. That season New York went 14–2 in the regular season and won the NFC title for a trip to the Rose Bowl in Pasadena for Super Bowl XXI. With a huge national audience watching, Parcells got doused again as the Giants beat the Denver Broncos 39–20, and, with zero marketing effort on the part of Gatorade, the tradition of American victory celebrations was changed forever.

A footnote to the story is that one year before Jim Burt soaked Bill Parcells, Chicago Bears coach Mike Ditka was actually the recipient of the NFL's first Gatorade shower. On November 25, 1984, after the Bears beat the Vikings 34–3 in Minnesota, linemen Steve McMichael and Dan Hampton were the culprits. But they didn't repeat the prank, and it didn't happen in front of a massive Super Bowl audience.

The sports that Americans watch on television directly affect the pursuits we choose for our leisure hours when the set is turned off. From an early age, the events and stars that children see on television can influence the decisions they make about what sports they will pursue, which in countless instances are decisions that will change the course of their lives. One need only check the enrollment figures

Table 14.2 US high school sports participation, 2010–11

Boys' Sports	Participants	Girls' Sports	Participants
1. Football (eleven-man)	1,108,441	1. Track & field	535,672
2. Track & field (indoor + outdoor)	649,591	2. Basketball	438,933
3. Basketball	545,844	3. Volleyball	409,332
4. Baseball	471,025	4. Softball (Fast Pitch and Slow Pitch combined)	400,974
5. Soccer	398,351	5. Soccer	361,556
6. Wrestling	273,732	6. Cross-country	204,653
7. Cross-country	246,948	7. Tennis	182,074
8. Tennis	161,367	8. Swimming & diving	160,881
9. Golf	156,866	9. Competitive spirit	96,718
10. Swimming & diving	133,900	10. Lacrosse	74,927

Source: National Federation of High School Associations 2010–11 High School Athletics Participation Survey

for local gymnastics schools after each Summer Olympics is televised to prove this hypothesis. And participation in a sport as a child is one of the primary factors determining fan allegiances as adults.

The hours each week that more than 30 million fantasy sports players spend drafting and trading players, managing their teams and doing research on the internet, is time they would spend doing something else if it weren't for sports on television. It is possible to play fantasy exclusively online using statistics, analysis, and projections, but scouting players and tracking their performances in live games is a large part of the appeal. Research done for the Fantasy Sports Trade Association (FSTA) projects that 19 percent of American males and 8 percent of females over the age of twelve play at least one fantasy sport. Fantasy football is the runaway favorite with over 60 percent of all players owning at least one team. Fantasy baseball is a distant second with just under 20 percent participation. The FSTA research done by Ipsos Public Affairs includes demographic profiles showing that fantasy players are more likely to be college educated than not, and are also more likely to be employed full-time than the general public.

What We Say

If you did not watch sports on television, would you speak a different language? To answer that question think about how often you use words or phrases from sports as metaphors or short-hand to make your listener quickly understand your point. The English language is filled with "sports-speak," which is nothing new. In *Romeo and Juliet*, Shakespeare wrote this line for Juliet when she was contemplating suicide: "A bloody knife shall play the umpire." It may not be new, but its prevalence and acceptance into common discourse are largely attributable to what is said on television.

What has also become all too common across the country is trash talking. In professional leagues, talking "trash" is a means toward sharpening the competitive edge over an adult opponent by finding and exploiting a sore spot or sensitivity.

Table 14.3 "Sports speak" How many of these expressions do you use in conversation?

1	Touch base with.	15	"Three strikes" law.	30	Slam dunk.
2	Monday morning quarterback.	16	Strike out.	31	Take your best shot.
		17	Pass the baton.	32	Drop the ball.
3	Screwball.	18	Touch and go.	33	Time out.
4	Out in left field.	19	Hit full stride.	34	Kick off.
5	Step up to the plate.	20	Put on a full press.	35	Throw a curveball.
6	Get to first base.	21	Heavy hitters.	36	Hail Mary.
7	Reach the goal line.	22	One on one.	37	Punt.
8	Heading for home.	23	Sticky wicket.	38	Jump the gun.
9	Double play.	24	Beat to the punch.	39	Go for the gold.
10	"Pinch hit for me."	25	The home stretch.	40	Make a pit stop.
11	"Go to bat" for me.	26	Game on!	41	Behind the eight-ball.
12	Up to par.	27	Batting 1.000.	42	Down for the count.
13	Extra innings.	28	Knock it out of the park.	43	Hit it out of the park.
14	Overtime.	29	Knockout blow.	44	"She's out of your league."

But it has been mimicked by children who watch TV and know how being cruel to others can reduce rivals to tears, which in turn may offer a better chance for victory. Incidents such as the October 2008 pee-wee football game in Pittsburgh's Mon River League, where parents had to pull the teams off the field because of fears that the trash-talking would lead to something dangerous, became so prevalent that many youth sports associations now include "no trash talking" clauses in their player/parent and coaches codes of ethics.

THE PASSION FOR SPORTS DRIVES BEHAVIOR

Perhaps nothing defines an individual better than his or her passions, the independent choices one makes in life. Octagon, the world's largest sponsorship consulting firm, started conducting studies in 2005 to better understand what drives different people to be passionate about different sports in ten different countries around the globe. Octagon's researchers, led by senior vice president for insights and strategy, Simon Wardle, who created the Passion Drivers® concept, interviewed thousands of sports fans and identified twelve separate factors that explain why people love sports. Almost all have sociological implications as they describe patterns of human behavior.

Octagon's Passion Drivers research, which went to version 3.0 in 2011, is sold to advertising, marketing, and media clients. Here is an overview of the motivating factors with none of Octagon's proprietary statistical analysis as to which are more or less important in any specific country or for any particular sport.

- *Active appreciation*—this is based on personal participation in the sport of which you are now a fan. You played the game in the backyard, with friends, or participate at any recreational or competitive level.

- *Love of the game*—you have loved the sport since childhood, more than likely attending or watching on television with a parent or siblings as you grew up.

- *Team devotion*—loyalty to your college team, to your regional favorite, or simply to a team for which you developed an obsession. Television has made it possible for these loyalties and obsessions to develop regardless of geography, such as the little boy in Connecticut who grows up loving the Cincinnati Bengals because he fixated on the team's orange and black tiger-striped helmets when he was three years old.

- *Player affinity*—fans draw human connections with, or identify with, players. A generation of baseball fans grew up in the 1950s and '60s idolizing Mickey Mantle and Willie Mays. In the 1980s and '90s Michael Jordan assumed the "affinity throne," but the player with whom a fan makes a connection need not be famous. Your choice of heroes can help explain who you are.

- *Talk and socializing*—sports fosters social interaction within peer groups and across generations and across gender and ethnic bounds. It creates conversation and connects the fan with friends and strangers alike.

- *All consuming*—a special event like March Madness or an annual event like the Super Bowl draws fans in because of its overwhelming social and media presence, regardless of whether they follow the sport during its regular season. One gets swept up in the tide of excitement and emotion that surrounds the game.

- *Nostalgia*—history and personal memories of bygone teams or players can be powerful motivators. Looking back fondly to connect special memories to the present works to keep the love of that sport alive for a lifetime.

- *Player excitement*—there are certain players in sport whose talent, ability, or superior performance command admiration. *SportsCenter* highlights of emphatic dunks, improbable catches or runbacks, amazing shots from tennis courts or golf courses can fuel this player excitement.

- *Gloating*—there are those who enjoy reveling in the agony of others, who need to feel superior. Think of the heated competitions among fantasy football players, or gamblers who have to announce their winnings (read: superior skill and judgment) to all their Facebook friends or co-workers.

- *Personal indulgence*—for their personal entertainment many fans are willing to make sacrifices, because the time they set aside to watch their favorite sport or the resources they commit to buying that season ticket is the one special thing they do for themselves. This may include some overt selfishness, but the indulgence is part of what defines who these individuals are in life.

- *Sense of belonging*—it's important for many fans to identify themselves as "part of the tribe," like "Red Sox Nation." There is a comfort in gathering with other like-minded individuals at games or in front of the television. It provides a social sense of connection: dressing, talking, and thinking like other tribe members helps people figure out how they fit into their social structure.

- *TV/media preference*—some fans make their choices based on consumption preferences. If they have established a connection or a bond with ESPN, or NBC, or any network or website as a credible source with congenial or entertaining talent, they may choose to watch more games or consume more video product from these media "friends."

Everyone's personality is shaped to some degree by the passions, sports-related or not, which are developed over a lifetime. Television coverage of sports plays a role in all of the motivational forces listed above with the only exception possibly being "active appreciation," and clearly the choices made by young people as to which sport to play are very often influenced by the games or athletes they see on TV at an early age.

THE PORTRAYAL OF WOMEN IN TV SPORTS

Televised sport has played an important role in changing the dominant ideas about gender in American society. Our cultural understanding of femininity has been radically altered by images of women with athletic skill, muscles, and endurance. In the America of the mid-20th century the individual sports that required grace, glamour, and self-sacrifice such as figure skating, tennis, golf, or gymnastics were seen as most suitable for women. Sports that demanded strength, stamina, and speed, any team sport involving contact and any sport such as auto racing that came with a degree of risk, were traditionally the domain of males only.

The version of basketball that was designed specifically for women one year after Dr. James Naismith published his original rules of the game in 1891 divided the court into three sections to limit the amount of running and exertion required of female players. In 1938 the three sections were reduced to two, with six players per team. Three players per team were restricted to each half of the court so that only three of the six ever got the chance to score a basket. The other three were full-time defenders at the opposite end of the floor. Girls were only allowed three dribbles per possession and "no snatching or batting the ball away from a player" was permitted. Basketball for women was meant to be a form of exercise that promoted socialization and cooperation, not strenuous competition. Full-court, five-on-five women's basketball was not officially sanctioned until 1971, but six-on-six basketball was widely played until 1993 at high schools in a few Midwestern states, most notably Iowa.

Women had experimented with and adapted most every sport by the end of the 20th century. The competition that they relished, coupled with the strength and endurance they built, represented a form of female empowerment to a society that for generations had accepted male domination as the natural order. To many men and women alike the changes were a threat to their pre-conceived notions of the ideal woman and mother. A female athlete with muscles did not fit what had been the cultural template, and neither did a woman who dared challenge a man on the field of play.

One of the true pioneers of gender equity did just that in 1973, and because of Billie Jean King barriers began to fall and previously unimagined opportunities began to open for women in sports. Her tennis match against former Wimbledon champion Bobby Riggs was called "the Battle of the Sexes," and it aired live from the Houston Astrodome in prime time on ABC television on September 23, 1973.

Riggs had won Wimbledon in 1939, but by 1973 he was a 55-year-old hustler hoping to get publicity and make a few bucks challenging the women professional tennis players of the era. He goaded them with "male chauvinist pig" rhetoric about how a woman's place was in the home "barefoot and pregnant" and how no woman athlete could beat a skilled man regardless of his age. Riggs' favorite T-shirt bore the acronym "WORMS" for a fictitious "World Organization for the Retention of Male Supremacy." Margaret Court took the bait and played Riggs on Mother's Day, 1973. The Australian star was twenty-five years younger than her opponent and had won seventeen grand slam singles titles, including all four majors in 1970, but she lost 6–2, 6–1 to Riggs in just fifty-seven minutes in a match in San Diego that aired on CBS.

Billie Jean King had resisted Riggs' taunts, but when she learned that Margaret Court had lost she resolved to play him so that her campaign for equal prize money for women players on the tennis tour would not be jeopardized for years to come. She was twenty-nine and had won the Wimbledon singles and doubles titles in 1973. In her career, Billie Jean King won a total of thirty-nine grand slam singles and doubles tournaments, but no victory would have a more momentous impact than "the Battle of the Sexes."

She arrived at the Astrodome court on a gold litter carried by four muscular men dressed as Roman slaves. Riggs, wearing a satin "Sugar Daddy" jacket for his hastily signed candy sponsor, was wheeled out to the court on a rickshaw pulled by sexily attired models he called "Bobby's Bosom Buddies." Howard

Figure 14.1 "The Battle of the Sexes" tennis match in 1973 was a media spectacle. Billie Jean King's victory over Bobby Riggs had a lasting impact on the image of women in American sport and society

Source: reprinted with permission of Getty Images

Cosell, ABC's provocative commentator from *Monday Night Football* and virtually every Muhammad Ali boxing match, added his dramatic observations to heighten the sense of theater.

Before a worldwide television audience estimated at 50 million, Billie Jean King out-hustled Bobby Riggs, winning 6–4, 6–3, 6–3, and in so doing "she convinced skeptics that a female athlete can survive pressure-filled situations and that men are as susceptible to nerves as women," wrote Neil Amdur of the *New York Times*. Martina Navratilova later said of King, "She was a crusader fighting a battle for all of us.

She was carrying the flag; it was all right to be a jock." *Life* Magazine named Billie Jean King one of the "100 Most Important Americans of the 20th Century." She was the only female athlete on the list.

Billie Jean King helped change how young women thought about themselves and how men thought about women. The role of sportscaster, which had been monopolized by men, was also beginning to change. Donna de Varona had been seen nationally reporting on *ABC's Wide World of Sports* and the network's Olympic telecasts, but, when Phyllis George debuted in 1975 as the co-host of *The NFL Today* on CBS alongside Brent Musburger and Irv Cross, the male-only domination of major team sports commentary in the United States started to crumble.

Phyllis George had toured the country as Miss America 1971, and she had impressed media executives with her personality, poise, and intelligence during her television guest appearances. She brought far more than a pretty face to the interviews, feature stories, and on-set reports that she did on CBS. Phyllis George added character and depth to story lines, often getting athletes to open up and show their personal side because of her comfortable humanity. Girls who loved sports but who were never going to achieve the international athletic success of Billie Jean King now had role models in George and de Varona, who via their visibility on television served as trailblazers in the process of redefining women in American culture.

THE IMPACT OF TELEVISION SPORTS ON RACIAL ATTITUDES

When the dramatic series *I Spy* premiered on NBC in the fall of 1965, Bill Cosby became the first African-American to have a starring role in a weekly television program in the United States. Up to that point the only minority stars that Americans saw on TV with any regularity were professional athletes such as Willie Mays of the San Francisco Giants, Bill Russell of the Boston Celtics, or heavyweight boxing champion Muhammad Ali. Their representation in the media helped the process of broadening and improving the understanding of diversity and race in this country.

Americans who grew up in the 1950s, as television penetration was exploding from less than 10 percent of homes at the beginning of the decade to nearly nine out of ten homes by 1960, came of age recognizing that people of different races played for the same teams. In 1946 the unwritten color ban in the NFL was broken when the Cleveland Rams moved to Los Angeles, and, as part of their lease agreement for the publicly owned Los Angeles Coliseum, agreed to add UCLA stars Kenny Washington and Woody Strode to their roster. The following year Jackie Robinson broke Major League Baseball's color barrier that had excluded players of color since 1889. The NBA's first black players made their debuts in 1950: Earl Lloyd for the Washington Capitols followed by Chuck Cooper of the Celtics and Nat Clifton of the New York Knicks. Their presence by no means implied that professional sports was a space devoid of racial discrimination, but it did begin to build a sense among those who saw them play in person and on television that players from diverse backgrounds would be selected based on merit and that their contributions to team success were valuable. The fan bases for teams and sports expanded to include more minorities in the decades since these pioneers made their mark. These increasingly diverse crowds and television audiences collectively cheering for victories and championships have helped bring people of all colors together.

Minorities Assume Leadership Positions

The opportunities for minorities in the major sports however were limited for years to the role of "performer." The presence of African-Americans or Hispanics on the playing field and their absence from any leadership positions such as coach, manager, captain, or quarterback reinforced a racial hierarchy that always put whites in charge. At its core, racism is about domination, one group exerting its control over others. As long as the leadership positions were "whites-only," sport in America was not a true meritocracy and therefore retained the vestiges of racism. This hierarchy was reaffirmed every time a television camera showed a quarterback calling signals or cut to the sidelines or dugout to show the managers and coaches, all of whom were white.

The athletic skill of minority players in the NFL had become inarguably evident in the years since the integration of the league began in 1946, but there was a perception among many white fans in America that they did not possess the combination of intellect and leadership required to be a quarterback. In 1953, the Chicago Bears had just two African-Americans on their roster; one was a rookie from Michigan State named Willie Thrower. On October 18, 1953, he entered the Bears' game against the San Francisco 49ers in relief of starter George Blanda. He threw eight passes, completing three before Blanda returned. Willie Thrower was the first black quarterback to play in the NFL since the league's color barrier fell, but his name is largely forgotten because those eight passes were the only ones he was ever allowed to throw in his career.

The first black quarterback to start a game in professional football was Marlin Briscoe, who took the first snap for the Denver Broncos in the fourth game of the 1968 season vs. the Cincinnati Bengals. He faltered in the first half and was replaced by Steve Tensi. The first African-American to start a season at quarterback for an NFL team was Joe Gilliam, Jr., who led the Pittsburgh Steelers for the first six games of the 1974 season. He too struggled and was replaced as the starter in game seven that year by Terry Bradshaw, who went on to win four Super Bowls with the Steelers and was elected to the Football Hall of Fame. The stumbles made by these early pioneers gave those who still believed in the old racial hierarchy what they saw as justification for their prejudice. The process of burying forever the myth that blacks couldn't succeed at quarterback gained momentum when Doug Williams quarterbacked the Washington Redskins to victory and was named the MVP of Super Bowl XXII before a television audience of millions in January of 1988.

The responsibilities and decision-making skills required to lead a team on the field are not insignificant, but they pale in comparison to those of a coach or manager. Bill Russell was the cornerstone for the Boston Celtics during their run of nine NBA championships in the ten years from 1956–66. He was named the team's player-coach for the 1966–67 season, succeeding the legendary Red Auerbach who was retiring. Russell thus became the first African-American to coach a team in any of the major American sports. He served as player-coach for three years and stepped aside after having led the Celtics to eleven NBA titles in his thirteen seasons. Russell was named the NBA's MVP five times and is a member of the Naismith Basketball Hall of Fame.

Major League Baseball's first black manager was perennial all-star Frank Robinson, who took the helm with the Cleveland Indians in 1974, just as his Hall of Fame playing career was coming to an end. The first minority head coach in the NFL was Hispanic. Tom Flores was promoted from assistant coach to head coach of the Oakland Raiders in 1979, and he proceeded to lead the silver and black to championships in Super Bowls XV and XVIII. When Flores retired in 1988 he was succeeded by Art Shell, making Shell the league's first African-American head coach.

As diversity spread from the player level to management, the identity of minorities in sport and throughout society underwent a reconstruction as America watched on television. A milestone came quietly in early 2007 when the coaches of the two teams in Super Bowl XLI were both African-American: Tony Dungy of the Indianapolis Colts and Lovie Smith of the Chicago Bears. These two men at the pinnacle of their sport were the leaders of men from many different ethnic backgrounds. They were the bosses. And at the conclusion of that 2006 regular season, 60 years after the NFL had begun to integrate, Dungy and Smith would be judged by the overwhelming majority of fans based on the quality of their work and their won–lost records, not the color of their skin.

CHANGING PERCEPTIONS

No one in the history of sport since the advent of television challenged racism more boldly than Muhammad Ali. Born Cassius Clay in Louisville, Kentucky, he won a gold medal as the Olympic light heavyweight champion at the Rome games in 1960. He was eighteen years old. At twenty-two he won the world heavyweight championship by knocking out Sonny Liston and announced to the world that he "must be the greatest." Shortly after the fight Ali made another announcement: that he had joined the Nation of Islam and was changing his name, first to Cassius X, then to Muhammad Ali. "I know where I'm going," he said, "and I know the truth and I don't have to be what you want me to be. I'm free to be what I want."

Figure 14.2 Muhammad Ali in one of his many interviews with Howard Cosell of ABC Sports
Source: reprinted with permission of Getty Images

Ali was stripped of his title in 1967 after he refused induction into the military on the grounds that he was a conscientious objector whose religion forbade taking up arms against others. Ali won his case against the US Justice Department three years later when the US Supreme Court found in his favor, but those were three years in which he had been unable to pursue his livelihood and compete in the ring. He regained his world title in 1974 by defeating then-champion George Foreman in "the Rumble in the Jungle" in Kinshasa, Zaire, which is now known as the Democratic Republic of the Congo. Ali would retire from boxing in 1981 having won the heavyweight championship three separate times.

Muhammad Ali's arrival on the sports scene was a watershed event. His impact on the sports media was immense because he was never afraid to speak, he looked confidently into the camera, he was controversial and quotable, never subservient. Ali dashed any semblance of racial hierarchy. He held his own and traded barbs over the course of several interviews with ABC's Howard Cosell, a man who had many more years of education than Ali, but no greater command of the language or understanding of the world around him. Muhammad Ali would not be dominated; his words and actions transmitted into homes across the country and around the world shook those who had complacently perpetuated the two-tier society that put whites on the top and everyone else beneath.

If sport is indeed going to completely shed the inequities of the past, there is still catching up to be done. Calling the plays on the field and calling the shots from the sideline or bench are one beachhead. Calling the games on television is quite another. The representation of minorities in the announce booth and the studio lags far behind their numbers on the field or court. Every year the University of Central Florida's Institute for Diversity and Ethics in Sports does a "race and gender report card" for each of the major sports in the US. The 2011 survey showed that, while 78 percent of the players in the NBA were African-American, only 17 percent of the radio and television talent covering the games were black. Seventy-two percent of NBA broadcasters that year were white. There was an even greater discrepancy in the NFL where 67 percent of the players but only 8 percent of the radio and television commentators and reporters were African-American. Seventy-nine percent of all broadcasters covering the NFL at the local and national level were white in 2011.

The argument is not that in order to achieve racial equity the ratio of minority broadcasters to players in any sport needs to be one-to-one. A case could in fact be made for the desirability of a one-to-one ethnic ratio not between players and sportscasters, but instead between the make-up of each sport's fan base and the sportscasters who serve those fans. Using that premise, if 79 percent of all NFL fans were white, then the same percentage of white NFL broadcasters would be equitable. What the argument is about is the end of racial discrimination and the accurate portrayal of minorities and women as equal partners in society, capable of achievement to the fullest extent of their talents and deserving of the opportunity to reach their goals.

One final point that demonstrates the power of television in molding our perceptions of sports reality: if you were to ask any group of adults, "Who was the first African-American to win a grand slam tennis title?" the answer you would undoubtedly hear most often is "Arthur Ashe." Ashe, a member of the International Tennis Hall of Fame, won the US Open in 1968 and the Wimbledon men's singles title in 1975. Both events were televised nationally. The first African-American to win a grand slam was actually Althea Gibson, the Wimbledon and US Open women's singles champion in both 1957 and 1958, but those tournaments were not on television. Althea Gibson was a pioneer, a remarkable athlete who, when her tennis playing days were over, became the first African-American to join the Ladies

Figure 14.3 Althea Gibson was the first African-American to win a major tennis title. She was
the Wimbledon and US Open women's singles champion in 1957 and 1958
Source: courtesy Notable Biographies

Figure 14.4 Arthur Ashe won the US Open men's singles in 1968, eleven years after Althea
Gibson's first grand slam championship. But Ashe's victory had far greater impact because it was
televised nationwide and Gibson's was not
Source: courtesy Hickok Sports

Professional Golf Association, and she too is a Hall of Famer. But her achievements made less of a lasting impact because what she did was not seen on TV.

SUMMARY

The passion for sports and its proliferation on television affect millions of people's personal decisions and preferences as to how they spend their time, the products they consume, the words and phrases they use, how they perceive themselves, and how they perceive and interact with others. Sports television has helped American society change by providing a platform upon which racial hierarchies and gender stereotypes could be challenged and overthrown, where personal initiative, skill, and determination could overcome every obstacle, even racial discrimination. The recognition that people of color were deserving of and capable of success in sports leadership positions, and their ascension to those jobs in increasing numbers, has been a major step forward in the drive for racial equity that began with the integration of player rosters in the 1940s and 1950s.

This is not to say that sport has become race-neutral or that racism and stereotyping don't still exist, or that work does not still need to be done to reach equitable participation at all levels. In fact the representation of African-Americans in the professional basketball and football games seen on television has created a false stereotype among minority youth who perceive sports as providing a vast potential for their personal upward mobility, when in fact the number of jobs as a "pro athlete" is infinitesimal compared with the work force as a whole.

Media coverage of sports has helped Americans understand the issues of race and gender, allowing them to construct collective and individual identities that reflect the growth of diversity and the higher standards for performance and competition that are its direct result. Television magnifies reality and at its best exposes inequities in sport, thus accelerating social and cultural change.

DISCUSSION TOPICS/ASSIGNMENTS

1   Do a self-assessment. How has your perception of the opposite gender and of races other than your own been influenced by the sports you see on television?

2   Research how the color barriers were broken in any of the sports you play or follow. Who took the initiative? What was the effect on the players, the team, and/or league in the first year of integration? What role did the media play?

3   Select a female pioneer from a traditionally male sport and write a profile that includes the obstacles and stereotypes she had to overcome, what level of support she received from the public and from within her sport, and the impact she made for other women who followed. Example: Janet Guthrie, who was the first woman ever to drive in the Indianapolis 500.

4   Do a tally of every member of a minority group who has ever served as head coach or manager in any of the major sports leagues. What trends can you identify? Has there been steady growth? Any reversals? Which sport has hired the fewest minority team leaders?

5 Find videos online of Muhammad Ali from the 1960s and 1970s. Compare his demeanor with that of other African-American celebrity athletes of the era. Discuss how Ali forced Americans to perceive blacks differently. How effective do you think his interviews with Howard Cosell were in changing perceptions of race?

6 Compare the careers of Althea Gibson and Arthur Ashe. How did Gibson open doors for Ashe? How did winning his first major title on television increase the impact that Ashe had in sport and society in the years afterward?

15 COMING UP NEXT

Uz.

(Early *SportsCenter* shorthand for "Stay with us.")

Table 15.1 Chapter 15: The Rundown

- The 21st century fan.
- 3D TV and technical innovations.
- TV everywhere.
- What's next?
- "*A la carte*" TV via broadband.
- Changing audiences and media convergence.
- Conclusion.

Technological innovation has been changing what it means to be a sports fan since the first days of broadcasting. At the beginning of the 20th century, being a fan meant going to see your favorite team in person and checking the scores in the newspaper, until radio brought the sounds and stories of live games into the home in the 1920s. Television added another dimension to being a fan, and it added more fans whose first exposure to sport was not at the ballpark or stadium, but in their homes. The evolution of the fan ever since has been a dynamic process connected to the rapid evolution of the communications media.

THE 21ST CENTURY FAN

Being a sports fan in the 21st century means watching games in person and on television, catching the edited highlights of every game on *SportsCenter* or any number of web-video sites, watching features on stars and strategies before games and interviews that dissect the results after each game, and subscribing to TV services that offer every game day and night. Being a modern sports fan also includes getting the latest scores on your smart phone, accessing live games and highlights on the phone or a tablet in places where you could never receive TV signals before, following analysis and commentary on sports websites, reading columns by your favorite bloggers, sharing your own impressions and experiences on social media sites, "liking" your favorite team on Facebook, following the Twitter feeds of your favorite players, listening to criticism on sports radio stations or calling in yourself, and playing fantasy sports in one or more leagues or multiple sports.

With each new year come new opportunities for fans across the globe to pursue their love of sports. The cable television networks and regional sports networks founded in the years after the first commercial communications satellite, RCA *Satcom I*, was launched in 1975 gave fans access to far more sports content than had ever before been available. Content options expanded again when the direct-broadcast satellite (DBS) services, DirecTV in 1994 followed by Dish Network in 1996, started beaming a multitude of channels directly to home dishes. The digital delivery of high-definition television via broadband internet connections and phone systems such as Verizon Fios and AT&T U-verse, collectively referred to as internet protocol TV (IPTV), are products of the 21st century that have created even more competition in the video distribution marketplace and more options for fans. Improved access to sports programming has been a significant driver for each of these television distribution innovations.

SPORTS FANS LOVE NEW TECHNOLOGY

Sports will be one of the primary forces contributing to the sale of 3D TVs in the coming years. The Consumer Electronics Association put the number of 3D sets sold in the United States at 3.6 million in 2011, up 192% over the previous year. The percentage of all 3D-enabled televisions sold compared with 2D sets is growing steadily and should continue to rise. "Sports fans are early adopters of technology," said Sean Bratches, ESPN executive vice president of sales and marketing, "and we think that the genre plays very well in terms of the technology." When the next technical innovation that further enhances the television viewing experience is introduced, we can expect sports fans to hold true to form and be the first in line.

Figure 15.1 Cameras shooting 3D TV are distinguished by each having two lenses, not one
Source: courtesy ESPN

The new technology we can expect to see in the coming years will not stop at 3D TV. New devices that will increase the functionality of digital television sets, computers, and all mobile devices, integrating them to enhance our options for television viewing and program storage, and broaden the range of content available anywhere, will also create new markets for hardware and software.

Technological advancements will also change the ways in which live sports events are covered on television. The miniaturization of cameras, microphones, and transmitters, and new systems that put them into motion, will give viewers more sights and sounds from previously inaccessible locations, limited only by the creativity of producers and directors and the vision of sports leagues and organizers who grant their approval for innovative coverage as a means of more intimately engaging their fans. Innovations in video recording and processing will continue to expand the variety of tools that television professionals can use to describe and analyze sports action. The super slow motion replays and telestrators that have become a staple of coverage could look antiquated in the not too distant future.

TV EVERYWHERE

The "TV Everywhere" initiatives undertaken by most digital communications providers allow access to sports and all other programming on mobile devices wherever wireless broadband internet is available. The new freedom to watch every channel to which you subscribe without having to sit in front of a television that is physically connected to a coaxial cable or satellite receiver harkens back to the era when the vast majority of Americans got their TV signals over the air at no cost. Instead of hundreds of channels there were only three or four back then. And while thousands of hours of recorded video are now available free on broadband, you must be a regular paying subscriber to gain access to services such as Comcast's "xfinity" that deliver live events and entertainment shows at their scheduled air times, giving you the option to watch them live or time-shift them on your DVR.

The Federal Communications Commission's (FCC) National Broadband Plan called "Connecting America," which was mandated by Congress in 2009, has set as its priority the expansion of wireless broadband nationwide. To do so the FCC is reclaiming those portions of public band spectrum that were being used for analog broadcast television signals. The more spectrum that is made available for broadband, the more video and data content will become accessible for Americans using wireless devices.

Greater access along with the ever-increasing amount of live streaming programs and recorded video that is aggregated on the internet has naturally led to greater usage. Online video achieved a milestone in the year 2010 when the number of Americans watching at least one video per month on the internet surged past 50 percent of the population. And most people watch far more than one video. The digital measurement and business analytics firm comScore reported that, at the end of 2011, over 183 million Americans were spending up to twenty hours per month watching video online. The total amount of video viewing on the internet started out as only a small fraction of the hours spent watching traditional television, but the annual trend is for double-digit increases in both the number of online viewers and their time spent viewing. This trend will be fueled by more innovations like "NCAA® March Madness on Demand"® from CBS Sports and Turner Sports, which puts every game from the NCAA Men's Basketball Tournament live on the internet. In 2011 there were 1.9 million unique users each day watching the games on broadband and nearly 700,000 more using their mobile devices to tune in. Both figures are huge increases over the previous year and should continue their strong growth for each successive tournament.

The trend toward more online video viewing has created the phenomenon known as "cord cutting." Subscribers cancel their cable or other television distribution services, stop paying a monthly bill, and do all of their TV viewing online. Television sets built with internet connectivity enhance the viewing experience and serve to encourage "cord cutting." The choice of free sports programming online is and always will be limited to advertiser-supported series and games that do not command huge rights fees. But the NFL and other valuable sports franchises do have exclusive long-term rights deals with broadband providers that make it possible for cord cutters to buy a season of live games without subscribing to a cable or DBS service.

"A LA CARTE" TELEVISION

The "*a la carte*" selection of TV programming is a trend that will gain momentum despite a number of powerful industry players who are lined up against it. The multi-system cable operators make their profits by packaging "tiers" of channels that must be purchased with no substitutions or deletions. They function as if they were restaurants where you have to order everything that's on the menu and pay for it all, even if you aren't very hungry. By so doing, the television distributors guarantee that they will cover their operating costs as well as the price that each channel charges for its programming, and still turn a sizable profit regardless of how good their service may be.

Viewer surveys have shown for years that most people watch a relatively small number of their favorite channels and not the eighty to a hundred or more channels that are available to them. If people could simply pick their ten or fifteen favorites from the cable, DBS, or IPTV menu "*à la carte*," they would have far greater control over their monthly bills. But, despite an occasional threat from a crusading lawmaker or two to force "*à la carte*" on the television distribution giants, the power of the industry lobby has proven too strong to overcome. Where they have failed, however, technology will succeed.

The delivery of television via broadband internet is overwhelmingly "*à la carte*." You choose what you want to watch, live or recorded, and you pay for only that programming if a price is charged. And you are free to watch whatever you choose whenever it's convenient. The growing multitude of television consumers who get more and more of their content from broadband will be the shifting tide that finally sends the tier system the way of the rabbit-ears antenna.

WHAT'S NEXT?

It is very possible that, in the future, leagues and other content owners could sell some or all of their television rights to YouTube, or a yet to be launched online video aggregator, which could then put all those games or events on a channel titled "NFL" or "NBA" and charge you a monthly fee to subscribe. You could select only the sports and entertainment shows you want to watch from the YouTube list of channels, and your total subscription fee would still be lower than your current monthly bill for television services. Google, which owns YouTube, is moving in that direction with "GoogleTV," an Android-based operating system that uses a

Google Chrome browser to bring online video to your television. GoogleTV has partnered with Dish Network and other television providers to make the service available, but as broadband penetration increases YouTube may become the only distributor that Google needs to become the ultimate source for "*à la carte*" television, including sports.

One by-product of expanded television distribution via broadband internet will be a level of usage tracking more accurate than ever before. Every computer and broadband-enabled mobile device or television will become a "people meter" providing data on which shows are viewed, live, or time-shifted, for exactly how long to the second, and by whom. The old Nielsen model of using a statistical cross-section of the US population to project what the entire country was watching will appear imprecise by comparison. The Nielsen Company has already begun to monitor web activity as it too seeks to improve its measurement techniques and keep pace with the ways in which technology is changing television viewing habits.

The more information that is available about who is watching what, and from where, the more customization becomes possible. The data that television providers can collect about you, including your location provided by the global positioning satellite (GPS) chip in your smart phone or tablet, will undoubtedly lead to the "hyper-localization" of advertising and promotion. Commercial messages will be focused specifically on the retail and services available in your area, even including directions to the nearest store that sells the product being advertised. Individual products and programs can be targeted at specific audiences identified and selected based upon their demographics, region, or current location, and viewing tendencies.

We can also expect to see far more advertising dollars being spent each year on hybrid ads that blend in with sports content, brand placement inside programming and on player uniforms, and on interactive commercials that allow you to order samples or products using your television remote while you continue watching the show.

SHIFTING AUDIENCES AND MEDIA CONVERGENCE

The more sports content that is available on an increasing variety of delivery platforms, the greater the trend will be toward a splintering of the audience into smaller segments. Fewer people will be watching the same programs at the same time in their homes on TV sets connected to a cable system or other television provider. The heightened competition for eyeballs is in the process of transforming the economic models and shifting the concentration of power in the television industry.

The segment of the population that currently watches the most online video is the 12–34 age group, which foreshadows a future in which a large percentage of adults will be much more comfortable choosing their programs from broadband internet menus on any number of devices, and less likely to consume television the way their parents did. They are also more apt to "co-watch" sports on two screens: their television sets and simultaneously on their internet-connected computers, which provide them access to a wider array of data about the game and its stars, or simply a means of communicating with friends and fellow fans.

There are some industry observers and insiders who see a gloomy future ahead for the sports that rely upon fan bases who remain loyal for a lifetime. They see new generations of young people who are more transient in changing jobs and moving from region to region, who won't retain the "live and die" loyalties their parents had for teams. Others believe that shifting lifestyles will only change how sports are delivered and consumed, but not the love that new generations will have for sports.

There is no guarantee however that the next generation will follow the same sports that are popular now, which means opportunity in the future for the development of new competitions and programs. The traditional sports that lose audience to newer ones with exciting action, a structure of quick action punctuated by natural breaks, and story lines that make them more television-friendly, or that lag behind in the diversification of their distribution, will gradually become relegated to second-level status.

The forces that are transforming sports television consumption should produce more disintermediation and a further consolidation of sports content ownership with distribution. Leagues and organizers that increase their power and create new revenue streams by establishing their own networks and internet protocol TV will be able to offset potential reductions in the rights payments they receive in new contracts with independently owned networks. The unwelcome side-effect of more disintermediation is the trend toward more one-sided messages being delivered to sports audiences, without the unbiased analysis of producers and reporters who don't owe their allegiance to the team or league they cover.

The media companies that will thrive in the era of shifting audiences will be those that take the utmost advantage of media convergence. Before the internet and digital distribution, different media covering sports were separate and distinct: television, radio, newspapers, and magazines. Radio shows weren't on television; newspapers and magazines didn't show videos on their websites. Convergence is the technology-driven unification of different media channels. It has blurred the lines that once separated each medium from the others. When television programming distributors such as Comcast diversify from cable into broadband, and unite with the owners of multiple networks like NBC Universal, they assure themselves steady growth even as the number of cable subscribers gradually declines.

Media convergence gives conglomerates the power to spread sports and entertainment content across all delivery systems, adding many splintered audiences together, reaching more people. And that means they can charge more for the advertising and sponsorships they sell. The communications firms that don't embrace convergence and stick with just one product will either be taken over by the stronger, diversified giants or face a future of dwindling profits and eventual extinction.

CONCLUSION

Sport has changed television, and television has changed sport. Coverage on television has made sports more pervasive, more popular, more powerful, and far more profitable. Events such as the Olympics and the Super Bowl that are a stage for politics, economics, and entertainment have changed television programming and the type of specialized talent and resources needed to produce the shows. The symbiotic relationship between sports and television is dynamic and evolving, each continuing the process of change in stages both overt and subtle.

Television cameras have never been mirrors that merely reflect what's happening in a sport back to viewers who can't attend in person. They are not neutral. The cameras' presence changes how performers and fans alike behave and react, and then it magnifies each action, adding drama and importance. The impact was evident from the very first sporting event ever televised, when Columbia's pitcher against Princeton on May 17, 1939, said some of his teammates were running out of position just so they could be seen on the one television camera that was in place at Baker Field in New York. Think of all the touchdown dances and fist pumps to the camera that have followed.

What is seen on television, and what is not seen, changes how the events and the participants are perceived, helping to shape social, cultural, and economic hierarchies. The decades-long absence of women and minorities from commentary booths and studios, as well as their absence from any sports leadership positions, made it very clear to the viewing public during those years who had power and who did not, whose aspirations could be fulfilled and whose could not.

By choosing which shots will go on the air, and the words used to describe each player and action, television changes reality into "dramatic reality." What the viewer sees and hears is reality that has gone through the filter of each producer, director, and commentator as well as the network and the owners of the league or event. Their judgment as to what is important and what is not will always affect the end product that fans receive. Heroes are celebrated with replays of their successes and smiling close-ups, while villains are castigated with unflattering words and pictures that can be edited to omit any positives or redeeming characteristics.

To this reality, however, sports fans willingly surrender. Regardless of who owns the network or which screen is the best available, we are drawn to the stories, the triumphs, the controversies, and disappointments that each game and each season brings. From generation to generation we remain interested in the people of sport: the electrifying rookie who bursts onto the scene, the seasoned veteran returning from injury or decline to win once more, the record-setter who goes higher, faster, farther than all who have come before, and the teams whose collective skill, determination, and personality reward them with victory, making avid followers of us all. Sport inspires and entertains us, it always will, and it makes great television.

DISCUSSION TOPICS/ASSIGNMENTS

1 Compare the sports channel offerings of one local cable system and one DBS service to the sports offerings from your broadband internet provider. Do a table listing what each service delivers, then discuss which you think is optimal for the sports that you follow.

2 Write a 4–5 page paper on what you see as the "Next Big Thing" in TV sports coverage or programming. What trend(s) do you expect in the next five to ten years? Why?

3 What sports will be more popular ten years from now when today's teenagers are in their twenties? What sports will have smaller audiences? How will this affect advertising and television rights fees?

4 What evidence do you see of how television has changed sports? Examine changes in the rules of different sports. Which ones do you think were instituted to enhance the sport on television or accommodate live coverage? Compare the average length of games from a variety of sports now with how long they lasted in 1960, 1970, and 1980.

5 How has sports changed television in the past twenty years? Compare the total hours of sports on television. How many different sports and events are available now that were not televised twenty years ago? What kind of television programming has been de-emphasized, if any, because of the increase in sports?

Bibliography

Akamai. "Akamai's HD Network Delivers for 2011 NCAA March Madness on Demand," news release, April 7, 2011.

Arledge, Roone. *Roone*, Harper Collins, 2003.

Baseball Reference.com.

Bradlow, Eric T., Ennen, Steve, and Fader, Peter S. "Wharton Interactive Media Initiative: Reflecting the Future," UPenn.edu, 2009.

Buchwald, Art. "Heidi Fans Next Game: Swiss Alps vs. Super Bowl," *Los Angeles Times*, November 24, 1968.

Carrington, Ben. "Fear of a Black Athlete: Masculinity, Politics and the Body," *New Formations* 45, winter 2001/02.

Castleman, Harry and Podrazik, Walter J. *Watching Television: Six Decades of American Television*, Syracuse University Press, 2003.

comScore. "The 2010 US Digital Year in Review."

comScore. "comScore Releases July 2011 US Online Video Rankings," press release, August 22, 2011.

comScore. "comScore Releases November 2011 US Online Video Rankings," press release, December 15, 2011.

"Congress Helped Found Saints, Super Bowl," *Washington Times*, January 29, 2010.

Cornell.edu/copyright cases 1991 Feist Publications vs. Rural Telephone Service.

Curran, Bob. *The $400,000 Quarterback or: The League That Came in from the Cold*, Macmillan Company, 1965.

Dougherty, Philip H. "New Sports Network's Clients," *New York Times*, September 25, 1979.

Eggerton, John. "Commissioners Vote 5–0 to Change Service Rules for TV Band," *Broadcasting & Cable*, November 30, 2010.

Evey, Stuart and Broughton, Irv. *ESPN: The No-Holds-Barred Story of Power, Ego, Money and Vision That Transformed a Culture*, Triumph Books, 2004.

Fantasy Sports Trade Association. "Fantasy Sports Participation Sets All-Time Record, Grows Past 32 Million Players," press release, June 10, 2011.

FCC. "Connecting America: The National Broadband Plan," 2010.

"FCC Votes to Launch Broadcast Spectrum Reclamation Initiative: Commissioners Vote 5-0 To Change Service Rules For TV Band John Eggerton—Multichannel News, 11/30/2010 1:10:58 PM".

Frost, John. "How Walt Disney Changed the Olympics Forever," Disney blog, January 24, 2010.

FundingUniverse.com.

Funt, Peter. "Tomorrow: 'A Video Supermarket,'" *New York Times*, July 22, 1979.

Gould, Jack. "Olympic Ceremonies Taped in California," *New York Times*, February 19, 1960.

Gould, Jack. "TV Review: Pro Football Kicks Off in ABC. Primetime," *New York Times*, September 22, 1970.

International Olympic Committee. "Olympic Broadcasting History," Olympics.org.

Keese, Parton. "Bristol Hits the Big League in Sports TV," *New York Times*, December 9, 1979.

Koppett, Leonard. "Baker Field: Birthplace of Sports Television," *Columbia Magazine*, 1999.

Lapchick, Richard. *Racial and Gender Report Card*, University of Central Florida Center for Diversity and Ethics in Sports, 2011.

Lowitt, Bruce. "Heidi Game Remains Best You Never Saw," *St Petersburg Times*, September 23, 1999.

MacCambridge, Michael. *America's Game: The Epic Story of How Pro Football Captured a Nation*, Anchor Books, 2004.

Mawson, L. Marlene and Bowler, William T. III. "The Effects of the 1984 Supreme Court Ruling on the Television Revenues of NCAA Division I Football Programs," *Journal of Sport Management*, Vol. 3, Issue 2, July 1989.

MLB.com.

Moore, Kenny. "A Courageous Stand in '68, Olympians Tommie Smith and John Carlos Raised Their Fists for Racial Justice," *Sports Illustrated*, August 5, 1991.

Museum of Broadcast Communications.

NASA National Space Science Data Center.

National Cable and Telecommunications Association. NCTA.com.

New York Times, May 18, 1939.

NBA.com.

"NBC, Versus Ink 10-Year, $2B Deal to Retain NHL TV Rights," *Sports Business Daily*, April 19, 2011.

Newspaper Association of America.

NFL.com.

NFL Films interview transcripts.

NHL.com.

Nielsen Company. "Cross Platform Report," 1st Quarter 1, 2010.

Nielsen Company. "Three Screen Report," Vol. 8, 1st Quarter, 2010.

Nielsen Company. "State of the Media: Year in Sports 2010."

Nielsen Company. "Cross Platform Report," 1st Quarter 1, 2011.

Nielsen Company. "State of the Media: Consumer Usage Report 2011," 2012.

Nike.com. Nike annual reports.

"Nike's annual revenue tops $10 billion," *Portland Business Journal*, June 26, 2003.

National Sports Law Institute of Marquette University Law School. *Sports Facility Reports*, Vol. 7, Appendix 1 & Appendix 3, 2006.

OBS.es. "Olympic Broadcasting History."

Olympic.org.

Oriard, Michael. *Brand NFL: Making and Selling America's Favorite Sport*, University of North Carolina Press, 2007.

Paley Center for Media. "Women Creating Television and Radio: Phyllis George, Television Sportscaster," SheMadeIt.org.

Paley Center for Media video archives.

Pro-Football Reference.com.

Radio Hall of Fame (Red Barber).

Rasmussen, Bill. *Sports Junkies Rejoice! The Birth of ESPN*, QV Publishing Inc., 1983.

Rhoden, William C. *Third and a Mile: From Fritz Pollard to Michael Vick—an Oral History of the Trials, Tears and Triumphs of the Black Quarterback*, ESPN Books, 2007.

Roberts, Selena. "Tennis's Other 'Battle of the Sexes,' before King–Riggs," *New York Times*, August 21, 2005.

Rogers, Thomas. "Jets Cut for 'Heidi'; TV Fans Complain," *New York Times*, November 18, 1968.

Rovell, Darren. *First in Thirst: How Gatorade Turned the Science of Sweat into a Cultural Phenomenon*, AMACOM Books, 2006.

"Rozelle Indicates Tomorrow's Super Bowl Contest Could be Next to Last," *New York Times*, January 11, 1969.

Sandomir, Richard. "PRO FOOTBALL; Citing NFL, ESPN Cancels 'Playmakers,'" *New York Times*, February 5, 2004.

Schwartz, Larry. "Billie Jean Won for All Women," *ESPN Sports Century*, ESPN.com.

"Small Amount of Loss is Offset by New Two-Cord Households," ESPN MediaZone.com, March 14, 2011.

Smith, Red. "Cable TV for Sports Junkies," *New York Times*, December 3, 1979.

Society of Satellite Professionals International. "Satellite Timeline."

Spence, Jim and Diles, Dave. *Up Close and Personal: The Inside Story of Network Television Sports*, Atheneum, 1988.

"Sport: Vinnie, Vidi, Vici," *Time*, December 21, 1962.

Stelter, Brian. "For a Second Quarter, Fewer Pay for TV," *New York Times*, November 18, 2011.

Stelter, Brian. "ESPN Says Study Shows Little Effort to Cut Cable," *New York Times*, December 6, 2011.

"Super Bowl More Ordinary Than Super," *New York Times*, January 16, 1967.

Swisher, Kara. "Proliferating Platforms: Disney's Robert Iger on Why It's a Good Time to be in the Content Business," *Wall Street Journal*, June 6, 2011.

Time Warner Inc. "2011 NCAA March Madness on Demand Sees 63% Increase in Total Visits and 17% Increase in Video Consumption across Multiple Platforms for the NCAA Division I Men's Basketball Championship," news release, April 5, 2011.

Turner Broadcasting System, Inc. "Company History," Turner.com.

United States Court of Appeals for the District of Columbia Circuit, 587 F.2d 1248: Home Box Office, Inc., et al., Petitioners, v. Federal Communications Commission and United States of America, Respondents, Metromedia, Inc., American Broadcasting Co., Inc., Forward Communications Corp., et al., National Association of Broadcasters, Paramount Pictures Corporation, CBS, Inc., National Broadcasting Company, Inc., Intervenors.

United States Court of Appeals for the Eighth Circuit. Oct. 16, 2007 Nos. 06–3357/3358. CBC Distribution and Marketing, Inc. vs. Major League Baseball Advanced Media.

United States Court of Appeals for the Eleventh Circuit. March 4, 1997 D. C. Docket Nos. 00–01128 CV-J-20-HTS, 00–01128 CV-3-J-20HTS. Morris Communications Corp. vs PGA Tour Inc.

United States Holocaust Memorial Museum. "The Movement to Boycott the Berlin Olympics of 1936."

US Bureau of the Census: Statistical Abstract of the United States—1940, Bureau of the Census

US Bureau of the Census. Statistical Abstract of the United States—1950.

Verna, Tony. *Instant Replay: The Day That Changed Sports Forever*, Creative Book Publishers International, 2008.

Wallace, William N. "Pro Football Gets Four-Year TV Pact," *New York Times*, January 27, 1970.

Whalen, David J. "Communications Satellites: Making the Global Village Possible," NASA.com.

Women's Basketball Hall of Fame. Historical Timeline: Notable Events in the History of Women's Basketball.

Index

Page numbers in *italics* denotes an illustration/table.